Why the hell Bother?

Carolyn,
With best wishes of all
prosperity.

Anie Sicheto

Oct '11   London

Why the hell Bother?

How climbing the Seven Summits
changed my life

Ania Lichota

Published by Pinnacle Inspirations Ltd
145-157 St John Street
EC1V 4PW London, United Kingdom

Orders: whythehellbother@gmail.com

Printed in the United States of America

ISBN 13: 978-0-9568819-0-8

Contents

I dedicate this book to life – as a thank you for putting all those irresistible opportunities in front of me, for introducing me to the people I have met, for all the lessons that will be with me forever, and for guiding me, sometimes painfully, when I have strayed from my path.

Acknowledgments

MY thanks to Nigel for making the first draft of this book readable and for cracking me up when pointing out some of the corrections he had to make to my Polish English:

I strip of everything waste up	*I strip off everything waist up.*
I am totally, utterly naked and just fall down into my sleeping back	*I am totally, utterly knackered and just fall down into my sleeping bag.*
For dinner we have wonderful soup, meaty main and for the desert a chocolate mouse	*For dinner we have wonderful soup, a meat main dish, and for dessert a chocolate mousse.*
My black toe from Denali has just cured	*My black toe from Denali has just healed.*

To Julia, who applied her pen and scalpel in editing this book.

And to all of you who have been on my back to have the guts to finally publish this book.

Introduction:
Mountains made me

AS I climb down Everest after a successful summit, I realise I haven't rested or peed for eighteen and a half hours of physical effort above 8,000m (26,246 feet). Luckily I have several energy bars and half a litre (0.87pint) of liquid. I am in a storm, the clouds are mixed up with the snow, the wind is blowing hard and visibility is limited to five meters (33 feet). I want to get to camp four as soon as possible, although I am very aware that safety is more important than speed. I have lost my peripheral vision, and I feel the overwhelming pain of blocked vertebrae between my shoulder blades and from bacteria eating my cheeks. I am crying from uncontrolled waves of pain overpowering my body. I remove my goggles as the tears have frozen on the plastic, blinding me. Cold wind provides a bit of relief, or perhaps it's the needles of ice stabbing my face that are keeping me awake. Time passes and I realise I can't hear, smell or taste anything, as if all my senses have switched off and I am in a heightened state of being – fully alert to what my hands and legs are doing.

I so want to lie down in my sleeping bag and finally rest. I come up with little routines to cheat the pain. I trust my equipment and my training without judgment, rope after rope. I lost track of my team after the last conversation with my Sherpa at the balcony. He stayed behind to help others – everybody needs to get to the camp.

In contrast to my body, my intuition is absolutely crystal clear. No hesitation with anything, no thinking. I know exactly what to do, how to secure myself, how wide my steps should be so I don't catch my pants, how to use the slope of the mountain to help me grab the next rope below the anchor, how to take over other climbers who are slower than me and being helped by others. I look down without fear at the immense space below me, which could just swallow me forever with one unfortunate move. Being unafraid opens up opportunities that I didn't know existed, to try new things with my gloves, my carabineer, the rope and my body, which I fully trust to the last cell. To keep moving I take energy from the surroundings. I breathe in the wind and cloud and I constantly put one foot in front of the other. No rest until I get to the camp.

Mid-way, I catch myself smiling a very peaceful smile. I pause for a milli-second. I feel fully content with the situation. I am totally on my own, one moment I can see the camp, the other only clouds racing around me; it's just me and nature. Suddenly I stop experiencing myself as separate from my surroundings. I am part of the snow, of the cold, the thin air, and of the rock. I am a mere particle of the universe. I am free from the sense of self.

I realise that through the mountains and nature I have tapped into a totally different perception of the world which, peak by peak, has totally changed the way I experience life. Through this altered perception, I have found the strength always to take full responsibility for my thoughts, words and actions. I have learnt not to be a hero, but to get up every day and remain humble and open to learn whatever life has in store for me.

On the pages that follow, I describe my story of the Seven Summits, with all its preparations, fears, family issues, farewells, supportive boyfriends or lack of. I write about the laughter and tears, as well as the pain and ailments that tormented me. Throughout this experience, I am undergoing a personal transformation that I am initially unaware of and which has nothing to do with my physical changes. I am so grateful for this opportunity. At first the lessons are like a slap on the face, like big 'aha moments', then they become increasingly subtle. I am still discovering them and, I am sure, will continue to do so throughout my scholarship of life.

I hope you find my story of the Seven Summit Challenge interesting, uplifting and entertaining. By buying this book you are contributing to my efforts to improve the education and life of children in Nepal. Thank you for your generosity.

PART ONE

Getting the basics right

CHAPTER 1

A walk in the park

January 2006
Africa, Mount Kilimanjaro – 5,895 metres (19,340 feet)

CLIMBING Kilimanjaro is a taster and perhaps a first step in the long journey of the Seven Summits. As it is my first significant mountain and the expedition is a major endeavour for me, I take my preparations very seriously. I am living in Russia and working crazy hours as a sales director for the retail banking arm of General Electric. Thank goodness Moscow is a thoroughly capitalist city with a twenty-four-hour economy, where I can go to the gym between six o'clock in the morning and eleven at night and have a private trainer who helps me to get fit in the luxurious environment of filtered and oxidized air. There you can buy light sport equipment at two in the morning and have a massage two hours later.

I train for six months, planning to climb Kilimanjaro with my boyfriend Nigel, who lives in the UK. However, much to my disappointment he has to cancel the trip for family reasons. I initially try to accommodate him by moving the dates, but then decide to go on my own over the Russian New Year holiday, as I had planned for over eighteen months.

So instead of an exhilarating trek up Kilimanjaro with the man I love, with a romantic rest on Zanzibar over New Year at the end of the trip, I board a flight to Africa shortly after Christmas with nine other strangers from my group.

I sleep most of the way and wake up as we land in the blazing sun of Africa. I had promised Nigel that I would capture every bit of the journey in the diary that he gave me as a present. I duly record my feelings and emotions, group conversations, meals, trek, tents, toilets... the whole shebang.

We are taken to our hotel in Moshi, Tanzania, where I spend most of the day by the (empty) pool. I share my room with an Irish lady called Clare. She is my mother's age, is a great adventurer and a good companion. There are several Londoners in our group and others from around the UK. For most of us it is the challenge of our lives. At dinner we discuss our motivations for going on this trip. I say that I have a love of mountains and that I hope to attempt Elbrus and Aconcagua if I do well here. For me, the first three of the Seven Summits are attainable, but whether I succeed in doing all three depends on how well I acclimatise. Prior to this trip I had already trekked at relatively high altitude in Nepal and Europe, and I like being well above sea level, particularly above 4,500 metres (14,500 feet). I find the mountain environment, and especially meeting the people who live there, very energizing. It recharges my life batteries and brings me a lot of joy. Physical effort of any kind, but particularly the strenuous effort of climbing a mountain, enables me to enjoy the simple pleasure of being human, stripped of the ego.

This is in total contrast to my life in London now, where I work for an investment bank, am surrounded by people who consider themselves to be masters of the universe, modern-day superheroes armed with BlackBerries and Porsches. And in our so called civilised world we are bombarded with 'celebrities', who appear larger than life, monopolise public attention and fill our television screens and magazines. When I am on a mountain with my climbing companions, battling the terrain and our physical frailties with our determination and skill, all artifice and ego is stripped away. We are just human.

Day One

We pack our things into a Jeep and set off at six o'clock in the morning. We are taking the least-used Rongai route up Kilimanjaro. This is the longest route up the mountain and therefore gives greater time for acclimatisation and a better chance to reach the summit. At the gate of the park we are registered.

Our loads are divided among the porters: they cannot carry more than 20 kilograms (44 pounds) each. Today's walk is an easy, three-hour stroll up a gently winding path. At the first camp the tents are erected, the sleeping pads blown up, the table set up in the mess tent, and the afternoon snack of freshly popped popcorn is ready for us to munch on. Wow! This is royal treatment. At this stage conversations among the trekkers are relatively superficial; likewise with the porters who have limited English. I am dutifully learning the 'Hakuna Matata' song. Yes, the one from *The Lion King*.

After a change of clothes in my tent I am ready for dinner. To our delight, we have proper tables complete with tablecloths, chairs and metal cutlery all the way up to Kibo Hut. This evening, dinner is amazing: three courses of delicious soup, rice with some meat (which I avoid because I'm a vegetarian), and chocolate mousse for dessert. However, because I am single and the group does not bond well at the beginning, I start feeling lonely and mentally berating Nigel for his absence.

Day Two

At exactly five forty-five in the morning, I hear a gentle wake-up call from a porter outside the tent. 'Wakey, wakey, washy, washy.' He brings two bowls of water for Clare and I to wash our faces. I am on a mountain, and I can wash my face with soap and water in the morning? This is great. After a five-star breakfast we are given packed snacks and we set off on our second day's walking, again up a gentle slope, but this time for eight hours. Lunch is set up on a table outside a cave with a tablecloth and chairs. What a feast.

The afternoon stroll takes us to our second camp where we can see the cone of Kilimanjaro for the first time. It is beautiful, faraway, remote and very high. It looks fantastically red, set against the blue cloudless sky. I have a tremendous appreciation for the mountain and the nature it offers. I know that if I do not respect it, it will punish me in some way. Before I left Moshi I bought a Kilimanjaro hat. However, out of respect for the highest single-standing volcano in the world, I will not wear it with its name at the front until I have climbed it. And I will not call it Kili before I have come off its summit safely.

Before going to bed I meet others going on our route: workers from the City of London; a couple from South Africa on honeymoon; and a Brazilian guy, Tasso, who climbs Mt. Elbrus with me six months later. Conversations are basic and brisk as we assess and compartmentalise each other.

I sorely miss Nigel and our conversations. We have talked on the phone every day for at least twelve months now. I talk with my tent-mate Clare. She has a great perspective and shares her life story. After three husbands and now on her own with her two children grown up, she is finally living the life of her dreams. She tells me to just be here now and fully in the present. My confusion with my boyfriend will either work itself out or not. Just be.

Easier said than done!

Talking to her, I realise I have subconsciously avoided becoming close to other women. After a childhood of fighting with my sister and mother, who were always trying to change me into somebody I am not, I have become highly suspicious of other women. By contrast, my dad, a very straightfor-ward person, just accepts me as I am. I find it much easier to relate to him. After spending time with Clare I conclude that I am missing something by not having more females around me; I will try to change this pattern.

Day Three

We continue the ascent, walking 'poli poli'. This is one of the first Tanzanian phrases we learn from the guides, meaning slowly, slowly.

Physically, I feel no effort at all and am usually ahead of the group. The plains below are receding. Because Kilimanjaro is a stand-alone mountain, from any point, one can see the villages at the bottom of it. As we ascend, the vegetation becomes more sparse, and I find the space and landscape exciting and liberating. I strive to connect with the natural surroundings, sometimes kneeling down to touch a flower or interesting foliage. Most importantly, we have the sun. Every day the round, yellow, smiley face wakes us up and puts us to bed. It's like a 'Be happy' badge, and that is exactly how I feel here. The environment gives me a fresh perspective on life and the slog I left behind in Moscow; it allows me to believe I can achieve anything I might dream. I walk without speaking to anybody for hours at a stretch. I quieten my mind and try to listen to myself. The pace of my feet becomes a sort of trance, very rhythmic, as it grounds me.

We stop for lunch, which is again a treat. In the afternoon I start with the group, but leave them behind pretty quickly and spend another afternoon on my own. I admire the natural beauty on this barren volcano. Little blades of grass, tiny flowers, and various colours of red, grey, black, white, and brown of lava hardened through the centuries. It amazes me how the lack of civilisation beautifies the surroundings.

My thoughts turn to my mother. I have a deep-seated guilt at having left Poland years ago for an unknown future. My mother nurtures my guilt and reinforces it every time we speak. She gives me examples of other sons and daughters who regularly visit their parents and make various expressions of love and gratitude, while I just call every so often and visit perhaps once a year. I am not sure what to do about it. I certainly love her, but I don't miss home, and I don't feel the need to call and share details of my life with my family.

On the mountain, we adhere to the natural light cycle in order to have the longest active days possible. I chat with the porters as they pass me and learn some of their language so I can engage in some small talk. These people are very poor. Some walk in flip-flops all the way up and without proper weather-resistant clothing, but they still have giant smiles on their faces. They look straight into your eyes when talking, hiding nothing and being totally engaged. This is in sharp contrast with London where people tend to engage through small talk, and it takes a long time to gain friends. On the London underground, people avoid looking at each other, and they cleverly use newspapers or books as a cover. Their faces look tired. Their rare smiles disappear immediately when their backs are turned. I like the thought that you are responsible for your own face and it will reflect who you really are and how you truly feel.

After reaching camp at approximately 4,200 metres (13,800 feet), we scramble up some rocks for two hours to acclimatise. Touching the rock and feeling its coolness calms me. My anxiety at being alone without Nigel is fading. I like being here. I breathe in my newly discovered freedom with the fresh air. We sit on the top of the hill for twenty minutes and talk about reaching the summit. The people in my group are determined to get to the top and take that all-important snapshot. Some are very fit, but altitude is a great equaliser. We are tired and anxious about summit day. For me, reaching the top is important, but it is only a first step in a potentially long journey.

Dinner tastes different today. It's as if, via my silent contemplation during the trek, my sense of taste has sharpened. I feel I am getting more energy and nourishment out of my food than I did yesterday.

Tomorrow is going to be a long day crossing the saddle and we are told to prepare for high winds. All wrapped up, I stand outside my tent. It's dark, but I can see everything around me quite clearly. I watch several clouds gracefully passing lower down the mountain. Above, the moon is enormous, surrounded by thousands of stars. The air is crystal clear. I can see for miles below me, where the villages surround the volcano with their fires alight as if the stars are looking down into a mirror on the ground. I am starting to feel a new type of connection with nature, which evokes a warm and happy sensation inside me.

Day Four

As we walk across the saddle we can see the camp for the following night in the very far distance. This motivates us, but it looks deceptively close and it takes eight tedious hours of walking on the flat, featureless plain to get there. The cone of the mountain ahead looks even more barren. I listen as people in my group start to complain about the physical difficulty and discomforts of this trip. Some are vomiting from altitude and others are swearing at the mountain. I watch wives and girlfriends shouting at their partners for dragging them out here. Some have burnt the insides of their mouths and lips, possibly from talking too much, or perhaps just from walking with their mouths open and breathing through their mouths rather than their noses. Some even have blisters on the roof of their mouths. I remain silent, as the journey has so far been pure fun for me.

We finally get to Kibo Hut, and are pleased to find it has proper brick built toilets, an emergency hut and a lot of tents. The last 100 vertical metres (328 feet) has tired me as I didn't do it 'poli, poli' in my haste to reach my tent and rest. I can feel the altitude properly now and how it surrounds me in cotton wool, making every movement an effort. The summit is 1,000 metres (3,300 feet) above us. We have a very early dinner and a thirst-quenching dessert of watermelon, which one of the porters has carried all the way up the mountain. We pack our snacks and water for the night summit attempt. I delight in using a 'real' toilet, and then wash myself as a present and motivational trick with a collection of wet wipes.

Day Five

At ten o'clock at night, we are woken up to a steaming bowl of porridge and lots of tea. I feel great, but it is cold, and there is a strong wind. I cannot see any stars as we seem to be in a cloud. Our group gets ready and stands in a line at the bottom of the final 1,000 metres (3,300 feet). I receive strict instructions from the lead guide about not going too fast. I am placed behind him at the front of our group. As we ascend very slowly up the scree-covered cone in zigzags we can see the headlights of lines of groups ahead and behind us. The pace is too slow for me, and I get very cold very quickly. The guide sees me shiver and hugs me at every stop, providing a little warming massage. We walk like little R2-D2s from *Star Wars*. Fifteen steps, turn left. Fifteen steps, turn right. Fifteen steps, turn left. Fifteen steps, turn right. The dance of steps and turns again puts me into a trance. It feels like the wind is blowing through my head. As it passes through, it takes the past with it and diffuses it into the dark space behind me. Emerging from every turn, I feel more and more just myself, without the layers of guilt, emotional dependency and attachments.

We pass people vomiting on the side of the trail; another, zombie-like, is being led down between two porters for safety. Nobody says much, saving all our energy for our legs. At some point I switch off my head torch and continue to shuffle in dark silence. We stop two-thirds of the way up before the bouldering section to catch our breath. I have an energy bar. I feel a strange warmth moving down my thigh and realise with alarm that my period has started unexpectedly. I inform the guide, and in total darkness, a discreet distance away from everybody, I attend to myself at 5,500 metres (18,000 feet). This proves to be challenging, but not impossible, as I had packed the right gear. I use bucketfuls of hand sanitizer to clean myself afterwards and swallow a large dose of painkillers to ward off any cramps.

My team is ready to move up. We separate somewhat. Bouldering is something that cannot be done in a line. Everybody selects what looks like a good strategy for him/her. Time has come to a standstill for us all. I have no idea how long the ascent has taken or what time it is. I don't feel tired at all, despite having had only three hours sleep in the evening. I am excited to be here and getting closer to the summit with every crawl and step. Again, the coolness of the stones calms any anxiety about the summit. I know I can get to the top now. It is just a matter of slow and patient progress. I like the smell of the stones as they are turned over and the little moisture that the cloud we are walking in gives us. The cloud makes it even colder, but I can now move more at my pace. That keeps me warm.

We get to Gilman's Point, where many people typically quit. It is still two hours to the summit, and some in the group are feeling really ill and tired. I can understand how easy it would be for those with bad headaches or nausea to turn around and return to the comforts of the camp. But I have no doubt that I want to keep going. We sit and drink hot tea. We miss out on seeing an amazing sunrise because of the cloud. It is still cold and almost dark. I take out my heavenly bitter raw chocolate with mint that I brought for moments of weakness. I indulge in every bite with immense pleasure. It secretes endorphins in my head and motivates me further.

The lead guide looks at me. 'Are you ready?'

Of course I am.

I get my own guide and we continue up. My guide says, 'You are very strong. I rarely see a white person walking so fast along the summit crater.' I accept the compliment, but don't get too confident — I am not at the summit yet. It starts snowing and the ground has become a bit slippery. I am cautious and grateful for my walking poles which help me to keep my balance. From the other direction I can see three silhouettes approaching in a strange embrace. It is a Japanese tourist being carried down between two porters. The guy seems unconscious. My guide exchanges some words with the others, and we press on.

The walk along the summit crater is a very deceiving gentle incline.

You keep seeing summit after summit, but frustratingly not the final one. Patience is rewarded when I finally see a wooden board appear through the falling snow and cloud 20 metres (65 feet) ahead. My guide and I smile at one another. I hand him my camera, he takes one picture ... and the film breaks! I have another roll in my pocket, so I impatiently rewind and load, by which time we are both frozen solid. He quickly takes a couple more pictures and then we start the brisk walk back. I don't even have time to reflect that I actually made it to the top. Somehow the rest of the team and I don't cross paths on my way back, but back at Gilman's I meet other groups I recognise and my new Brazilian friend. I tell them it is all doable, and to just keep walking. The mist is starting to lift, which will help everybody.

My guide lets me descend on my own after the boulder section while he goes back up to help others. Great! With every step down, and I am almost running by now, I feel warmer. I can see the camp and I think of the warm mug of tea waiting for me and the nap I can have while waiting for the others. The whole descent takes me well under two hours. I get to the kitchen tent to the welcome of the smiling faces of our cooks. They treat me like a queen and give me freshly roasted peanuts and loads of liquid. I take a couple of sandwiches in each hand and go to my tent to have a nap. Bliss.

I don't know how long I sleep for, but I feel very good when I wake up. It starts to dawn on me that I am safely back from the summit, and I feel ecstatic. Outside the tent I start jumping up and down and squealing with delight. Others have arrived back and had their snacks. We pack to go further down the mountain. I feel light. On the way to the last camp I jump up and down slightly with every step, like Pippi Longstocking. I am thrilled.

Before we leave Kibo Hut we hear a rumour about a death on the mountain, and two days later we learn that an American tourist and two local guides died on the other side of the mountain that night in a stone avalanche. All the Americans in our groups plan to call their families the moment they can get to a phone to reassure them that they are alive. I have no doubt that my mother will have heard the news and will pester those around her relentlessly to find out from the internet whether any Poles died.

The evening at the camp is very brief. People are tired after such a long day so we just eat and crash. Tomorrow is the last day of walking, and it will be through the forest.

Day Six

We get up to a day of fantastic sunshine again. I feel dizzy with delight as it dawns on me that I have made the first step in my long journey. After breakfast we have the porter tipping ceremony. There are strict instructions about how much money goes to whom: cook, assistant cook, porter, junior porter, senior porter, lead porter, and guides. And the list goes on. We need to pay around $150 each to cover it all. It seems a lot to me, but then I remember the watermelon, my private summit guide, and the congratulations when I got back. At least I know that those dollars will go directly to the people in front of me and ease their difficult lives. We also leave some unwanted clothing in the middle of the field for the porters to take. I start the home run. I have a smile on my face as I walk through the forest.

Where is Nigel in all this? Where is anybody else in my happiness? Right now there is nobody. Wow, so I can be happy, fulfilled and charged up on my own. I feel liberated. I am alone, but not lonely anymore. This is fantastic. I can control my own emotions.

At the celebration dinner we receive our certificates. Some of my group get very drunk and vow never to climb a mountain again.

✦✦✦

My euphoria is short-lived and my mood drops when I reach Zanzibar. I pace around the swimming pool until the sun has burnt my feet. I hate Nigel again for not being there. I fall tired onto a deck chair. Loneliness strikes hard. Here I am in a romantic resort with couples holding hands and canoodling, and I am alone. I decide to end our relationship, which I would communicate to Nigel at the end of January. But what do I do now? I don't like beach holidays and yet here I am on my own for four long days – I am stuck. I am tired, so I decide to have a massage, a good dinner and go to bed. Tomorrow is another day.

The next day I decide to take full responsibility for every decision, action and state of mind I experience. I decided to climb Kili on my own, and in so doing I have made my first step towards emotional independence. I need to carry on with the process.

***

On my return to London I notice that my friends are interested in the story and pictures, but nobody, except Nigel, goes deeper into my obvious excitement. I am disappointed that I fail to interest others in my heightened state of awareness. I feel as if I have been born again. When we are brought into the world as babies, we don't know that we are separate from our mothers. Like a child who starts pointing at herself and calling herself by her own name, on Kilimanjaro I feel that I learnt my own name again. I start to stand on my own.

This trip triggers in me self awareness and emotional independence. It takes four years to truly understand this and become sufficiently self-aware to prevent myself from being manipulated by others to feel emotions and feelings that I don't want to experience. The feeling of being in far greater control of my own body, mind and emotions is highly liberating.

CHAPTER 2

It's not that easy after all

June 2006
Europe, Mount Elbrus – 5,642 metres (18,510 feet)

I am still living in Moscow. I am on a kind of gardening leave after almost being made redundant. My American employers don't like the idea of my going to Elbrus, and say that going to the so-called war zone between Russia and Georgia is not a smart move for a company director. Well, I am going anyway.

I end my relationship with Nigel at the beginning of May. It happens on a platform at Waterloo station in London after a passionate night together. I am supposed to go to an interview that day. We both cry. Over the next year or so we practise parting a couple more times before separating for good eighteen months later.

A few weeks earlier I submitted my PhD dissertation, with great hopes of closing the study period of my life at least for a while. It has been six months since I completed Kili, but I keep up my exercise routine. Tasso, the Brazilian I met in Africa, who lost a bet with me about which is the highest mountain in Europe, is coming over to climb it with me. This is the cheapest of all my climbs, done with a local company called Pilgrim Tours. Thanks to my fluent Russian, I pay a local rate for the logistics as well. After the ease in which I climbed Kili, I am greatly encouraged, confident and … yes, … utterly ignorant. The mountain will teach me a lesson.

Day One

On my arrival at Sheremetyevo airport in Moscow I immediately spot Tasso with his daypack. We sit in a café and catch up on the six months since Kili. Then, one by one, we pick out of the crowd, recognisable from their attire and backpacks, all the other climbers who are on the same expedition. There are four Americans, an Englishman, a Canadian lady and a couple from France.

Oxana, the lead guide, joins us at Mineralnye Vody, the very small, regional airport closest to Mt. Elbrus. She checks our papers and it turns out that I don't have the right stamp in my passport. To avoid delaying the expedition, I need to slip unnoticed across the green border between two ex-Russian republics. I went local some time ago in terms of customs through living and working in Russia. The core strategy is that one does anything to beat the system. I casually walk around the airport buildings and through some shrubs with an assistant guide. I walk as if I do this every day of my life. My heart doesn't beat any faster, despite my being aware that I am doing something highly illegal. In the middle of the walk we stop for a pee. Then we keep going. After a thirty-minute walk we are reunited with the others in a little van beyond the airport.

We drive for a while and get to know each other. There is an immediate spark between Shaun, one of the Americans, and I – on the very last day of the trip in Moscow, Shaun and I snog briefly in a lift as I escort my group to a taxi.

We stop at a shop, which in true USSR style has virtually nothing to sell. This seems a very long way away from the splendid supermarkets in central Moscow. We arrive at a horrible concrete hotel next to a giant, working cable car. The hotel inside is well furnished with good kitchen facilities and a kind of club downstairs, where we later consume lots of vodka. Every room is decorated in a theme. I share a moon room with the Canadian lady. I sense Tasso's disappointment that we are not sharing a room. He says he didn't come here for a hike. *Hmm, I'm afraid I did.* This isn't the first or last time that my openness has been misinterpreted as an invitation.

We have a team talk. It is immediately apparent that the local guides don't speak good English and my foreign companions don't speak any Russian. So I am nominated as an official expedition interpreter. I enjoy this position as it gives me a lot of flexibility. Sometimes I am a local; other times a foreign tourist.

We set off to rent equipment we need. I need loads because I have been reluctant to invest in a lot of expensive kit before I was sure that high mountains are indeed for me. Somewhat to our surprise, the local shops are fantastically well equipped. Loaded up with our gear we go for a short practice walk, which turns out to be a five-hour hike. Nobody complains though.

Dinner is typical Caucasian cuisine with expertly prepared vegetable stews for the vegetarians (me) and grilled meat for the carnivores. As we talk I realise that I am the least experienced member on the team, which starts to dent my pre-trip confidence. I haven't climbed many mountains, yet some of these guys have done Aconcagua already. The French couple, who look like they are made of pure muscle, live in the Alps. My roommate severely criticises my equipment. Yes, my stuff is amateurish, but for now I am simply an amateur on a steep learning curve. Listening to the others' mountaineering stories, I realise how limited my track record is, and feel diminished.

Day Two

For our acclimatisation walk to Sheget, we take a ski lift halfway up the mountain and then walk. The weather is beautiful, with just a couple of fluffy clouds and a bright yellow sun. It is so comfortable in terms of temperature that we spend a good forty minutes eating, drinking and telling stories on the summit. I stick close to the guides to be better informed and translate for the others if need be. Shaun, who runs an entertainment company, turns out to be quite a comedian. We laugh our socks off when he sings, tells jokes, and turns every situation into a little comedy.

Returning, we slide down the snow at high speed on our backsides using our backpacks, plastic bags or waterproof trousers. This is a dangerous ploy before a major hike, but the words 'Russian' and 'safety' don't fit well together in a sentence. We have tremendous fun. Who would want to walk down anyway?

My dual role as local when I speak with the guides and foreign tourist provides me with insight from both worlds. It also stretches my sense of identity and allows me to question once again my own philosophy of life. The members in our group converse with the locals as much as possible. Tasso is a real rarity here because he is from faraway Brazil. People want to touch him for being so exotic. The three Americans from Los Angeles ('Ah, Hollywood', all the locals exclaim) are also in high demand.

We have an early dinner with plenty of freshly grilled lamb and local fish. There is no nightlife in the town, so we go to the downstairs club at our hotel and engage with locals who are celebrating somebody's birthday. We learn some local dances and a couple of words. I am very aware of an amazing mix of Mongolian, Tartar and Turkish blood surrounding us. The smiles are not white. They are perfect rows of solid gold or silver. Perhaps it's an interesting version of portable pension schemes. Everybody is very friendly toward our small group of foreigners. Most of these people don't even speak Russian but their own valley dialect. We dance away until midnight. As most of us have been to Kili before, we sing the 'Hakuna Matata'. Unlike my experience on Kili, our group bonding is fast and furious.

The others' descriptions of how fit they are worry me. Some do triathlons, some marathons, whereas I have just been to the gym. My roommate has just completed Mount McKinley and is en route to the Himalayas. I feel seriously out of place. Last time I was on a glacier was over two years ago. I can hardly remember anything we did. I think about my physical confidence on Kili and vow never again to be overly confident of my abilities. A growing anxiety makes me very focused.

My roommate turns out to be an awkward customer on the trip. On summit day, for example, she decides not to take overboots, which prevents her from making it to the summit. She then tries to go on her own the next night but turns around at the saddle, a bleak and windswept place approximately 200 vertical metres (600 feet) from the top. So, the most experienced person on the trip doesn't make it after all.

Day Three

Even in summer, Elbrus is a ski resort. We decide that, if we get a chance, we will ski after the summit. In the morning, we go up the cable car to the barrels, our accommodation. Six of us are packed into each one. Our barrels look and feel like giant metal petrol or gas storage devices lying on their sides on brick and wood trestles so they don't roll off the mountain. There are several small steps to get to the door and one window cut through what would be the bottom of the barrel. We have a separate barrel as kitchen and dining room. The lady who cooks for us manages to produce wonders on two tiny gas stoves above 3,000 metres (10,000 feet). We overeat, if that is at all possible on a mountain. The food is so good. There's always a soup for dinner and delicious, local, main courses. The toilet is the worst facility: a smelly, overflowing hole in the ground behind a wooden door.

We go for a very short walk just to get used to the white snow, the crampons, and our surroundings. I bless the phenomenon called 'muscle memory' or even 'body memory.' Even though I have not been on snow for a while, I seem to be able to walk intuitively with wide strides on crampons and grab the ice axe in the right way. I have no problem organising myself.

The contrast between yesterday's greenery and today's whiteness is stunning. I stare into the distance of the mountain range and can see Georgian valleys bathed in sun. I imagine people growing vines for their famous wines, which are currently embargoed in Russia for political reasons. I turn to see the twin summits of Elbrus, like the humps of a camel, luxuriating in the sun, blue sky and summer. The air is clean and sharp. Elevated to serious altitude too quickly, I have a headache, but try to breathe deeply, appreciate where I am, and slow down all my movements in order to adapt. In front of the barrels we can see the path we hope to take tomorrow for a proper acclimatisation walk.

Dinner is superb. We start calling our cook 'Babushka', Russian for grandmother, because she looks ancient. She is very kind and looks after us like our own grandmas would. Due to my Russian abilities, she spoils me rotten. She even ends up calling me 'Ań', which indicates a close relationship in Russia.

The time when we are not walking on this mountain flies by with talking, singing, doing silly competitions we invent for ourselves and, of course, playing cards. The team has divided into two distinct groups. Myself, Tasso and the Americans are in one, while the French contingent and Tony from the United Kingdom are in the other. We discuss why we do all this walking up and down hills. We talk at length about the Seven Summits. It seems that I am the only one among us who, very shyly, is considering it. The others say anything is possible – you just have to buy some equipment, book the trips, have some determination, get fit, get lucky with the weather, get rich, and take six months to a year off. And anybody can probably do it. *Yeah, right.* On average, it takes people eight years to do all the Seven Summits. It costs in total well over $150,000 and means you actually spend six months on various mountains. It takes over 100 hours of flying to get to those places. I will certainly take it step by step.

Despite all the comforts, food and proper hydration, my slight headache has by now become a slow, regular hammering, although it does not alarm me at this stage. When I lie down the room is spinning. I want to vomit, so I prepare a plastic bag just in case. Before falling asleep I think about what a climber from another group told me today. Around a month ago there was a terrible mountaineering accident here. Eleven people died in a single day of climbing to the summit. It seems their death was simply due to their determination to be on the summit on a specific day of the year, World War II victory day. However, the weather was bad that day. I wonder if I should share this story with my expedition companions or withhold the information for now. There is no weather forecast here – we rely on mobile phone conversations that our guides have with guys watching TV back at the hotel. I decide not to share.

Day Four

I wake up with the same headache as last night. I let the team know that I might not be the best companion today. I receive 'get well' hugs. We gear up, have a mighty breakfast, then set off to Pastuhova Rocks at 4,600 metres (15,000 feet) for an acclimatisation hike. I am slow, and the others seem to be running past me.

Oh, sugar. Am I really up for this? Perhaps I should go back home and take up knitting instead of traversing a glacier with mostly rental equipment, afraid that it is too steep and icy.

Plus, the elements are testing me, as if throwing down a gauntlet. The weather is simply atrocious with high winds, snowfall, and thick, grey clouds covering the horizon. It is unimaginably cold. The path is extremely steep and we are not roped to each other. I do a mental simulation of what it would mean if I fell. I turn around and see a long path back to the barrels at the end of a cliff that is 2,000 metres high (6,561 feet). So, if I fell, I would slide down, gathering speed up to the barrels. Then I would be catapulted up into the air and come back down to earth, maybe back in Moscow. I become scared and tense up. I start noticing how fragile my crampon grip is. I am basically perched on twelve sharp spikes of steel on each foot, which are barely penetrating the ice. They just scratch the surface and suspend me between the grey sky and the blue ice. I concentrate on every step. I listen to the crunching ice underneath me and carefully craft every step from now on.

Coming up to the halfway point, I realise I am drenched with sweat underneath all my layers. We stop for drinks and I start to tremble with the cold. My synthetic underwear is not keeping me warm. In a desperate attempt to continue the climb, I strip off from the waist up in minus 25 degrees Celsius (-12 Fahrenheit), put on my icebreaker shirt, put the other layers back on, and close my eyes. I pray that I will get the feeling back in my toes, fingers and the skin that was exposed. Oxana gives me her mitts and turns around to keep going as if there is nothing to worry about. I slowly start feeling warmer and start the slog again, which lasts for two more hours. We stop above Pastuhova Rocks. Shaun has totally frozen fingers. The team gathers around him and he sticks his hands underneath his companion's armpits, the warmest easily available place. I am too cold to wait for everybody.

Oxana shows us how to walk on crampons downhill. We take big steps, lock the knees, and use only the heels on such a steep slope. I follow her, but she soon turns around to order the others down and tells me to keep going. I am on my own. The wind is howling, and I am still cold despite being totally wrapped up with goggles, face mask, and every dry article of clothing I have. I speed up my steps with renewed confidence in my ability to descend without killing myself.

While on my own, I reflect. Getting help from Oxana and seeing Shaun being looked after so caringly takes me back to Nepal in 1994 where I was trekking with my boyfriend. One day when we were drying our T-shirts on the bushes, a skinny local dressed in rags walks by and asks us to give him one shirt. I look at my boyfriend, and he says no. The guy asks us again and again, but we stick to our decision. He just wanted one T-shirt. It took me years to forgive myself for being so damn selfish and point-blank stupid then. I reconcile that the current me, regardless of my companion's view, would have shared. I am relieved.

I also reflect on myself in comparison to my group in terms of experience, equipment, pace, preparedness, and level of determination. Everybody has such different histories, legacies, life plans and ambitions. I tell myself that I should not be comparing myself to anybody. I had a headache in the morning, but I still went. I got very cold, but remedied the situation. I did not know how to walk safely on crampons, but now I do. I need to stick to my guns here, no matter what people around me may think, say, or do. I need to be true to myself.

Back at the barrels, after having stripped off all wet clothes, I put on some wonderfully warm, dry, woollen layers and dive into my sleeping bag. The feeling of getting warm again after having been chilled to the bone is fantastic. You can feel every inch of yourself coming back to life, bit by bit, as if each cell has been in suspended animation due to the freeze, as if holding one's breath, anticipating the possibility of breathing again. My cheeks are amazingly red. I wriggle like a caterpillar in my sleeping bag to warm myself up and eagerly chew on dry fruit. The simple pleasures of life.

I examine my wardrobe as I unpack my gear. I conclude that wool and silk are the warmest fabrics. Then there's cotton and linen, but cotton is not suitable for high exertion. I wonder why that is. I imagine how the different fabrics are produced. I imagine the warm balls of cotton on a sunny slope in some country; I see a smiling sheep in New Zealand keeping cool in the summer and warm in the winter; and a snug silkworm in its cocoon. And the synthetic stuff just gets made in a factory. But where would the synthetic stuff derive its warmth from in the first place, being man-made? I get it. From now on my wardrobe on the mountain and elsewhere would be all natural and, ideally, organic.

Day Five

For the last several days we have been deliberating whether, on the summit day, to take a snow-cat up to 4,200 metres (13,800 feet) and from there walk the next vertical 1,300 metres (4,300 feet), or walk straight from the barrels, which would prolong the trek by two to three hours. We finally decide on the quicker, snow-cat option. The barrels are too low to properly acclimatise for the height of the summit, so we hope to get to the summit and back down again before altitude sickness kicks in.

Today is glacier training day, where we try to master the skills of self-arrest and self-rescue. It is tremendous fun. I forget about my sore head for a while. With the fresh air and being high on the mountain, I feel fully alive again with lots of energy and a huge smile. The mountainous horizon is liberating, beautiful and slightly intimidating. We spend the afternoon resting, eating and playing poker. We will go for the summit overnight as the weather looks good.

Right after dinner I get so anxious that I call Nigel, even though we have not spoken for over a month since our breakup. He is very patient, listens carefully, and tries to give me some advice, but I don't really feel any better. That only reinforces my determination not to rely on someone else to fix my own emotions. I need to work through my own fears and anxieties.

I feel as if I have a fever, alternating between hot and cold without knowing why. Perhaps my body is just coming to terms with the altitude. This is very different from my perfect conditioning on Kili. The thought of climbing the Seven Summits feels totally impossible at this stage. I am convinced that Aconcagua should be next because I have no love of the cold, the snow and the wet – i.e. Denali. Aconcagua is almost 7,000 metres (23,000 feet) high. How will I acclimatise to that? I'm not sure right now. However, with every step I take on this mountain I become increasingly confident with the skills needed; I therefore decide to aim for Denali twelve months from now.

Before we retire to our barrels, our guide tells us not to take more than half a litre (one pint) of water and one snack for the summit attempt! We calculate the amount of hours of walking ahead of us and totally ignore her advice.

I have a stomach upset, so when we get up at three forty-five in the morning I lose my whole breakfast before even starting the summit day. We start the climb below the Pastuhova Rocks. There is no snow at all; it is all clear, blue ice. The slope is steep, and the whole thing is very difficult for me. I stubbornly place one foot in front of the other. I switch off my head torch because a fantastic moon illuminates the way. The air is clear and very cold. I cannot wait for the sun to come up. After two hours of very slow progress, we get to snow-covered ice that makes it a bit easier, but it is still physically very demanding for me. We come to a long traverse bearing right. The sun is shining down on us, but it is still cold. I don't remove my goggles and mask. I feel like a horse, patiently plodding my way up. I see with some surprise that on the traverse I have managed to catch up with the others, although I was really slow on the way up. We reach the saddle. Tony is vomiting violently. We give him water, but it comes out instantly. Oxana takes him on a short rope because he insists on going up. I feel good, apart from the steady drum of my headache, which I have got used to. Luckily it is not increasing. I am just so slow going up compared with the other guys (the runners). The proud and physically confident person on Kili has gone. I take every step carefully, aware what a tremendous effort each step is.

The wall in front of us is close to vertical and looks very daunting, but the good news is that it is the last 200 vertical metres (656 feet) to climb. I see Denise (one of the Americans) peeing while standing up. I am impressed and ask her how that is humanly possible, and she shows me her funnel contraption.

Right! I have so much more to learn!

We start our ascent of the wall after fifteen minutes. If we have too many people with altitude sickness too soon, we won't be able to reach the summit. We are not roped again. I squeeze my ice axe in the left hand and try not to lose balance to the right because it would mean a nice speedy slide back to the rocks of the saddle. This part is particularly slow for all of us. After an excruciating hour, although in tremendous weather, I reach the summit plateau. I can see the summit around thirty minutes from me. I slog along, wishing I had my poles, which we left at the saddle to help my legs. My head-ache is so vivid that I cannot think, so I switch off everything but my legs and keep going. Some of the group is still behind me, which buoys me somewhat.

As I approach the summit pyramid I hear people cheering for me and clapping. They come off the summit to line up with me, and we all complete the last ten steps together. That feels good. I am being carried on the team morale and strength. Thanks guys. Everybody poses for pictures. I look around and see the world at my feet. Fluffy clouds laze around. There's almost no wind. I breathe in the stillness, the peaks of the range and the clouds. I am deeply grateful for the sun and the people around me. I am part of an international community on the highest peak of Europe, which we have to ourselves. But it is cold, and when I look at those photos later, I see that only the tip of my nose was visible. It burns badly.

We start the descent. Tasso is swaying a bit from altitude sickness. Shaun and I take him between the two of us. It is amazing how my tiredness and headache instantly vanishes when I need to help another. Tasso cannot operate his ice axe and seems to have forgotten how to walk on crampons. We give him a quick reminder and keep descending. However, I realise that if Tasso makes one mistake, we will both fall. I examine my thoughts to establish whether I am really ready to help him without limits. The answer is *yes!* If I have a chance to help him at my own risk, I will. Going down the wall, again with no ropes, is as scary as going up, so we progress slowly down to the saddle. I don't think Tony is conscious anymore. He wants to do the Seven Summits. I don't think I would even try knowing that my body doesn't acclimatise well.

At the saddle where we pick up our poles, Oxana starts deliberating which way we should go down. The left of the mountain is ice that is as smooth as glass, which we negotiated going up. Going there now with the sun, which has polished the ice even more, is unappealing. On the other hand, on the right side of the mountain there are crevasses. The guide starts to the right. Again, we are not roped. All of us follow suit. Tony is catching his crampons every step and looks totally unstable. If Oxana was not as strong as she is, he would have fallen down a long time ago. We occasionally pass over small crevasses. I learn to recognise snow bridges over deep spaces. I like my new skill as a crevasse spotter. We need to meander a bit to avoid a couple of bigger ones. The American contingent mumbles that it is unacceptable that we are not roped in such terrain. And where are the ropes? Well, we just have one. After an hour, I can see the barrels. They are small dots at the moment, but that comforts my body and mind. We are getting closer with every step.

Just keep going.

Mid-slope, we witness a horrifying scene on the left-hand side of the mountain. A person has fallen and is speeding down toward the Pastuhova Rocks. Everybody freezes and just waits for the inevitable. I feel cold sweat streaming down my back and have tears in my eyes. I dig my crampons into the snow for him or her as if creating a connection between us to stop the body in flight. The little silhouette continues to slide. The silence is unbelievable, as if the whole world has stopped in its tracks to witness the event. Suddenly, the body stops perhaps 50 metres (150 feet) from the black spots of the rocks. We can see the rest of the team running down, mindless of their own safety, to get to their companion. We are in shock, but with two team members of our own in questionable condition, we need to keep descending. After a while, we turn down at an angle so we are unable to see what is happening on the other side.

I realize now that it is not important whether I am slow, fast, first, or last on the mountain... or in my city life for that matter. I realize how much I love and appreciate life, just breathing every day, seeing things, and experiencing the good and the bad. I appreciate people around me and the sun, wind and snow. I feel deep gratitude for everything. The world gives us a chance every day, and I am going to make the most of it.

We reach the snow-cat tracks and take off our crampons. I help Tasso, and we start walking faster. After an hour we reach the barrels. I sit on my bed. Tasso is next to me and we are hugging. The others are doing the same, satisfying the need for human contact after the tremendous physical and emotional effort of the last 24 hours. We sit in silence for a while and then take off our mountain gear. It's a great feeling.

Meanwhile, Babushka has cooked up a chicken soup for dinner. What else would you need after a day like today? The good mood returns on the news that the person who fell has survived and is joining us for dinner. When he joins us he is still in shock, black and blue from bruises and with most of his fingernails and two fingers broken through his down mitts as a legacy of his fight for life. We hug this total Scottish stranger and bless the world for saving him. The feeling of camaraderie is immense.

He recalls the accident: 'I was falling. I was totally aware that if I hit the rocks, I was gone. I could see my daughter. She was shouting "Daddy, Daddy!" I somehow turned around, dug the heels of my crampons into the ice and snow, and stopped.' He is crying. We are quiet and humbled.

My first shower is heavenly. I play with the water like a child, wishing I had some rubber ducks to entertain me. My roommate seems unhappy that I made it and she didn't. I organise my 'unprofessional' gear, feeling enormous satisfaction at my achievement, while my roommate – this strong and wilful woman who is on her way to climb a peak of 8,000 metres (26,000 feet) – sits on her bed in silence.

Day Six

We ski the whole of the next day because the trip has finished early. Tasso experiences his first time on skis and we have great fun. The celebration dinner is very Russian style with amazing amounts of vodka and food. Later, in the disco, I take my first belly dancing classes from a very free-thinking woman, Molly, a teacher from Carolina. I like how she moves in a very feminine fashion, but has just climbed the same mountain as me. We are engaged in a very deep conversation.

She asks me, 'What would you want your obituary to say when you die? What are the three most important things to you?'

I say, 'Learning, human interaction and nature'.

I still haven't written my obituary. Perhaps one day.

★★★

Back in Moscow most of the people from my team stay on the floor in my flat for a week. I give Andrei, my trainer, a big thank-you hug because I have no muscle pains whatsoever. The only part of me suffering badly is the burnt tip of my nose.

I return from Elbrus with greater knowledge of myself. I learned there that if I seem less experienced or slower than the rest of the team at the outset or any part of a trip, this does not reflect on my ability to keep going or succeed. I shared a room with the most experienced person on the expedition. I was the least experienced and slowest and yet I still made it in good time and good health to the top and back. My initial loss of self-confidence, caused by comparing myself with those around me, was misplaced. Everyone has different experiences and different strengths: mine are determination and willpower. I later learn that success in mountaineering depends up to 75 percent on mental attitude and only 25 percent on physical abilities.

If you compare yourself to somebody else, your satisfaction or otherwise lasts only as long as the object of your comparison is there. When the object of your comparison disappears, your opinion of yourself changes, but in fact you have not changed at all. Comparing yourself to others makes you dependent on them. You will strive to have the same type of clothes, figure, professional position, stature, house, spouse, kids and so on. I conclude that the only useful way of assessing your own progress through all aspects of life is by looking back and seeing how far you have moved from your starting point.

CHAPTER 3

Hard work can be so much fun!

January 2007
South America, Aconcagua –
6,964 metres (22,848 feet)

THREE months before my expedition to Aconcagua, I move from Moscow to London where I start a new job in an investment bank. My first two ongoing projects to run are in Moscow and Mexico, which means being on a plane constantly for seventy-two days. I go to the gym at every opportunity in every hotel I stay in. I had warned my employers that I would be taking time off during Christmas for three weeks and then again in June 2007, if I dare to book Denali. This is nonnegotiable for me. My boss has no problems with this, provided I deliver on my work commitments. Thank you, Franco!

My journey to my next mountaineering venture starts at three o'clock on a Saturday morning on my arrival back from a work-related trip to Moscow, where I had been babysitting our first-ever trade in the new bank there – a very exciting project indeed. I repack my bags for a four p.m. flight to Argentina the following day. On the way, I have to go to the office, send emails and reports that I completed on the flight from Moscow, and leave a bag with my office clothes and a laptop with a colleague who will take it to Mexico City for me. I will be going straight from my climb to set up the operations department in our local branch there.

I'm really looking forward to this mountain. It's a trekking route, which I like the most. It's not technical, but high at almost 7,000 metres (23,000 feet). This is my altitude test. If I can acclimatise well to that height, then I might have a chance at Everest one day. I know the most difficult part of it is the last 200 vertical metres (656 feet), called, rather romantically, the Canaletta. It is a steep, scree-covered slope. If you walk in the middle of the couloir, you are risking too much. At the bottom of the Canaletta is the psychologically weak point, where most people give up. I have been rehearsing in my head how I will deal with this – by not looking up at the challenge, but just putting one leg in front of the other until there is nowhere else to go. The summit success rate is around 38 percent, mainly due to the bad and capricious weather. Only eight percent of women get to the top on the first attempt. I am going with Exodus again because my experience with them on Kili was excellent.

Day One

I get to London Bridge with two backpacks. The larger one is 18 kilograms (39 pounds), which is almost too much for me. After having missed one train to Gatwick, I need to wait for thirty minutes. I just sit there on the platform because I don't dare to take my burden off. I am glad we can use porters for at least part of Aconcagua for some of the luggage. The load on my back slows my pace significantly.

After sleeping through all fifteen hours of the various flights, we land in Buenos Aires. We have a quick tour around the city with the main attractions being the house of Eva Peron, the old colonial part of the city, and then lunch at the oldest, most amazing-looking café. Most of us have prosciutto crudo with melon and superb local bread. I settle for some smelly cheese, which is delicious. I have another good night's sleep. I am certainly on the road to recovery after my work marathon.

Day Two

We fly to Mendoza, the wine country. My group drink alcohol, whereas I stick to my tradition of being a teetotaller before every trip. Among the team of twelve there are eleven Brits and me. I am relieved to see another female to share a tent with, Ann from Scotland. We become very close. We have similar equipment, share a similar sense of humour, and are very down-to-earth. We become like twins on the trip, sharing everything from life stories to food, water and tiredness. We are both trying to figure out the relationship side of our lives. During our trip we have a serious conversation over who would be best suited to one of our team members as a potential boyfriend. We decide that Ann is the right person. Three years later I am dancing at their wedding in Scotland.

I have my first-ever equipment check, which involves unpacking everything and a guide going through the pile on the bed. I am responding to questions on my gear strategies. This annoys me because I had packed everything beautifully at home, but Elan, our lead guide, insists on seeing everything. This time I have invested in a state-of-the-art expedition sleeping bag because I get so cold. I have bought a professional down jacket for freezing evenings and the summit day. I have also purchased a great rain jacket by Arc'teryx, which apparently looks quite sexy on me. Elan instructs me to save a clean pair of socks just for the summit day and to have my favourite bite of food for the extra effort on the summit night. I oblige. With a rather long list of things still to rent and buy, we go shopping. We also purchase our individual climbing permits, which means parting with another $330.

During lunch we discover dulce de leche, a kind of condensed milk with toffee or caramel. This stuff has an impressive calorie count per 100 grams. We pack loads for the mountain. During the trip, most of us, including me, lose around 8 kilograms (18 pounds), but Ann, who falls in love with dulce de leche, sees no weight loss. To consume it on the mountain, we freeze the sachets outside our tents and lick it like ice cream.

The local restaurants serve huge steaks, which my companions heartily consume, washed down with lots of local wine. Being a vegetarian I choose salad, though the concept of salad doesn't really exist in Argentina. It usually involves a plate of disassociated veggies with olive oil and balsamic vinegar on the side. The taste, however, is fantastic. The tomatoes actually taste of tomatoes and are packed with succulent flesh. The cucumber smells fresh and is moist and crunchy. I indulge big time.

I draw close to three other expedition members. One is Dan, who later marries Ann. I love his sense of humour and his strong Welsh accent, especially when he pronounces 'arse' with a very strong, rolled RRRRR.

Ian and Chris, father and son, are also great fun, and very masculine. It is so great to watch a fully supportive and respectful relationship between proud fatherhood and strong youth. I contrast this with my dysfunctional family, with its masks and lack of mutual acceptance. Around my family I learnt to cover up my true personality so well that, at some point along the way, I lost the knowledge of who I really was. I believe that is true for many people – through life we are trained to behave in a certain way that is socially acceptable, and through this we develop a cult of average behaviour.

Day Three

We travel to Los Penitentes by bus along a bumpy road. That is it for transportation. From now on, we walk. We go for an acclimatisation walk for three and a half hours. It is pleasantly warm. We have a three-course meal with a heap of ice cream for dessert. We start talking about life and through this the team bonds. We invent nicknames for everybody. There is Scrooge, Double D (two down jackets at once, not a bra measure), Wind-suit and Burberry, a very posh guy with perfectly matching kit. I'm Giggles, and I certainly live up to it. They are all very fit, and their talk of marathon runs and mountaineering in Scotland leaves me feeling weak and underprepared once again.

Day Four

We rise early to a wonderful breakfast. We hold an international ping-pong tournament and I end up beating Chris, which almost results in a Polish-English conflict – being a 'bloke' and more than ten years younger than me, he doesn't appreciate being beaten. In the early afternoon we leave the comforts of civilisation behind us and start walking to Confluencia, our first camp at 3,390 metres (11,122 feet). At the gate of the park, the team is given loo bags, all three of them. We need to bring them back nicely filled up.

That will be interesting. Twelve people sharing three bags.

The path is comfortable, and the day is easy. We walk through the sites

44

where they filmed *Seven Years in Tibet*. The camp is very exposed to wind, but has a shower box, proper toilets, and great eating tents for the whole team. In the evening the wind picks up. During the night a sandstorm hits us, and the elements keep waking me up, despite the earplugs. The tent is no longer stable. If I were not inside, it would have blown away. Everything moves and makes an incredibly loud noise. Waves of sand hit the walls and then roll down as if it were raining. The sand gets everywhere, into my eyes, mouth, ears, and sleeping bag. I end up wearing my sunglasses and buff over my face. I sleep on my belly with my face squeezed into my inflatable closed cell pad. Apart from that, what a great night.

I need to figure out how to warm up my sleeping bag before I get into it, without losing so much energy myself. It is freezing every evening. I am surprised. I have so much down, but only if I ignite it with my own warmth does it provide any warmth back. Reciprocity theory at its best!

Day Five

Today is acclimatisation day, all eight hours of it! We walk up to a lookout at 4,080 metres (13,385 feet). Again, the walking is easy, just a matter of keeping on plodding for me. We get to the end of the path where the view onto the north face of Aconcagua is stunning. This side is the most challenging climb. Only a handful of people have ever climbed it, and there are still those unlucky ones stuck to the wall of ice from Japanese and Brazilian teams. The wall is amazing: 3,000 metres (9842 feet) high and 4,500 metres (14,762 feet) wide. It has a vertical rock face covered in ice and snow. This has no attraction for me at all. I intend to stick to the easiest route I can, as it is already challenging enough and none of the peaks I climb are a goal in themselves, but rather all part of my life journey.

We create a picnic with all our sandwiches in a central place: the simplest sandwiches taste so good, little carrot sticks are a delicacy, and we cherish the simplest warm cup of Lipton tea. I, like most of us, have a slight headache on the way down, and a somewhat sore throat. I get a stomach bug and lose my lunch on the way back. I drink 4 litres (1 gallon) of water a day, hoping it is enough to stay hydrated.

Some say the Andes are not very beautiful and the Aconcagua climb is not very rewarding when it comes to views. It is totally barren with almost no vegetation, but for me the combination of glaciers, colourful rock formations, valleys and waterways look absolutely amazing set against the background of a perfectly blue sky.

Dan, Ann and I break from the main team and run down. We drink lots of water, have snacks and toast, and go to bed for a recovery afternoon snooze. Dinner is wonderful, with two bowls of soups each and pasta. Somebody puts on an iPod with little speakers and the disco starts. We play cards passionately, we laugh and spirits are high. Chris teaches us a 'villagers, police, and Mafia' game. To defend one's position, it is necessary to lie or invent false personalities. After losing numerous times, I am glad to discover that I cannot lie with a straight face. I don't want to lie anymore.

Day Six

Today is a rest day, with sun and blue sky. I take a shower in the morning ($6), possibly the quickest ever in my life. I do my washing and proudly hang everything on my pegless line, which makes the washing immune to wind. Things dry in less than thirty minutes. For lunch, we have fresh vegetables and grilled eggplant. I am in heaven. In the afternoon we go for a short walk, during which we discover the remains of some mountain animal. We spend hours trying to reconstruct it. The pelvic bone of the poor thing becomes our team's totem and ends up going to the top of the mountain with us. My headache has gone but I have a strange new ailment to take its place. Due to the sand getting everywhere the night before, I have a belly button infection that is bleeding and painful, made more uncomfortable by my pants and the rucksack belt pressing against it. After carefully disinfecting the whole area, I consider taking antibiotics. I decide to wait a day but in the meantime I apply some antibiotic cream and an antiseptic plaster. It heals within two days. That would be the weirdest mountaineering injury ever. Did you suffer from blisters? No. Did you break a leg? No. Why didn't you make it then? I couldn't continue the climb because of my belly button. Yeah, right!

I realise I have stopped thinking about work, therefore my external shutters must have kicked in. The internal part of me is being exposed to the elements of real life again, and I am delighted. My thoughts are drawn back to Nigel – we had hooked up again in New York for a day and night. I don't seem to be able to let go of him and I simply don't understand why. Ann has a similar problem with her boyfriend, so we analyze every angle of both relationships. We can each see clearly why the other should not be with her guy, but we are unable to see our own situations clearly.

It is too hot and dusty to sleep in the tent during the day. Some of us develop bad chest coughs due to the dry air and omnipresent sand. Thankfully, I remain immune to that. I snooze on the dining table, with others on chairs and the floor. Somebody is reading, somebody is playing cards, somebody is listening to music, and others just gaze into the distance and reflect. We go to bed early because tomorrow is a big day. We are moving up to base camp.

Day Seven

We set off at eight, just after the sun hits the path. It is very windy. I have my new super jacket on, and I am totally covered up, with my sunglasses on and my nose and mouth behind a buff. I have terrible diarrhoea, which means I have no choice but to stop frequently, hide behind rocks, and then catch up. The path is tricky because we are walking on a vast riverbed, which becomes a huge river in the spring. I take care not to twist my ankle. We need to cross small streams by jumping over them or climbing higher. I get weaker with every hour because no food stays inside me. Today we need to walk for eight hours and I am last to every stop. Moreover, my belly button still hurts, but I have no alternative than to keep going. At the last stop I am swaying somewhat. I take two Imodium tablets, which don't help at all. We have a steep 200 vertical metres (656 feet) of zigzagging to go. I start counting steps but lose count at a hundred. I start again. Through the rhythm of steps and listening to my heavy breathing, I numb my perception and self-pity. I notice that if I don't apply any judgment to my situation, it becomes just a situation. It is not bad or very bad. It just is. It seems an excellent recipe for just accepting whatever happens and responding to whatever life brings.

I finally see the sign for base camp, and I am so relieved. I hug the little wooden plank with joy. My tent has already been set up. Today I am certainly the weakest link in the team. Inside my new fragile home, I unpack, blow up my pad, and collapse inside my sleeping bag. The others decide between themselves where to set up more tents, but I am sound asleep by then. I am truly exhausted, possibly for the first time in my life. Somebody brings me hot plain rice some time later. I polish off the bowl and go back to sleep, having drunk another bucketful of warm water. My thoughts meander to tomorrow, a rest day, when I can gather enough strength to walk the day after. With that, I fall fast asleep again.

Day Eight (Christmas Eve)

I awake to both good news – a cured stomach – and to bad news – a head full of cold. I have breakfast along with honey and lemon before going back to my tent, the temple of healing, where I stay in my sleeping bag and sweat the cold out. I try to visualise myself being healthy and walking tomorrow, with a heavy backpack, up to Canada Camp, 700 vertical metres (2,300 feet) up the mountain. Right now it hardly seems possible.

On all my trips I take pieces of equipment and clothing that I don't use any longer but are in a good enough condition to pass on to the locals. This time is no different. I hand over a fantastic fleece, which I hardly used because I don't like pink, and a Patagonia wind and rain breaker. Luck has it that my gear goes to the main cook, a stunning Argentinean girl, who cooks hearty pizzas and home-baked cakes at 4,250 metres (14,000 feet). As I go to the kitchen one more time to get yet more lemon and honey, she is proudly wearing my gear. She knows it is from me, so my pleading eyes are met with her grateful eyes for my donation. She hugs me, sits me down by the warm stove and gives me hot fresh tea with lots of lemon and a jar of honey. I sit Turkish style on a chair, enjoying the warmth and great flavour. We cannot really communicate other than by looking at each other and smiling. I eat a garlic sandwich that she has made to aid my recovery. Touched by her kindness, I leave the kitchen tent, where visits by tourist climbers are strictly forbidden, with tears in my eyes. I sleep most of the afternoon in my tent. In the evening I sit alone in a corner of the dining tent.... strangely nobody wants to sit next to the garlic muncher.

In the early evening I call my mother on a satellite phone in the communication tent and wish her a 'Merry Christmas', as the Poles celebrate on Christmas Eve. It's the most expensive phone call I have ever made in my life.

Through the receiver I can hear the bustling of Christmas preparations and carols being played in the background. The whole family is gathered. They will soon sit down to dinner, followed by presents, midnight mass, and then they will start eating all over again at two in the morning – I have done that so many times. Some grab the receiver and shout 'Good luck' and 'Wesołych Świąt' (Polish for 'Merry Christmas') I tell my mum that her handwritten letter, which I received just before leaving for Argentina, brought tears to my eyes. Attached to the letter, the white, fragile *opłatek*[1] we traditionally share around the Christmas table as a sign of peace takes me back to my childhood. I feel very close to all of them.

My mother asks me to describe where I am. I do. There's silence.

She asks, 'Do you like it there?'

With all the energy and enthusiasm one can put in two words through a crackling phone line, I say, 'Oh, yes!'

She is silent for a while. 'All the best, and come back safely.'

It's as if, for the first time, she has fully accepted my choice in life, to be on a freezing mountain far away from home. I am happy I made that call and grateful for being accepted. As I return to my tent I consider how far I have travelled from home, not only physically, but mentally, professionally, traditionally and culturally. I conclude that I don't belong to that community in Poland anymore. I cut the umbilical cord a long time ago.

I sleep like a log.

Day Nine (Christmas Day)

I wake up feeling well, and express my gratitude with a little shout and lots of giggling to make sure everybody knows. Before carrying half the load up to Canada Camp, we go to the base camp doctor, who studiously measures the oxygen saturation in our blood, pulse and heart rate. He listens to our lungs and gives me and some of my team the go-ahead.

To others, he says seriously, 'No coffee and no salt. Come back tomorrow for a recheck.'

Hmm, so it is quite a serious height we are doing.

---

[1] A holy wafer – Catholic symbol of new life and peace

After breakfast, we pose for a team photo, and then off we go. My backpack is a manageable 12 kilograms (26 pounds). The 700 metre (2,300 feet) vertical ascent is via zigzags on stone steps. It takes around three and a half hours including all the breaks we take. The pace is slow, thankfully. My shoulders hurt. I am shaking from the effort, excitement and cold. At the top I change my sweaty shirt at camp and snuggle into warm, dry layers. We shelter behind some stone walls and have lunch, which tastes fantastic. We are in good spirits and perform a little celebration dance and a high altitude group hug. After a quick and uneventful descent we have Christmas dinner of turkey with baked potatoes and tiramisu for dessert, along with a local wine. What a feast, and what a wonderful way to recover after a hard day. Tomorrow is the last planned rest day on this expedition.

The day after will be a test for me. I have not paid for porterage ($550) above base camp so I can establish whether I can carry heavy loads at high altitude. This will help me determine whether I can attempt Denali, my next planned mountain.

Day Ten

It's a rest day. I go to the hostel, a rather unpleasant concrete bunker, to shower. Then I sit in a kind of restaurant eating several cheesecakes and wait for the others to make their calls on a pay phone. I call Nigel. I want to tell him so much but don't want to just ramble on as usual. Anyway, it is good to hear his voice and affection. I do miss his warmth and understanding. We are very close indeed. Walking to and from the hostel, we have to gingerly cross a giant field of Penitentes, hard snow formations made by the snagging wind and sand. They form amazing shapes of birds, planes, and pine trees on the top of giant hard, snow stalagmites. On reflection, Penitentes look like an army of Ku Klux Klan dressed in traditional white with spiky hats on, or the penitents walking the streets of Spain during Holy Week as penance for their yearly sins. Perhaps in this cold, treacherous environment we are also being purified from our sins.

In the afternoon, we observe the helicopter evacuation of sick climbers. We also meet an American team, a father and daughter trying to climb this peak for the third time. They have slept in an oxygen chamber back home to aid acclimatisation. They are very determined to do it because their mother died here a couple years ago. He is seventy-three; later we learn that they succeed and get a helicopter ride back to Mendoza from base camp.

There is also camp maintenance going on today involving lots of helicopters flying back and forth as they take away the toilet barrels and drop food supplies. As the evening progresses, we have another laughter-filled night play cards, telling stories and tango dancing. I teach my team the polka, my national dance. Outside the tent the landscape is magical. All the mess and kitchen tents are lit up inside, forming domes of light of different colours against the black sky and rock. Some are blue, others white, red or green.

Day Eleven

Today we start the climb to the top. We put on our double plastic boots, which weigh a ton and are basically like skiing boots. They are warm, but totally stiff. We will do the whole ascent twice: first moving up a cache to the next camp and then moving the camp. We go to Canada where we cached two days ago. My backpack is 17 kilograms (37 pounds), and it is a burden from the very beginning. I am very slow. It reminds me of Elbrus on summit day when I was last. I wasn't a hero then, and I am not one now.

I can hear David behind me, breathing in my ear constantly, 'You can do it. Keep going. You are doing great.' That mantra helps me. I start repeating it to myself. It lightens my step, but I don't dare to take off my pack at any time. I am too scared that I won't be able to put it back on. I finally stagger the last few steps into camp. I throw off my burden and support myself on a rock to catch my breath. That was a much harder day than I anticipated. There is an enormous difference between carrying up to 12 kilograms (26 pounds) and over 15 kilograms (33 pounds). For Denali, I will have to train bloody hard in pack carrying, or I won't even stand a chance. I will have to carry up to half my body weight – 33 kilograms (71 pounds) – for over 15 days. This has been a worthwhile lesson. I turn around and realise something else. There are no tents or barrels set up as on Kili and Elbrus, and there are no warm snacks and tea waiting. Nobody is welcoming us.

This is a big step up in expedition protocol; we are no longer the pampered clients, and now have to put in much more effort ourselves. We pitch our own tents and divide up the team gear. Only then can we sort ourselves out. Elan instructs us on using the high-altitude toilet. This is just fantastic. There is a normal plastic toilet seat with a bag suspended underneath. All of it is perched on a metal structure somewhat like a throne. When you sit on the throne your legs dangle over a cliff 2,000 metres (6,561 feet) high. It's truly a toilet with a view, and prompts a photo session.

True to form I discover I am getting my period at a most inconvenient time. I tell Elan and he agrees that I shouldn't carry the heavy pack for a few days. I return to my tent, now sharing with Ann. We discuss how difficult climbing is for women and compare notes on funnel usage. I covet the ingenious Freshette she managed to purchase in the United States. It looks much easier to use than my tiny bit of plastic. She tells me the story of her family from a very strict Scottish island, where men are still very domineering. I am astonished because it sounds more like an orthodox Muslim country than Western Europe.

Before dinner, the guides tell us that John, who has had a constant headache for several days, needs to go down. It is dark already. We all admire his decision to give up on fulfilling his lifelong dream. We give him hugs and words of support and watch the two little headlamp lights touching the void as he walks down with one of the guides. We eat our delayed supper in silence.

Day Twelve

We go to the cache at Nido de Condores camp at 5,350 metres (17,500 feet). The walking is easy as we do several massive zigzags and arrive at a stone-walled plateau, our home for the next two nights. We drop our team gear, which some of us carried, me included. Relieved of our burdens, we sit around a plastic bag, our improvised tablecloth, and have lunch of dried olives, tinned meat and fish, and defrosted bread. The mountain is totally empty because everybody sane celebrates Christmas with their families or has gone skiing to the Alps for the New Year. But I'm glad to be here now. It is peaceful, it is dry, I have great company, and I have good guides and team leaders. The sunset is amazing, displayed in front of us like on a giant screen. We follow the red ball of sun going behind the horizon, which, for us, means 'seek cover (warmth) now'. From Canada Camp, we can see the main massif of Aconcagua proudly crowning the Andes and can identify where we will traverse through the windy pass to the bottom of the Canaletta on the summit day. At sunsets, the rock is bright red reflecting the sun.

Day Thirteen

We move to Nido camp. Everything goes to plan. We have another dancing session in the evening. I do my stretching exercises, and some follow suit. Everybody is in good spirits. The food is now a dehydrated mixture in a plastic bag with a bit of hot water.

Food is never really hot. The water to make tea is also lukewarm because it takes ages to boil and distribute. We take turns to transport the snow for melting in big, black bags. This year, the whole area is very dry due to El Niño, which has swept the snow almost completely from the whole mountain. That means we need to walk for over an hour in some places to gather the life-giving snow. We have great appetites, much to Elan's surprise. He says that his groups usually stop eating at Nido. At Berlin camp the next day, very few people have a full meal but I still have a great appetite, thankfully.

I drink 4 litres (1 gallon) a day. I don't like drinking from wide mouth bottles because I sometimes spill the liquid over myself, but a camel bag is of little use here and higher. I learn that you can buy little inserts for bottles to create a mouth-sized hole. I use them on all my future expeditions. I also learn to protect liquids overnight with my own body heat in my sleeping bag. This is uncomfortable, but absolutely necessary. I later develop massive bruises from that and my rucksack hip belt. I also learn to cherish the additional warmth after one pees into the pee-bottle, which has to go back into the sleeping bag with you so it is not frozen in the morning and can be emptied.

Day Fourteen (New Year's Eve 2006)

We decide to single carry to Berlin Camp at almost 6,000 metres (19,700 feet). On the way, the guides decide I should walk in front of the group. Apparently, my pace is perfect for this altitude and I don't speed up. Somewhat intimidated by eleven people stronger than me scratching at my heels, I carry on. We come to an emergency shelter and a simple metal cross as a reminder of where we are. We get to our camp, which is 100 metres (328 feet) above Berlin Camp, a little ledge on a cliff falling off into noth-ingness several kilometres down. Our tiny tents seem very vulnerable to the elements. The place is magical. Our seven little two-sheet homes are just little dots on this planet and we are totally isolated. This altitude is my personal record and tonight will be my first high mountain night. This is the equivalent of sleeping on top of Kilimanjaro.

I am so glad I have no symptoms of altitude sickness. Ann, however, is struggling. She has stopped eating and drinking, but her stubborn Scottish nature and determination keep her going. I have both her and my portions for dinner. Lying between two mountains of down formed from two giant sleeping bags, we exchange New Year's wishes and shout to the other tents how wonderful the imaginary fireworks were.

We are supposed to start the summit attempt in the middle of the night as Aconcagua has a very strict cut-off time: if the summit isn't reached by a certain time in the morning, then climbers should return to high camp. We eat our porridge and wait for the howling wind to subside, but after two hours the summit attempt is called off. On the one hand it is good news as we will be better acclimatised tomorrow, but on the other hand we will have only one more extra day to attempt the summit.

It is a bad night for Ann, who wakes up and needs a lot of help with everything she does, including holding her pee-bottle and propping her up as she kneels above her sleeping bag. She cannot coordinate her movements and stay upright. I tell her to drink more and take Diamox. This drug helps to acclimatise and can prevent or help with altitude sickness. It is designed to drain the bodily fluids out so they don't drown the lungs or swell the brain.

Day Fifteen

Before breakfast, I inform Elan about Ann and he comes to our tent with breakfast and insists on watching Ann eat it all. She struggles, but manages not to vomit. He leaves three bottles of liquid for her that he says need to be gone before lunch. I leave the tent to give her space and join Ian and Chris. We play cards the whole day. At some point I live up to my nickname when I have a laughing attack, start crying, and cannot control myself. The laughter is contagious – the others start shaking and we all lose it.

Ann slowly recovers. She even manages to go to the toilet on her own, which is a big win. In the afternoon, the wind abates. Everybody is buoyed in anticipation of another summit attempt. We sit outside and eat dinner. Below us, in a wonderful cover of thick clouds, a storm with lightning is being played out before us as our evening movie. We watch a flash of lightning cut across the cover of clouds and hit the ground. We can hear only a very distant roar each time. The spectacle is fascinating. At sunset, we form a group of monkey-like figures, strangely twisted. Those poses make great pictures.The sky here is totally fascinating with its zillions of stars. Michel, who apparently knows his stuff, explains, or is perhaps just bluffing, about constellations, strength of light, and size of stars. We hang on to his every word like children.

I organise myself much better for the night, by packing my summit day clothes into my sleeping bag to keep them warm for the midnight call. I again eat two portions of supper as Ann gives up after a couple spoonfuls. She survives on energy gels, which are easier to digest. The call comes. We dress much quicker than last night and form a little train of people with head torches on. It is pitch-black, as there is no moon. After an hour ascending, David needs to return. He says he does not have it in his legs. After another hour Ian makes the same decision. He stands in front of his son and says, 'Keep going for you and me. I will keep the sleeping bag warm for you. Get to the top, son.' Everybody gets a little emotional. We hug the guys, turn around and keep going. A guide assists them back to camp. I am struggling to reconcile the fact that three strong guys turned around and I am still going up. I am feeling well, although my hands are super cold. I tell Elan, who puts my walking poles aside and tells me to keep squeezing my palms until the next stop. I do, but it helps very little. I don't dare to take off my gloves and put in a sachet of hand warmers[2], which, of course, is a mistake. I keep going for now. It gets light, so I look forward to the first rays of the sun.

---

[2] Hand warmers are an invention I bless every time I use them. They are little sachets of chemicals, activated by air, which you put into your mittens or boots. They keep warm for up to eight hours.

The next stop is behind a kind of a rock shelf, which gives some shelter from the strong wind. Elan instructs us to drink a litre (1 quart) of liquid here and now. I do so, knowing I might not be able to drink or eat higher up. He checks on everybody. My hands are frozen solid. The assistant guide, the local version of Antonio Banderas, takes off my gloves, puts the palms of my hands under his armpits and smiles at me. I find out later that he is the boyfriend of the main cook, the girl from base camp who got my fleece and jacket. He has promised her to look after me. After a while I can feel the warmth of blood coming back to the smallest blood vessels. I feel pain, but it is welcome this time as it means I don't have frostbite. He inserts two packets of hand warmers into each mitt for me. We need to move and walk fast now for an hour to get out of the wind. We all wrap up really well with goggles, face masks and puffy pants. I eat an energy bar.

Keep going. The toughest bit is still ahead of you.

We are off. After a battle against very strong wind for an hour, we are on the Windy Pass. It is a flat, 2,000-metre (6,561-feet) stretch, where the wind blasts relentlessly. The path is perhaps a metre wide. To the right, you have a straight slope back down to base camp (a drop of 2,000 metres or 6,561 feet) nicely exposed. We walk slowly. The team has split into three parts. I am in the middle. My hands and legs are fine and I don't have a headache. Elan tells me that I need to walk faster today and presents me with a Snickers bar.

I sit down on a stone and start chewing. This little bar of chocolate would take a couple minutes to eat at sea level, but here, because it is frozen solid and my jaws hurt after two bites, it takes me ten minutes to get through. It nevertheless gives me a little rest. I manage to catch up with the group up front after my energy boost. After ascending steeply for an hour, I ask Elan where the Canaletta is. He turns and smiles at me. 'You just walked up it. We are five minutes from the top.' My look of astonishment sets off his laughter, and he jumps a couple steps up. 'This is the top!'

We all rush up, and yes, we are on the flat top with a silver cross. We have made it! I start dancing with Chris. I take my UNICEF T-shirt out of my backpack and pose for a picture. I am so happy that my first charity hike is successful. I have a story to tell my supporters. The wind has subsided. We eat, drink, and wait for the others. The 360-degree panorama is astonishing.

For miles and miles we can see the Andes rising and falling into the distance. Blue sky and scattered clouds rush around. But soon it's time to go back down. I am very careful because 75 percent of accidents happen on the descent. Halfway down the Canaletta we meet Ann and Wind-suit coming up. We tell them that it is not long and they can certainly make it. The descent takes a surprisingly long time. Again, the group forms behind me. We plod, left, right, left, right. We trace our steps back through the Windy Pass, and downwards. Finally we can see the seven yellow tents an hour away in the distance.

Yippee! We made it!

David and Ian come out and congratulate everybody. We are very tired. I take off my boots and dive into my sleeping bag in full gear where I instantly fall asleep. I sleep through supper and breakfast.

Day Sixteen

Somebody eventually wakes me up. It is time to pack up the tent and return to base camp. We drag our feet a bit, but are finally off. What took five days up takes two hours down. The mountain gets busier and busier the lower we go with snakes of people slowly crawling their way up. We reach base camp and it is celebration time. We eat an amazing three-course dinner and then go to the bar tent that we had no clue about before. We drink to the bottom of bottle after bottle after bottle. It is three in the morning when we stagger across to our tents.

Day Seventeen

The walk out of base camp is long and painful. Fatigue suddenly sets in after such a tremendous effort on summit day, combined with serious hangovers and sleep deprivation. The wind is unforgiving and relentless, and the sand returns with a vengeance. The river has swollen a bit so we need to scramble up loose rocks in some places to stay dry. After six hours we reach the first camp, where refreshing juice and sandwiches are served. After three more hours of walking, there, in front of us, is the park gate. Jeeps are waiting for us with cold beer. Ann staggers to the jeep, as her knees have had it – it takes years for them to heal. We reach the hotel at two in the morning. I have a quick shower and crash.

Day Eighteen

My bath in the morning feels like heaven. I look at my seriously slimmed and bruised legs and kiss my knees as a thank you for their strength. I change my flights to Mexico City for the next morning. In the evening we have our celebration dinner in a 120-year-old local winery in a little castle. The guests are wearing black tie, while we are in shorts and sandals. The food – eggplant salad, grilled octopus, and a selection of desserts I share with Ian – along with 20-year-old bottles of Malbec, is the best dinner I have ever had. Then we hit the town. Chris, Ann, Dan and I end up playing pool in some dodgy suburbs until seven in the morning.

Day Nineteen

After sleeping for one hour, at eight thirty I am by the front door, ready to share a taxi with Chris to the airport. We jump on the plane to Santiago de Chile. There, I have a day of sightseeing while Chris heads back to the Emirates. After a full day I have a shower in the business class lounge. Because the whole lounge is empty, I stretch out and fall asleep, using my backpack as a pillow on comfy-looking chairs. I wake up in the middle of a smartly dressed crowd, eyeballing my tired body sprawled over four seats. I sit up and greet them, but strangely nobody is inclined to respond.

Day Twenty

It is Sunday evening in Mexico City. My colleague, who was supposed to bring my laptop and office clothes, has arrived, but our bags have gone to the United States. For now he is in jeans and T-shirt. I am in my dirt-encrusted hiking gear. We are supposedly coming from the European headquarters to meet the senior management team to help them plan to set up the branch.

I order overnight cleaning and ironing of my trekking pants and shirt, and with my backpack as a handbag, we enter the office at eight o'clock sharp. What a professional crew! Our impeccably-dressed colleagues explode with laughter. We spend most of the day with the CEO. At the end of the day our bags still haven't arrived, so we go to a local Zara and buy one change of everything for tomorrow. I still have that suit. I smile every time I wear it.

***

On Aconcagua, I learned to give without expecting something in return. If you want or choose to give or help, just do so. Don't attach any strings or conditions and don't expect people to say thank you or do something for you in exchange. Giving and sharing cannot be conditional because that contradicts the very fundamentals of giving. I have come to believe strongly that a universal exchange is going on in the world. The more you give, the more will come back your way if your intentions are pure.

I had to learn one more thing, though – to just receive. And it took me two more years after Aconcagua to learn not to feel the need to reciprocate instantly or to feel guilty.

I don't agree that "there is no free lunch". Society has made everything exchangeable, tradable and conditional upon both sides participating. We have built up an expectation of reward and reciprocation. But gratitude and love cannot be demanded or made conditional in my view.

PART TWO

Taking it to the next level

CHAPTER 4

The tipping point

June – July 2007
North America, Mount McKinley (Denali, the Big One) –
6,194 metres (20,320 feet)

I know that if I succeed with Denali then I will seriously consider attempting the other three mountains, and thereby complete the Seven Summits challenge. Denali proves to be a tipping point for me, the most challenging thing I had ever done — a true test for me as a mountaineer, person and team member.

I book the expedition with Mountain Trip, an American company. It has great local knowledge and experience and is one of the most respected companies on the mountain. What a crew! Bill and Todd, the owners, still guide, which means they don't lose touch with the reality of guiding in extreme conditions. The client care is just amazing, ranging from surprising cooking ideas at 4,000 metres (13,123 feet), such as burritos, enchiladas, pizzas, ice cream and cheesecake, to having fun and, most importantly, taking safety and security on the mountain very seriously. After Denali, I go with Mountain Trip to both Antarctica and Everest.

My Denali expedition starts for me in February 2007, three and a half months before the actual summit day. My research into Mount McKinley tells me I need to go at the warmest time because temperatures can drop down to -30 degrees Celsius (-22 degrees Fahrenheit), even without the wind chill effect. I aim for midsummer, the end of June. I am already fit after having climbed three mountains in a year. But I need to add load-carrying exercises and design a training routine where I go out with a backpack full of water (dead weight) every weekend and increase the content of the rucksack from 5 to 30 kilograms (11 to 66 pounds) to match the load on the climb itself. My ultimate test is to complete the Big Black Mountain Challenge in the SAS playground of the Brecon Beacons in Wales in mid-May. I plan to carry 30 kilograms (66 pounds) for eight hours in one go with Nigel as a bodyguard. He carries lunch for both of us. What a gent! I am working full time, so I end up walking with the load to work and back every day for a month. Initially it takes me ninety minutes; over the weeks I get it down to fifty minutes. All the security guys at work know the sound of my steps and the sight of my towering red rucksack as I enter the gleaming office at dawn and leave at dusk.

The spring weather is against me. It rains on most of my training days, and I am set back with a cold. I put on all my rain gear and backpack full of water and set off into London for five to six hours of walking at six o'clock in the morning on Saturdays and Sundays. Every second weekend, I train with my boyfriend out of town. It is so much easier to have somebody with me. When it's raining I get soaked right through, I'm cold as hell, my lips are blue and on top of that my knees hurt from the load. It is miserable when I am alone, and I want to give up. Few can understand why I put myself through all this preparation, pay a lot of money to run myself into the ground and still call it a holiday. I just keep putting one foot in front of the other. I try to look for fun in this craziness. For example, I go on the London buses and stand in the buggy area without holding onto anything and try to keep my balance only with my legs as we go round corners and stop and start in the London traffic.

On one of the walks in the woods, I practise using the peeing funnel, which enables ladies to pee standing up when trekking in a harness or kneeling down in a tent. I have to totally master this skill so that it becomes second nature. At first I do it in the shower, then over the toilet, and then outside. I complain to Nigel that it does not feel as comfortable to me as he looks when doing it. We compare postures: spread of legs and direction of slope. All are important. I practise it on a regular basis. Eventually the day comes when I finally discover the full satisfaction of a naturally emptied bladder standing up. It's a wonderful feeling. I envy you guys.

The walk back home from my London walks is always easier and seems quicker than getting to the destination. Hence, I always push myself to go as far as I have planned. From there I have no alternative but to return home one way or the other. Nigel says I'm like a donkey – I speed up as I get closer to food, water and shelter.

On Denali, I know I will have to carry half of my own body weight and pull a sled going uphill. Yet here I am, struggling to carry 15, 20, or 30 kilograms (33, 44, or 66 pounds) on my back while walking on the flat through London.

I often have visitors staying with me. I am usually back from my five-hour walk at the weekend before they've even woken up after having partied the whole night. I hardly get to see some of them at all. My mum comes to visit. She watches me eat my full breakfast at five thirty and then put my backpack on. To do this, I prop the pack against the wall, sit in front of it, put it on, and then turn onto all fours. I slowly lift myself up, grabbing stools and cupboards to help my knees. I leave the flat. As I walk past the windows, I see my mum glued to the window. Our roles have changed. I remember doing that as a child in Poland, when she was leaving the house and I was insecure about her coming back, even though she always did.

Walking in the early morning around London is mostly fun. The streets are empty, and I have the town to myself. Fridays are different, however, with the stink of vomit around the corners of the pubs. I learn which corners are the worst and adjust my route accordingly.

Every second day I go to the gym at six thirty at night and bike like mad for two and a half or three hours. When I get off, my legs are shaking and I am trembling all over. My backside hurts from being on the saddle for too long. At the beginning it takes me fifteen minutes to recover, enough just to be able to go and have a shower. I do this religiously for two months until my thighs are rock-solid. It feels good!

In March, two months before D-day, I notice something is not right with my right arm. It goes numb after an hour of walking with my heavy load. I go to a physiotherapist, Rosy Mews, the best therapist I know. I have a trapped nerve on the top of my shoulder. She puts it back in place, but recovery takes time. I need to watch for the numbness when I train and stop every hour to release my arm from the load. I need to add padding to the backpack strap as well.

One weekend I do the 1066 Walk, one of my favourite walks close to London, with Nigel. It goes from Pevensey to Rye via Battle. We march in the footsteps of William the Conqueror and his Norman army. But in 2006 we meet sheep and bulls rather than the Saxons of Wessex. We set off early. After five hours we decide to go into a local pub. Some twenty metres from the pub, Nigel turns to me and says, 'Quick! Give me your pack so they don't think I'm a complete wuss.' The locals in the pub aren't fooled though, and are merciless. Halfway through my pint of water I start examining the map to see how far we still have to go.

The crowd cheers, 'Ah, so she's not only strong as an ox but she can read a map, too.' 'Can she drive as well?'

'Of course.'

'What else can she do?

We look at each other because we both know the answer. 'She can also pee standing up.' The pub erupts into laughter and I earn myself another drink.

I am afraid of two things on this expedition. One is the cold, so I buy good quality equipment and way too many hand warmers. I think through my layering strategy carefully. My second fear is the Head Wall, 300 metres (984 feet) of fixed ropes to be negotiated. I want to practise this in London, to get to know my limit. I enrol in an ice climbing course at Ellis Brigham shop in Covent Garden and go during my lunch breaks. Their wall is vertical and 7 metres (23 feet) high. On my first attempt, I get halfway up and then bang the ice axe on my lip. It starts bleeding. To stop the bleeding, I touch my lip on the ice. It gets stuck, and when I pull it off I rip several more layers of skin from my lip. I check my teeth with my tongue. I still have them all! I am still stuck to that wall though and cannot move a muscle from panic. I bang my knees against the hard ice and finally shout to the trainer to lower me down. I look up and see my blood on the wall. I need to warm up and have another go. My shins hurt – I must have banged them too. My arms hurt. Hacking into the solid ice with two heavy ice axes is really hard going. I try again, but after ten minutes of struggle and a few more minor injuries, I decide I've had enough. I pack my bag, tuck my tail between my legs, and go back to the office. As sod's law would have it, I have meetings back to back for the whole afternoon. It's an early night for me as I need to recover from this disastrous test. I realise I have hit an important physical barrier.

The list of equipment for Denali is long. Everything has to be top quality. If you skimp on anything, it can cost you dearly, a frostbitten finger or even your life. I have purchased most of it and have some from earlier trips. In all, it is worth around $3,000. It weighs 27 kilograms (59 pounds) and fits into two bags. Everything I need is lying around on my living room floor in logical heaps: legs, upper body, head, supplements, accessories, sleeping, hygiene, food, and a very separate little pile for the summit day. I won't unpack that particular sack until probably thirty days from now. The summit pack is like your life-support kit. It has to be pristine until you need it. I have a clean pair of pants (you can't just show up on a summit in dirty pants after fourteen days without washing), my summit socks, hand and feet warmers, special energy and recovery bars, super warm summit mitts, UNICEF T-shirt, one-time camera, spare batteries for my normal camera, and spare lip salve. The packing is meticulous. You need to think everything through in the finest detail. When the guides check your equipment before you set off, they will question your logic of taking this set rather than another set of layers, hand equipment, and sock combinations. It will be like an interview. If you are missing something, they will give you a chance to buy it.

Before I go, I write my will for the fourth time in my life and put it in an envelope with my mum's contact details. This turns out to be the last time I do this before an expedition. With time, I learn to accept what comes. I don't even write a will before Everest. What will be will be.

I write my last email to my sponsors:

Dear All, Here I go again. It is the fourth peak out of the Seven Summits, which I am climbing to raise funds for UNICEF. I have completed Kilimanjaro in Africa, Elbrus in Europe, and Aconcagua in South America within twelve months. This one is Mt. McKinley in Alaska, the highest peak in North America. It is 6,194 metres (20,320 feet) high, and trekking is in absolutely extreme conditions of snow, ice, glaciers, crevasses, and cold. It will take a full eighteen days to get to the top and down, weather permitting. We need to carry all the equipment and food for the whole duration ourselves.

I am leaving on Saturday, June 16, and have left sending this request for support quite late. I was scared that I wouldn't be able to train myself up to the necessary level of fitness (biking 90 kilometres in under four hours) and be able to carry 30 kilograms (66 pounds) on my back for more than five hours a day. But now I am ready and confident that I can do it. So please give generously.

I leave my London flat with just my duffel bag and a giant rucksack, and fly from London to San Francisco on Saturday, June 16, 2007. I do some sightseeing – Fisherman's Wharf, Alcatraz, and the Golden Gate Bridge. After a wonderful seafood lunch... or perhaps it's dinner, or maybe breakfast ... my body clock is confused... I take the fast train to the airport and board my flight to Alaska.

It's well past midnight when I land, but, of course, being so close to the Arctic Circle, there is still light outside. One of my bags goes to San Diego rather than Anchorage. That's just the sort of stress I need! I pray that I get it back before we set off for Denali. I take a taxi to the bed-and-breakfast and find my room and my male roommate, a total stranger, snoring loudly. I try not to make any noise and sleep like a log.

Day One

On Sunday morning the team assembles. They look fun and international. Jens is Danish. Paul and Denise (I already know them from Elbrus), Chad, Cheryl, Charles and Bill are Americans. Our lead guide, Zach, turns out to be first class: very mature, emotionally intelligent, great fun, incredibly physically strong with good intuition and judgement, and totally committed to getting us up that mountain.

After a serious equipment check we go for a shopping bonanza to REI, a very well-stocked outdoor and sports shop in the United States. I still don't have my other bag. If it does not come by seven o'clock tomorrow, I will have to buy all the stuff I have so carefully packed at home. I am worried, but sleep well.

Day Two

Much to my relief my luggage arrives at five thirty on Monday morning, enabling us to set off at seven thirty. Before we go, we leave all our valuable possessions at the bed-and-breakfast in sealed containers. I like the moment I switch off my BlackBerry – it means I am leaving my other life behind and nobody can contact me. The only connection with the outside world will be the blog, which Mountain Trip maintains, and a very occasional satellite phone call. I have a clear mind with no distractions.

A large van takes us to Talkeetna where we register with the national park officials and pay $210 in cash for the pleasure of climbing 'The Big One,' as the local people call Mount McKinley. Then we have an orientation talk with the ranger and are shown a very scary movie about frostbite, altitude sickness, and human waste disposal management. On the mountain we will poo into green buckets and pee into snow pee-holes or pee-bottles. We do some last-minute shopping at the supermarket where I buy a kilogram (2.2 pounds) of carrots, which the team will savour for three days, defrosting them one by one.

At the local airport a Twin Otter plane is waiting to take us to the starting point on the glacier. Our pilot ensures the flight is a spectacular event. Within thirty-five short minutes, we are transported from greenery and midsummer heat to the white snow-covered ice cap of the Talkeetna Glacier. From the plane we get a fantastic glimpse of the top of Mount McKinley. What a daunting sight. No wonder they call it 'The Big One.' We are told that most people who give up do it here on the landing strip, after that first glimpse of the challenge ahead.

The first base camp is located at 2,200 metres (7,200 feet). We are taught how to pitch tents on the snow, rope up sleds and ourselves, and how to pull the sledges. As we set up camp, the glacier moves as if we are in the epicentre of a light earthquake. It's pretty scary and we all look to Zach for an explanation. He says with great authority, 'The mountain is saying hello.'

That night I crawl into my Marmot -40 Celsius (-40 Fahrenheit) sleeping bag. I feel as snug as a bug in a rug. I have my earplugs and eyeshades handy, and I sleep well!

Day Three

On Tuesday, we get up at four in the morning to avoid walking in the heat of the day. However it takes us three and a half hours to break camp and we are told that this is unacceptable, as at midday the snow bridges over crevasses would be too weak to support us. In fact, a large part of climbing this mountain will be done at night. It takes us five hours to travel the six miles to camp one at 2,400 metres (7,800 feet). It's hard work, but with such spectacular weather, it is a treat. Our only stops are pee-breaks – I pass my standing-up test with flying colours.

Warning sticks are set around the perimeter of the camp. We are not allowed to go outside them because only around 160 square metres (525 square feet) of the camp area is crevasse-free. So, one step too far when you're going to the toilet and you can end up 200 metres (656 feet) below in an eternal fridge. Brrrr. We have pizza for dinner and go to bed early for a three-thirty start.

I share a two-man tent with Paul and Denise, my teammates from Elbrus. It is the first time I have ever shared such a small space with two near strangers, and one of them a man as well. But we quickly get accustomed to each other's smells, snoring, morning and evening routines, and, yes, peeing-inside-a-tent routine.

Day Four

Zach decides to single carry again, which means our loads are bigger, but we do the whole thing only once instead of carrying half a load partway up to the next camp, and then going back down to move the camp. With the double carry system, you end up climbing the mountain about three times. I can see the route ahead. Today will be harder than yesterday for sure.

Wow, what a day. I have repacked my backpack. It's much easier for my shoulders, but the sled is so heavy. I don't feel the sled that much when walking in a straight line; it only becomes a nuisance when it is stuck on a snow ramp or when we traverse a slope. Rather than follow you in logical horizontal succession, the sled slides sideways and not only pulls you down the slope you're trying to cross, but also goes against its own design. That makes it tough. Everybody is responsible for managing the sled in front of him or her by adjusting the tension of the rope. We cross several, very scarily deep, crevasses. My heart races, and I'm seriously out of breath when doing so. The snow bridges are very fragile. Good job that I'm not the heaviest person here, even with my heavy pack. I do not eat enough on the way and sit and shiver from exhaustion and cold when we get to camp. *Stupid woman!*

I snuggle up in my heavenly sleeping bag for three hours before dinner. We have burritos! As I said earlier, Mountain Trip is the best! In the tent, I stuff myself with chocolate bars and cashew nuts to get some energy back. Tomorrow, we will again single carry because Zach thinks we are a strong team. *Yeah, right! He didn't ask me!* The good news is that, by single carrying, we are saving days, which will give us a better chance at the summit. The bad news is that we are carrying more than normal, which means we could get too tired too soon.

The place names on the mountain are a mixture of quirky (Motorcycle Hill and Squirrel Hill) and serious (Windy Corner), which we will need to negotiate before getting to the second base camp, and the Head Wall with 300 metres (984 feet) of fixed ropes. Fixed ropes are solid mountaineering lines that the park rangers fix to the slope every season. Without them, the route would have been much more dangerous. I bless the rangers and the person who came up with such a grand idea. There are also names for places where a number of lives have been lost by particular nationalities, so there is an Autobahn, British Airways, and Orient Express.

Day Five

It is another three thirty wake-up time, followed by bagels with cream cheese and hot water for breakfast. It takes over three and a half hours to break camp. I am hungry again before even starting our snowshoe march. I eat some nuts and energy bars. That will have to do until dinner. It is slightly windy, and my hands freeze in a couple of minutes. Thank goodness I have hand warmers.

This mountain is so different to everything I have done before. It is such a very lonely experience. Our team consists of four ropes, and there are twelve of us in total. We are all roped up with large gaps between us to allow for the large crevasses we are crossing. We have to shout to each other if we want to stop to drink, eat, or pee. You have nobody to share thoughts with. You keep your frustrations to yourself, and you cannot seek emotional or moral support from others. Only in the evenings in camp can you vent and share, but on our march days we are all too tired to talk. It feels similar to those lonely, rainy, training days back in London and because of that, I am ready for my solitude.

We walk for five to eight hours a day. All I can see is the inch of rope disappearing in front of my feet. I stare at it and put one foot in front of the other. Chwap, chwap, chwap. It is desperately cold. This was my biggest fear when coming here. I have good gear and I don't freeze, but it is very unpleasant. The only time I really warm up is in my sleeping bag at night or in the kitchen tent when a meal is being prepared and all twelve of us are in there warming it up with our breath. When I am literally freezing, I question why I am here. I'm someone who normally sleeps in full pyjamas and socks at home during winter. I have never (willingly) taken a cold shower in my life. And unlike most Brits, I put on a hat, coat and scarf, even when it is only zero degrees back home. And here I am freezing my butt off on a regular basis.... Literally, because in my utter stupidity, instead of packing some big, woollen underpants, I took my skimpy, nylon thongs.

I have never had snowshoes on, I have never pulled a sled, and I have never camped on snow. The nature is incredible, and the views spectacular, but this venture is much harder for me than I had ever anticipated in my wildest dreams. I must deal with it as best as I can through learning and observing our guides. They know best. For example, I am adept at peeing through the funnel, but never with a harness and two pairs of trousers on. I didn't practise having to negotiate two carabiners, a dangling rope, a zip, my pants, and everything exposed to the wind, with three strange blokes on the rope and other people walking by. It is too much for me, so on some days I don't pee for seven hours. Because of that, I don't drink enough on route and become a water junkie in every camp. It is essential that your urine isn't yellow, the best sign of whether you are drinking enough or not. Good hydration is vital out here.

It is a tough learning curve, but every day brings some kind of personal discovery. Even the smallest experience helps craft my character to the core, questioning what I know, my attitude to things, my judgment and my beliefs. During the march I go into an altered state of mind, or kind of meditation. I go back to various situations in my life and straighten out memories, disassociate myself from things I don't want to remember, and see myself achieving things I want to achieve in the future. And I consciously work on my character by experiencing the most extreme conditions ever. I deal with my fear of exposure and falling. I am doing something against the very instinct of survival. I'm exhausted and still go on. I face the anxiety of every day. I discipline myself to get up, pack my stuff, be ready on time, and help others. I rarely think of the world outside of here and I don't carry pictures of anybody. This is my zone. I feel like I'm in perfect isolation, free to consult my soul on anything that comes to mind.

My philosophy is that it is the journey that counts, not getting to the summit. I take every single minute as a gift and savour it. I learn how to live in the here and now, hour by hour, and day by day. I don't think about the whole seventeen-day trek in one go. I think to myself, 'Can you get through today? No? Can you get through to lunch? No? Then, can you get to that little black dot out there? No? Can you do the next ten steps then? No? Then just do one step and then another and another.' This step-by-step strategy becomes my mantra, and it sees me through the whole Seven Summit Challenge.

On Denali, 85 percent of climbers are male. They dig large steps into the slopes, and I have to match them, which tires me no end. As a result, my natural stride lengthens significantly. I go slowly, especially uphill. I know I need to conserve energy for that worst moment to come, never knowing when it's going to strike. I use the rest step technique, where you give each leg a microsecond of rest between steps and you tune your step to your natural breathing. That way, I rarely get out of breath and can almost do without rest breaks.

It is interesting how the needs of a human being are exaggerated in the so-called civilized world. In truth we need so little, as on this trip: food, planning the water intake, pee breaks, rest, a bit of proper warmth every so often, small chats with strangers, and sleep.

I dance the polka today, and we laugh a lot in camp. Those moments when all barriers come down between climbers are very precious. It's as though we're all naked in front of each other. Nobody is wearing a mask; nobody is playing any games.

I meet Troy from Minnesota today. He's an enzyme expert, an industry figure. He stops in our kitchen tent on the way back from a successful summit attempt. This three-hour conversation changes me a lot regarding how and what to eat, how to restore strength to my body, and how to supplement my diet with digestive, systemic enzymes and probiotic bacteria. On my return to London I start doing fasts and detox diets, Troy introduces me to colloidal silver and its properties, I change my philosophy of how I combine the foods I eat, and with time, I give up dairy products and my current staple diet of seafood.

For now, we are in a whiteout, and the cold is unrelenting. I am dreaming of diving holidays on a boat with Nigel on the Red Sea. In the mornings, everything is frosted inside the tent. To get up, we first need to scrub snow off the walls and ceiling of the tent. Otherwise, it falls on you and wets your sleeping bag and clothes. By the time you've done that, you've lost the heat of the night and start shivering. I sleep with everything in my sleeping bag: night pee-bottle, water bottles for the next day, inner boots, and clothes to put on the next day. In fact, my sleeping bag is so full that I can hardly move. I raise my sleeping pad with my backpack underneath to an almost half-sitting position, which helps me breathe at altitude and guarantees relatively peaceful nights.

This is certainly the most difficult and exhausting trip I have ever done. When I walk every day, I can almost feel my love handles melt away. I actually lose over 9 kilograms (20 pounds) on this trip, and the weight yo-yo effect accompanies me for the four and a half years I do the Seven Summit challenge. I have to watch carefully what I eat, on and off the mountains.

Day Six

Today is the first day of summer. We are stuck in camp in a snowstorm at 3,400 metres (11,000 feet). We are all crowded into the kitchen tent, huddling together for warmth and hot water. Unfortunately, we have lost a day. We have blueberry pancakes for breakfast though and plenty of water to aid acclimatisation. We have all started smelling pretty bad. I promise myself a wet wipe bath when we get to the second base camp. Thanks to the rest day, I recover from my tiredness. Tomorrow will be another difficult day as we decide to single carry again.

Back in the tent I apply menthol ibuprofen gel. It works wonders on the aching muscles in my thighs and shoulders. It warms me up before I snuggle into my sleeping bag and helps me breathe clearly at altitude. Bless you Nigel for giving me this!

Day Seven

We wake up at four o'clock in the morning but the weather is bad so we go back to sleep. At twelve thirty, we decide to move camp up to 4,300 metres (14,000 feet). And what a day it is! We go up Motorcycle Hill, which is shorter and steeper than it looks. Then we turn right and start ascending Squirrel Hill. But instead of it being one hill, it turns out to be three! Perhaps that's how the name came about. All stashed away to surprise you, it's just not fair! By this time, the weather is turning ugly. The speed of the wind has increased dramatically and it is snowing heavily. I zip up, put hand warmers into my mitts, put on my goggles, face mask, and all the windbreaker layers I have. Then we have to negotiate Windy Corner. This is the only place on the mountain where you need a helmet, and you really do. The pieces of ice and rock flying around are lethal. We can't see a thing. I don't know how the guides find the way in such conditions. Carrying a heavy pack and pulling a sled in the howling gale is pure agony, but I am most worried about falling into a crevasse and getting lost. I start praying that we can keep finding our way. I stuff myself with super energy bars and drink frozen water from a bottle that makes me even colder on one of the stops. I say the Lord's Prayer out loud about a million times and really believe that only God can save us. We regularly trip over the rope. People fall. It is a total mess. Yet step by step, we get closer to our destination.

The most amazing thing, though, is that once we finally turn the Windy Corner and are out of danger of falling rock and ice, the weather is beautiful, sunny and even quite warm. We all stop to catch our breath and undress. We have been fighting with the wind for seven hours, and have two more hours to go. Jens, the Danish Viking, the strongest guy I have ever met with a great big heart, takes some of my group equipment to ease my journey. I have tears of gratitude in my eyes, it is such a great help. We get to camp at around ten o'clock at night, and it instantly starts to get really cold because the sun has disappeared. We are so weak from sheer exhaustion. I was on the last rope, which means my mates Denise and Paul have already pitched our tent. But we can't find our stoves, which means no hot drinks. I tremble from exhaustion and cold in my sleeping bag for ages until we finally have an instant noodle soup each and crash. Today felt like a summit day, and it will take its toll on the team.

Day Eight

Today is a well-deserved rest day for all of us. We all sleep in. What the hell! We are on holiday after all! After breakfast, I solve the world's problems with Jens and Meryl, and we're doing just great. After lunch, we go to the end of the world for the most spectacular views. The end of the world is where our base camp plateau disappears abruptly into nothingness. We are trained in self-arrest. This involves being thrown down a steep hill headfirst, and your job is to turn yourself upside down and stop falling using your ice axe. *Easier said than done!*

We have a lot of fun though. Then we practise fixed rope work. This involves great coordination between rope teams, which we will need for the Head Wall and summit day. We all patiently form a line. Everybody is fully geared up. The first one screams 'Anchor!' at the point where the rope is fixed to the mountain, and then 'Clear!' when he or she manages to swap to the next rope above the anchor. We practise until we can do it in our big mitts, with our eyes closed, and our muscles remember the moves. The whole day feels like scout camp for adults. We have to repeat our moves to the satisfaction of our guides, who are obviously amused at our floundering and are clearly enjoying bossing us around. I am changing my views about Americans, who I have known mostly through the corporate world. This trip is full of Americans and I am thoroughly enjoying their company!

Day Nine

Today we have to carry the cache to the top of the fixed lines at 4,800 metres (16,000 feet), and then return to camp. We leave at nine forty-five in the morning and trek up the ski slope. Yes, real skiing is going on. Halfway up the slope Meryl starts crying. She is not going to make it up. The Windy Corner storm day exhausted her to the limit. She says how sorry she is. We divide her group gear between the rest of us. She plods, sobbing, back down to base camp. Thankfully she can go down on her own without an escort on this part of the route.

We get to the bottom of the fixed ropes on the Head Wall, where we have to change gear for the rope work. During the two-hour hike my legs and glutes have been severely tested. I need to lift my legs up higher than normal to match the length of men's steps. The steps are sometimes so high that I need to prop my arm on my higher thigh. Only then can I lift my body with the backpack, while pressing down my other hand on a walking pole. We take a rest on a ledge barely wide enough for my bottom and the rucksack. I am shit scared. I am shivering from fear and my legs are wobbling from fatigue. Somebody drops something from higher up. All heads turn at once as we watch the item gather incredible speed and smash to pieces at the bottom. I am holding Jens' knee in despair, as if that is a good anchor! I eat a protein bar, have a drink of very cold water, and try to pee, but cannot concentrate enough.

It's time to go. I have feared this part of the climb the most, where I expect to be tested to the limit. I get to the first anchor and try to let my fear go. I have practised this. I have it in me. Just this time, it's almost vertical. I go into my altered mind zone where what counts is just me being safe and progressing up. It becomes like the practice exercise of the day before. I shout, 'On the fixed rope!' I take twenty-five steps. I shout, 'Anchor!' I manipulate the safety cara-biner and ascender. I shout, 'Clear!' I take twenty-five steps. I shout, 'Anchor!' I manipulate the safety carabiner and ascender. I shout, 'Clear!' I take twenty-five steps. I shout, 'Anchor!' I manipulate the safety carabiner and ascender. I shout, 'Clear!' That goes on for about two hours solidly without a rest for 300 metres (984 feet) of rope. I finally reach the cache place. *Phew!* That was tough but okay, nothing like the ice wall I climbed, or rather tried to climb in the shop in Covent Garden. I am so relieved.

Going down the fixed ropes is fun, and it goes quickly if your team is coordinating well. We return to base camp to find pizza on the table for dinner. Oh yum, yum! We have seconds. We are told to eat well tonight and tomorrow morning. From now on, we will be on high-altitude food, which is pretty basic.

Meryl calls her husband on the satellite phone. She is crying. She doesn't want to be a failure. The next day we say our good-byes to her.

Day Ten

Today we climb to high camp. This proves to be physically the toughest day of my life so far: I will fall apart and then reassemble myself emotionally; I will cry uncontrollably and keep going far beyond what I ever thought would be my limit.

At the start my backpack weighs 28 kilograms (61 pounds). This is almost half of my body weight because I have already lost some weight on the trip. We follow the route we know well from yesterday, up the ski slope and then up the fixed ropes. People in front of me have kicked in steps into the sixty-degree slope. I am struggling, but it feels easier today because I'm more familiar with the exposure and steepness of the route. Our rope team is strong, but, most of all, we're better acclimatized after yesterday's cache drop. At the top of the Head Wall, however, we pick up the cache from yesterday, which adds around 7 kilograms (15 pounds) to the 28 (61 pounds) I already have on. It is much too heavy for my liking.

It is very windy, and we need to negotiate the edge. That means walking on a shelf that is less than 1 metre (3 feet) wide and bendy. The tight bends mean that, being in the middle of the rope team, I am constantly lurching around dangerously. Charles is pulling me forward into the abyss; Jens is pulling me backwards. My steps are much shorter than the guys', so I have to keep running. I am scared again. I'm walking on the bench-like hard rock with a 1,000 metres (3,280 feet) drop on both sides. I try not to look sideways. My full focus is on keeping my balance on this tiny shelf. Before Washburn's Thumb (a very steep rock formation, which we need to negotiate using fixed ropes again), my emotions and body give up on me. I sit down and start crying. After thirty seconds I cannot control my sobbing.

Zach, the lead guide, asks if I can keep going. I look at him, but cannot see anything through snot, tears, sunscreen, and tangled-up goggles. 'Yes.' Then I start really wailing because I don't know where I will find enough strength to take even one more step. I feel totally humiliated by the power of Mother Nature, that big, beautiful piece of snow and rock. I feel beaten up. Zach's professionalism comes to the fore. There is no compassion and no time for bullshit, as if he is thinking, 'I need to make a quick, efficient decision. The weather is turning on us, and we need to proceed.' He offers no reassurance that I can make it. He just wants to know what state I am in. Next to me a guy is vomiting blood because of altitude sickness. It looks scary. He cannot breathe, but is convulsed by his illness. The blood comes from his lungs, not his stomach. His face is bluish and in sharp contrast to the red blood on the white snow. He could die if he doesn't go lower soon. Guides are silently preparing to take him down.

My rope team looks at the scene with horror because they know that if I cannot keep going, they will have to come down with me. Jens helps to take off my backpack and I get a group hug. I drink some tea and feel warmer. Finally I calm down fifteen minutes after my fit. I need to pee. Everybody in my group turns around as I present my funnel. They are used to it by now. But a seven-strong Japanese group coming up behind us have never seen a girl peeing standing up before and start pointing in my direction. They take out their cameras and start taking pictures and videos. Strangely enough I lose the urge to pee and cannot stop laughing. Now I am crying from laughter. Well, we all are. Don't you just love the Japanese tourists!

In the meantime, the weather is deteriorating. The wind has picked up speed, it is snowing, and the clouds are closing in. It is really cold, and we have at least three more hours to high camp. I put my burden back on my shoulders, my ascender in my left hand, and my ice axe in the right. We start on another stretch of fixed ropes. It's the now-familiar routine. 'On the fixed rope.' Take twenty-five steps. 'Anchor!' Manipulate the safety carabiner and ascender. 'Clear!'

An hour before camp I feel weak, hungry, thirsty, cold, miserable and extremely tired. My shoulders are just a tight disaster cramped under my much too heavy pack. The palms of my hands are freezing. But I know that going forward is the only option. We get to camp as the last rope, probably because of me plodding rather than walking. Thankfully, my tent is already up. As I crawl in, Denise and Paul hand me a special recovery electrolyte, a warm drink at last. Nobody says a word. I unpack the group gear, blow up my mattress, unroll my sleeping bag, crawl into it, and quietly shiver with the upmost satisfaction.

I analyze the day. I know I hit and overcame a mental barrier. I pray. I touch my golden cross dangling on my chest and say my thank yous to the spirit of the mountain and God. I cry again as I confirm my understanding of what I've just been through. I have reached the threshold of exhaustion and could not go on anymore. Through my tears, I switched off reason. No explanation was possible using my intellect. Rationally, I did not know how I could have taken another step. But through my heart and through seeing the outstanding beauty all around me, I felt I connected with the universe. I allowed the experience to happen. Just being there gave me the strength to continue for three more hours of climbing before reaching the camp.

What a day, nine long and unremitting hours of complete and utter exhaustion. We finally eat dinner at midnight, a pack of noodles each with hot water. There is constant light because we are close to the Arctic Circle. I like that as a sign of hope and some greater force caring for us. I put on my eyeshades and fall fast asleep in an instant. Tomorrow, the only option for me is a rest day.

Day Eleven

We wake up at seven, just in case the weather is good enough for a summit bid. It isn't. When I peep out of the tent, I can see a massive, beautifully-formed, elliptically-shaped lenticular cloud, which means high winds. We shouldn't go anywhere near the summit. I say my prayers in a big 'Thank you, God,' because I desperately need one day off to restore my muscles, senses, feelings, and emotional strength. I massage the wonder menthol and ibuprofen gel all over and snuggle back into my sleeping bag.

I wake up just in time for breakfast at ten thirty. We have bagels with cream cheese for a kind of brunch. *Delicious!* We talk some nonsense, walk around the camp, and take pictures until dinner. In the middle of the day, Mike, who had altitude sickness even at base camp, asks for the satellite phone. The whole camp can hear him. He calls his girlfriend and asks her to marry him. He says, 'I am done with the fucking mountains. I don't want to go to Everest any more. Go to the shop, and select an engagement ring. We are buying a house with the money I saved, and let's have a family.' She must have said yes because he looks absolutely delighted. He turns around and says simply, 'Zach, please, I need to go down now.'

We search for other parties going down. Yes, there is one, and the guide agrees to take Mike down to base camp, where Meryl and the assistant guide are waiting for us to return. I reflect on myself. No, I don't want to call anybody and go anywhere. I love being here, stranded at the end of the world, where my immediate worries are whether I am warm, if I can make it to the next camp, if I have an appetite, and if the other guys are okay. This is it. There's none of the craziness of the city, there are no choices to make, no corporate politics, and no demanding family members. Nothing. There is peace of mind and full freedom of the soul. I breathe in the spectacular views, the white snow against the blue sky. I feel good. I belong here.

Dinner, a bag of potato puree each, is the first disappointment on this trip. We are supposed to reach the summit on this tomorrow? We start talking about tipping, which is always a difficult subject because everybody is on a different level financially. We want to make it as fair as possible. I prepare for tomorrow's summit day mentally and physically. All my gear is nicely lined up in my sleeping bag.

Day Twelve

Today is our summit bid. We get up at seven and prepare. I have severe diarrhoea, but too bad, I'm going. We have oats for breakfast. We are all in standby mode, waiting until the wind dies down. It's eleven, and we are still waiting for the weather to improve. We are fully geared up and ready to start moving at any time. We can see some groups already going up, but not us. It's as if Zach has a hint of something in the air. For now, he just says that the conditions up on the ridge above the Autobahn are frostbite weather.

Because we made up days by single carrying, he is not bothered. So we keep warm and patiently wait. My intuition says that today is not the day, but I keep my thoughts to myself.

At eleven forty-five, we hear over the walkie-talkie that a guy going up in front of several rope teams has passed out. It's Stefan from Germany. This particular Autobahn is a one-way street, so everybody has to turn around to get him off. Zach asks us if we would give up our summit attempt today so he and the other guides can go and help save Stefan's life. He gets a resounding yes. Everybody in camp gets out of their tents and takes position – just like in the movies. Some of the guides have gone up to fetch him. If he has to be carried down, there will be a lot of help needed. Other guides start preparing the evacuation. We contact base camp. The whole mountain is on high alert. The evacuation will take place in an orange bucket-like vehicle that is lowered down on a giant rope, 1,000 metres (3,280 feet) long, through a sheer gully, straight down to base camp. Hmm, on reflection, I'm not sure if I would feel safer in that bucket or on my own wobbly feet. We are too high for a helicopter to come. After strong DEX (steroid that helps with oedema caused by altitude sickness) injections and an hour of nerve-wracking waiting, Stefan regains consciousness and seems fit to be led down on a short rope. Everybody on the Autobahn re-ropes. We can see the snake of people finally coming down.

So we have another afternoon at camp. We have read all the books, told each other all the stories and solved all the world's problems. We clearly need something new to do. We decide to make a deck of cards out of my note pad and play Egyptian rat screw with passion for the next five hours until the noise of empty stomachs forces us to stop and forage for some food. There is more potato puree. It's not my favourite, but the only option. I'm not going to eat my private summit day supplies now. I crawl into my sleeping bag and put my eyeshades on and earplugs in. There's lots of snoring out here. I pray for good weather. I feel that tomorrow will be the day. Yes, it must be tomorrow.

Day Thirteen

We wake up at seven and get halfway ready because the weather is marginal. We have all learnt patience by now and know there is no point getting angry or agitated. We are on mountain time, and the mountain rules here. The only consolation is that we still have a good number of spare days because we single carried most of the way and there is light twenty-four hours a day. Finally, around eleven thirty, Zach decides we are going to go for it. It takes us sixty minutes to get fully ready, and we start our snail's pace ascent up the Autobahn. We have the whole mountain to ourselves because the other groups are either having a rest day after an unsuccessful summit bid yesterday or going back down without even trying to get to the top because they are out of food and time. We all settle back in to the well-known rhythm of 'Anchor' and 'Clear' shouts. It's fun. When it's your turn to shout, you know that you have made at least twenty-five steps of progress. It connects you to the other people on the rope.

It takes two and a half hours to traverse up the steep slope. I fall once onto my knees in the powder snow with my arms into the snow and my face bathing in the white fluff. That is pretty scary, but I manage to arrest myself as taught. On the Windy Pass, we have to put on more clothes because the wind is fierce and frostbite rules. We meet the Japanese group that had filmed me trying to pee; they need to go down after failing to make the summit. From here on, it is a slow plod upwards with mini fixed ropes. The route is not difficult. We reach the middle of the so-called Football Pitch, a vast flat expanse of snow where the summit ridge seems deceptively close but is in fact still miles away. I am cold. The palms of my hands seem nonexistent and I'm losing feeling. We are so close, and I don't want to give up easily, but I need to warm up my hands. We stop. In two seconds a strategy is defined. Kneeling down in front of me, Jens is putting my puffy pants on me. Davide, our guide, warms up my hands under his armpits while standing over Jens. The scene must look totally comical, but nobody is laughing. We all want to get to the top. My being cold is the obstacle, so the team pulls together. I activate new sachets of hand warmers and add them to my summit mitts. That works and I feel much better. I eat natural energy gel and drink a half-litre

(1 pint) of almost-frozen water. We are good to go. The wind is picking up, however.

We finally get to the bottom of the summit ridge. It is an almost-vertical 150 metres (492 feet). We zigzag our way up to the ridge. We have 300 metres (984 feet) of a very gentle incline to the top. This very gentle incline is, however, on a top of a cornice, a snow wave built by the wind, so you effectively walk on 5 metres (16 feet) of snow hanging over nothing, actually over 3,000 metres (9,842 feet) of nothing. We can see the first team taking summit photos. But the wind is bad, and Davide is not sure what we should do. He wants to turn around. Jens and I exchange frightened looks.

He says, 'If we're going to do this, we have to run to the top and back. But I prefer to wait here for Zach and seek his advice.' There is no way I can run 300 metres (984 feet) at above 6,000 metres (19,685 feet) of altitude. We embrace to keep warm and wait for Zach. My thoughts are scary, but very clear. I know I'm the weakest link on this rope. I know it will be my fault if Jens and Davide don't make it to the summit. I know that, without me, they could.

All considered, I turn around and tell Jens, 'You should go. I will stay and wait here. You are much stronger than I am, and you can make it for sure.'

He quickly replies. 'No, we will do it together.'

'Jens, I don't run even at sea level. You need to go because you are the stronger one. You carried my group gear. You deserve to make it. I will go back down with Zach's team.'

We tighten the group hug. Davide gives me another energy wonder bar. Finally, Zach arrives with Denise and Paul. There is a quick dialogue between the guides. We don't say anything while awaiting our fate. My heart is in my mouth. I so want to continue. Zach decides we are good to go. He tells us that he has seen much worse winds. My heart starts racing as I realise that I might get a chance to stand on the top of the fourth summit after all. After thirteen days of slogging, pain and fatigue, and after eight and a half hours today already, we set off. In the middle of the suspended snow edge, we tread carefully. Then we meet the second team coming down. One of the guys seems to be unconscious, but still walking. The guide has him on a short rope for safety.

We reach the summit at eleven forty-five in the evening of June 30, 2007. I present my UNICEF T-shirt for photos, and we enjoy an amazing view for several moments. We are well above the clouds. The horizon is white, and the clouds and glacier become one. The sun is suspended between heaven and earth and colours the top of the clouds with a golden lining. We all hug, kiss, and prepare for the way down. Peace descends on me. I am reconciled. I leave my ego here. I don't need it anymore.

Armed with the knowledge that seventy five percent of accidents in the mountains happen on the way down, I never congratulate myself or anybody else on the summit. Until you are back down safely at sea level, you are vulnerable. Descending is difficult because it is tough on your knees and muscles. The adrenaline to reach the top is gone. You are totally knackered. The only thought to keep you going is that first shower or beer, or whatever else. For me, coming down is a time for consolidating the experience and internalizing my lessons. I always make sure I leave enough fuel (physical energy and motivation) in me for the descent. I always like to hold back my excitement and congratulations until I am safely down, then the joy is twice as big.

Trekking back to high camp, we pass the second team at the end of the Football Pitch, with the sick guy. They look in disarray. There is cursing and tension between the four of them. Our guides exchange medicine and advice, and we press on. The weather has turned ugly, it's a total whiteout! On the Autobahn, if not for the fixed ropes, we would not know where the way to camp is. I am cold and weak again. We cannot stop though because the rope between us has to be tight to make sure we can save one another in the event of falling. We cannot even hear each other shouting. The only communication is the loosening and tightening of the rope between us. The wind is howling, the snow is blowing, and the visibility is not even one-third of the rope length. In a word, the conditions are shocking. I know camp is close, but I cannot see it. I have one small wish, one thought on which I put all my focus and mind. I want to get back to my tent and feel my hands again. I am trying to concentrate on my steps. Although I am very careful how I walk, my crampons catch my trousers twice. I land headfirst with my face in the snow. I am petrified to move, so I don't slip down the Autobahn, 5,000 metres (16,404 feet) to the valley below. It takes me a good five minutes to achieve a decent propped-up position on my legs so I feel brave enough to stand up. I start to despair a bit because it seems that I want to pee, drink, eat and rest all at the same time. They are simple things, but so unattainable at this very moment.

Its three thirty in the morning. I have been awake for over twenty hours. I finally reach my tent. Denise and Paul are already there, snuggled up. We congratulate each other, but moderately because we are not off the mountain yet. Jens brings me hot chocolate. I remove my crampons and outer boots. Everything else goes with me into my sleeping bag. I touch the cross on my chest and thank God for a safe and successful summit. Suddenly, I don't hear the roaring of the wind, Paul's snoring, or when the third team makes it finally back to camp at five thirty. I wake up at ten, amazingly hungry. Ah, yes, stashed away for this very moment is my favourite Polish chocolate bar, Prince Polo. I munch on it in my sleeping bag. In fact, I have a second one straight away, and it is divine. I so deserve this indulgence.

I examine the soles of my feet. They are both a puffy mass of blister over blister. My right big toenail is blue-red-black. *Nice.* I regret taking off my socks and becoming aware of the situation. I put on triple layers of Compeet blister plasters and know that getting back down to the airstrip will be the most painful walk of my life. I smile. It's another endurance test ahead of me.

Day Fourteen

We have been trying to break camp since eleven o'clock, but people are simply not cooperating. There is no drive anymore. There's just the slog of getting back down. I'm still in my down booties, trying to save my feet from more torture. I eventually break my tent and then help with the other guys' tent. We are left with one more to do. I enter and try to negotiate with Chad to get him moving. He is too tired. Yes, we all are. I remove my gloves and help him dress and gear up – this time it's my turn to help somebody to keep going. At one thirty we are finally ready and start the descent. The weather is marginal again, and we might need to stop at anytime to pitch tents, but I simply don't want to even entertain that thought. I try to walk so the soles of my feet don't hurt, but it is impossible. The pain is excruciating, and I will have two full days of this. Suddenly, lost in thought or rather pitying myself, I fall and slip several metres off the ridge. The guys react perfectly, just as we have practised, and arrest the rope.

We all shout to each other, 'Rope secure!'

'Ania okay!'

'Get back in position!'

Easier said than done!

In falling, I hit my right cheekbone on the rock. I have my goggles on rather than sunglasses and that probably saves my face from a nasty open wound. I also now have my 30-plus kilograms (more than 66 pounds) rucksack, so getting up is tortuous, especially because I am on a scree-like slope covered with 10 centimetres (about 4 inches) of fresh snow. I finally make it onto my knees and look up. I can see Jens, who, of course, cannot move to help me get up because he is securing the rope so I don't fall even further down and take him with me. But he has a giant smile on his face as if all this experience is just about learning on both sides. And it is. I finally stand up and crawl back up to the line. The rope tightens again, and we start our plodding afresh.

'No more falling. No more self-pity,' I tell myself. 'You made this choice. You like being here, so accept whatever comes. Yes, that's right. Focus, think, act, woman!'

With traffic on the fixed ropes and the sick guy with pulmonary oedema on rope two, it takes us nine hours to reach camp. The sun is behind the mountain, and it is freezing. Jens, Davide, and I arrive first. We crawl into the kitchen tent and light the stove to warm up and prepare hot drinks for the other guys. We don't pitch tents because we might be going down further tonight. By the time everybody is back and we've had a cup of powdered soup each, it is two o'clock in the morning. We will not have enough time to reach the airstrip. The crevasses start to open up during the day, so the only way is to go overnight. We don't have much to eat, but we need to establish a camp. Finally at five thirty in the morning, we have instant rice with more powdered soup. The wind is very strong so we strengthen the ice walls around the camp. We are shattered. At seven in the morning, we finally crash.

Day Fifteen

I wake up at one in the afternoon and have a brunch of burritos. Oh yes, we are back on the gourmet food. We also have ice cream (made of snow, of course) and a cheesecake for dessert. Everything has to be eaten, whatever is left in the advanced base camp cache. We are the second last team on the mountain and the season is ending. That means we sit and eat complete and utter rubbish – M&Ms by the bag, stacks of Pringles crisps, Hershey's chocolate, and yet more biscuits. We have lots of tea to drink as well. We visit igloos and the rangers' station, where they are treating frostbite on a Japanese man who has very black, bloody, swollen fingers on one hand. I hope he won't lose them. This sight makes me seriously dizzy. I need to retreat back to the fresh air. For five minutes I can't stand straight. So that's how decaying flesh looks and smells. I so hope to avoid such a fate.

An afternoon siesta is ordered because we will start our descent around nine o'clock in the evening. It will take us around twelve hours straight. So prepare your snacks and take plenty of water. And off we go.

Our trek down proves to be the most beautiful night of my life. The wind has died down, the horizon is filled with white and ice-formed pinnacles, snow overhangs form some amazing structures, which play farfetched stories in my imagination. The colours of the sky are mixed, where the dawn meets the sunset and the sunset meets the dawn at the same time. It reminds me of a sorbet stand in Italy, a rainbow of colours, very carefully selected and then diluted. I can see the sun and the moon at the same time. They are talking about the caterpillar of wrecked mountaineers slowly crawling in a wriggling line down through the vast, white valley. The shimmering of snow under my snowshoes adds to the magic. I breathe in the beauty, the atmosphere.

The soles of my feet are killing me – it's like walking on hot coals. I walk through amazing pain, often with tear-filled eyes. When we stop, I don't dare to move and aggravate the pain. Several times my sled ends up in a crevasse because Charles does not keep the rope tight enough. We struggle each time, but succeed in extricating it. And then there is Heartbreak Hill stretching out in front of us, which needs to be climbed to get us to the airstrip. This is agony. Not only are we totally exhausted, but our motivation is at such a low that nobody is walking anymore. We are all simply crawling on our knees. I feel like I am pulling Charles behind me. I have no clue what is going on. My only wish is to get to the air traffic control tent and establish if there is flying weather or not. We are finally there. Everyone is silent. The guys find a container of beer, Coke, and more crisps. We all sit on our sleds like zombies. I put my head on Jens' knee and fall fast asleep.

Next thing I know, people are shouting, 'Yes, the plane is coming. Quick! Let's get into position.' This unfortunately means walking up the hill for another 1,600 metres (5,249 feet). I'm totally dreading it. But when we hear the quiet murmur of the engines, giant smiles spread across our faces. Yes, yes, yes, we are going back to Talkeetna today!

Day Sixteen

We land safely. The first thing I do is take off my boots. We realise how bad we all smell. It's embarrassing. We need to unload everything and categorise the loads. Only then are we allowed to search for a shower. But today is July the 3rd. Everything is booked up because of American Independence Day. We walk from one end of the small village to the other, but no chance.

Some woman takes pity on seven ghostlike people running around and shouting nervously, 'Shower?! Shower?! Please, somebody help. Shower?!' She points us to the local laundrette. A shower at last. We buy a token each, which allows three minutes of running water. We decide on the sequence of pleasure. I sit down on the floor, awaiting my turn. I'm afraid to look at my feet. The shower feels heavenly after seventeen days with only the occasional wet wipe. As I wash myself, I wonder where the rest of me is. I locate some scales and find I have lost almost 9 kilograms (20 pounds) in weight.

Due to the lack of accommodation in town, most of us decide to change flights and try to get home earlier. Over lunch I change my travel plans. With a day wait in Salt Lake City, I will be landing at Gatwick at six thirty in the morning on Thursday, July 5.

We have our celebration dinner in an Italian joint, where everybody orders two main dishes in a row. We polish our plates clean. Then we go to the best bakery in town and indulge in triple desserts. I feel seriously sick from overeating. Everybody, except me, has vast amounts of beer called Ice

Axe, with seven percent alcohol content. We exchange addresses, emails, good wishes, and hugs. And that's it. The team is officially disbanded.

Day Seventeen

I sleep through the flight. I sleep through most of the day in the airport as well on a bench. I sleep again through the second flight. I'm on autopilot. I don't know where I am or why. Meeting Nigel at Gatwick, I say I just want to have a shower and go straight to the office.

He looks at me with compassion shakes my shoulders and says: 'Listen, I've taken a day off work, so stop being overambitious superwoman. You can have one day of rest. Yes, really, you can.'

I cannot reconcile this place with my state of mind. I have an amazing out-of-body experience. Crossing streets, I almost get run over by traffic. Thank you, Nigel, for saving me. In the supermarket, all the choice and the noise of civilisation are totally overwhelming. I am lost, deprived of the simplicity of life on the mountain. All those colours and unnecessary choices of yogurt, chocolate and milk. What for? Simple and natural is good.

When we get home we make love, but I'm still not there. I find myself in a bath full of hot water and muscle relaxant looking at my bruised and hairy legs. I start to examine the damage. All is good apart from the massacre of my feet and ankles. In fact, I cannot see my feet because blisters fully cover them. And my ankles are like balloons rather than my own flesh. The skin up to my knees looks like that of a lizard. Very sexy! I spend hours in the bath, constantly adding hot water and relating the adventure to Nigel while he comfortably sits on the toilet seat. Then we eat salmon brought all the way from Alaska for lunch ... or dinner. I don't know which. I wake up in bed with crisp white sheets. I smell nice, but am still unable to appreciate it.

Next morning is Friday. I struggle to the office wearing flip-flops and some rather weird, baggy trousers. I get lots of hugs, handshakes, and free lunch and dinner. People are so happy to see me back in one piece. I have over 3,500 unread emails sitting in my inbox. I don't know if I replied to a single one of them that day.

I select photos to share with all those who were supporting me and contributed to UNICEF. I write the following email.

Dear All, I was lucky with the weather and managed to complete my climb to the summit of Denali (Mount McKinley) in Alaska sooner than planned. This has been the most physically and mentally challenging seventeen days of my life, but an incredible experience I will never forget. The climb up Denali started on the Kahiltna Glacier, flying into base camp in a light aircraft with all our kit and supplies that we would take up the mountain. We mainly moved at night to avoid the dangers of crevasses and unstable snow in the Alaskan summer.

These were long, strenuous climbs through snow, and I was glad for my hard core training. The cold, thin air and high wind penetrated right to my bones. From the third camp came the hardest part of the climb as we went up the Head Wall, a steep wall of snow and ice from 4,724 metres (15,500 feet) to 4,907 metres (16,100 feet), attached to fixed ropes for safety as we hauled ourselves up, digging our crampons into the ice, step by step, up the sixty- to eighty-degree slope. This was so hard that I wept, humiliated by nature and feeling totally insignificant against the altitude, wind, and sheer cold. The ridge after the Head Wall then had big, knife-edged rock formations falling dramatically away to the snow and rocks below. From high camp at 5,242 metres (17,200 feet), we made our attempt for the summit. But we had to abort to support a climber with severe altitude sickness, bringing him back to high camp. They call this stretch 'The Autobahn,' because you can slide away at high speed if you lose your grip. We were fortunate with the weather though, and it held out long enough for us to make another attempt. I finally reached the 6,194 metres (20,320 feet) high summit at eleven forty-five at night, on June 30.

My muscles ache from climbing and carrying such heavy loads, erecting and breaking down tents, cutting ice blocks to form a shelter from the snow and wind, and not being able to stretch out in my sleep because I was so cramped in our tent. My fingers are battered and bruised from the ropes, and my toes are black and blue from bashing against my boots. (And I think one of my toe nails is lost!) Twelve-hour days were not exceptional, and we had no set times, climbing during the day or night to take advantage of conditions or avoid danger. And in my mind's eye, I can still see the rope snaking away in front of me to the next climber in the team, leading the way safely.

But I'm home (and clean again at last), and I'm amazed at how green everything is after close to three weeks in a beautiful and awe-inspiring wilderness of snow and rock, black and white. Your donations for UNICEF and goodwill kept me going to the top and safely down. Thank you very much for all your support.

***

I need a full weekend at home to fully reunite my mind, body and soul. A week after getting back, my neck goes into a spasm one morning while putting my hair up. I can't move it and am in absolute agony. I take a taxi to the physiotherapy clinic and Rosy comes to my rescue again. I managed to climb Denali without injuring myself, but doing my hair up has left me with four dislocated neck vertebrae. Rosy fixes me in three sessions and prescribes some rest. I do as I'm told for once. Obviously, getting this injury is closely linked with sleeping in the cold, being contorted into unimaginable positions during my sleep, and carrying loads. Anyway, I'm not booking the next expedition before next year, so I have plenty of time to recover.

I have one ugly, black, big toenail. It comes off with time, and takes a year to fully recover. My blisters are so severe that all I can wear to the office are some half-covered, soft shoes. It takes a month to get my feet and ankles back to their normal size and three months before I can wear high heels.

After my experience on Denali I focus much less on the short-term goal of each trip, that is, getting to the top. Likewise in life, I don't look to tick off another achievement. Life to me is about being in the present. Prior to this I had always looked into the future. I lived in the future, in my plans. I had a year plan, a month plan, a week plan, and a day plan. I always looked to tomorrow, but tomorrow never really comes. Life alters our plans all the time. Things just don't happen as we plan them. Life has its own unpredictable logic. By living in the future, I was missing the joy of the current moment. Or as John Lennon said 'Life is what happens when you are busy making other plans'.

Being totally in the moment on Denali taught me to engage fully my whole existence in any activity I do. I now do things mindfully: my actions have purpose. When I eat, I chew slowly to appreciate the taste. I notice the different textures of the food in my mouth and think about the nutrients entering my body. When I'm on the phone, I'm solely on the phone. When I make love, I make love. And when I work, I work. I believe that doing any task with the full intensity of my being enables me to find excitement in everything I do, whatever it is.

CHAPTER 5

Between a rock and a hard place

September 2008
Australasia, Carstensz Pyramid –
4,884 metres (16,023 feet)

I return from my Denali expedition in early July 2007, having completed the fourth of the Seven Summits. During the eighteen months it took me to do these summits, I lived a relatively normal life. I moved countries, changed jobs and employers, bought my own flat after nine years of moving round Europe with my fifty-two relocation carbon boxes, changed boyfriends, lived with one of them, read books, attended personal and professional training, went to church every Sunday and saw my family. The physical training, booking and preparation for expeditions become part of my life and a personal journey.

I have three more mountains on the list:

- The most technical climb out of the seven, Carstensz Pyramid (Papua Island, Indonesia)
- The coldest and the most remote, Mt. Vinson (Antarctica)
- The highest, toughest, and still unattainable (in my mind), Mt. Everest (Nepal)

Carstensz's summit day is a pure rock climb, and I have only scrambled to date. I read as much as I can about the rock climb, research the difficulty level, and sign up for climbing lessons. I also do a cash flow model for myself. With serious austerity, I believe I can save up for Carstensz in seven to eight months.

United Kingdom health and safety regulations don't allow indoor practising of what you need for Carstensz, because it's … too dangerous. Thankfully, my instructor, Peter, has previously trained somebody else for the same challenge, and he knows where and how he could bend the rules. Of course, he's Polish, too. The first time I come down a free hanging rope in the Castle Climbing Centre from the top of the tower (around 20 metres or 65 feet in height), my legs are like cotton wool, and my heart is racing madly. I am sweaty and prefer not to look down, but, following my instructor, I slowly lower myself to the ground. By the fifth time I am doing it with one hand. Peter is very patient. I master climbing the free hanging rope using a complicated (to me anyway) prussik and leg loop and jumar and God knows what else. I rappel down using a figure of eight – a little aluminium tool. We also practise basic rock climbing techniques. I do all that in my own climbing gear and full kit (rucksack, helmet, heavy full leather boots, and heavy-duty gloves) in the climbing centre. I am getting some very curious looks from the other clients and staff. I no doubt look odd, but I know that the more I practise as if it is the real thing, the more comfortable I will be in the real situation.

There is one more thing I need to confess. I don't actually know any of the mountaineering knots for the rope, not even the figure eight, the easiest. On expeditions where we need to be rigged up, I am shown the technique but I can just about remember it for a day, and then it's gone. I have tried to practise, I have tried to draw them and I have tried to memorise. Nothing stays in, period. On the mountain, I'm very honest about it and always get others to help me. But I know I'll never be good enough to go on technical routes without a guide. Without knowledge of knots, I would be totally improvising if an emergency happened. And that can be dangerous.

I know there will be no heavy loads to carry, but I still need upper body strength, which is not a female's strong point. So I purchase a chin pull-up bar and install it in my bedroom. I exercise religiously: push-ups and pull-ups for my arms and chest; and the plank which involves hovering over the ground suspended only on my forearms and feet, for core strength. Every day I do a short Pilates and yoga session to improve my flexibility.

In January I book with Adventure Indonesia, a local company (and therefore cheaper), for a trip in late March 2008 and pay my deposit. However, my trip is pushed forward twice. The first delay occurs when my boss asks me to postpone my three-week holiday until later in the year, ideally after the summer, because I am running a large change programme in operations for the derivatives department in the bank. I'm truly gutted. I write to the organisers of the expedition and ask them to keep the deposit and move the date two months forward.

The second delay happens on the Friday morning before leaving for Jakarta, when I am confronted with the news that the planned approach to the mountain might be closed due to some local illegalities. I travel to Jakarta, but end up rebooking the expedition for September. After a week's holiday in Indonesia and Bali, I start looking for partners for my planned climb. A couple I shared a tent with on Mt. McKinley, Paul and Denise from America, agree to come. I have a team. Because there are three of us, we even get a discount. Great!

I know from my Chakra's enlightenment course on Java that, not only do I need to be fit and able to rock climb, but I also need to work on my communication skills, i.e. to express myself better and listen to others. And that's hard for me! I sign up for a negotiation and persuasion skills course, as well as belly and jazz dancing classes. I plan to give a belly dance performance for my friends, just to make sure I have mastered self-expression. The first couple of belly dancing lessons are a total disaster, but with time and my teacher's perseverance, I'm ready. She performs the dance with me in front of twenty people. Bless and thank you, Shorma.

September comes fast. I have to leave in the middle of an IT strategy meeting at three thirty on Friday, September 12, to catch a plane. I send my usual email:

> Dear All, Here I go again. It is the fifth peak out of the Seven Summits (highest peak on every continent), which I am climbing to raise funds for UNICEF. I have completed Kilimanjaro in Africa, Elbrus in Europe, Aconcagua in South America, and Mount McKinley in North America.
>
> This one is Carstensz Pyramid in Papua Indonesia, the highest peak in Australasia. It is almost 4,890 metres high (16,100 feet). Not only will I have to negotiate my way through cannibal villages, but also face the most technical climb of my life. It involves a free hanging rope climb for 15 metres (49 feet) and conquering a gap 30 metres (98 feet) wide in the summit ridge. It will rain most of the day, every day. It will be hot and humid, and I still call it a holiday. Please give generously.

As I leave the office, one of my colleagues is tearful as she hugs me good-bye. Everybody is gathered around me. I squeeze multiple hands. As is my habit by now, I'm wearing my trekking gear, and carrying my big, red, 80-litre (21-gallon) best friend of a rucksack. I also have the luxury of a suitcase on wheels. Why carry any more than necessary? I board the same plane as last time. Everything feels like déjà vu. I go to the same bar for lunch in Dubai on route, go through the same bureaucratic process to obtain a visa at the airport, and the same people greet me in Jakarta. It's the same heat wave, same driver, same car, same hotel, same degree of tiredness after an overnight and day flight, and multiple changes of time zone. This time round, though, I know there is a team, so no cancellation is possible.

I sleep like a log that night, and in the morning I learn that four more people are joining our little group. It is a free day so I have spa treatments and visit the old part of Jakarta, which is smallish and rather colonial. Around midnight on the second night, Paul and Denise telephone me to say that they are delayed leaving Los Angeles due to a typhoon in Taipei. They have to wait one extra day because all the flights have been cancelled. I reveal to them that four more people are on the expedition and all the transfer flights have already been booked for us for tomorrow. I'm not sure I can arrange the postponement. Waiting for them would also mean that we would have one day less to get to the summit.

Nothing goes smoothly in life, does it? I have an awkward situation, and I need to manage it. I speak to the organizers. They say it is not their fault, we cannot wait. My friends will have to forfeit all their money. I speak to the other team members, and they say they would wait, but only if that does not jeopardise their summit attempt, which I cannot promise, of course. My friends are begging me to negotiate a postponement for one day. Emotionally, I am stretched. This is my second time here. I want to have a chance at the summit, but Paul and Denise are coming because of me. It's supposed to be an expedition for the three of us. So I'm stuck between a rock and a hard place. I muster up all my negotiation skills and bring them up to a whole new level. I have individual discussions, group discussions, telephone discussions, SMS discussions, and email discussions. Paul offers to pay all our hotel bills for the extra day. I buy lunch for everybody, but the organisers say we need to go immediately because the flight tickets from Jakarta to Timika are hard to get. It's a full, long day of talking, schmoozing, and trying to make everybody happy. During supper, we decide to wait one day for them, provided I can prove the progress of their travels from Los Angeles to Jakarta bit by bit. We decide to wait in Sugapa, the village in the middle of the bush where the trek starts, just in case they don't catch up and we will have to start trekking without them.

Day One

We fly out of Jakarta via Bali to Timika on an overnight flight. On leaving the hotel, we are given $7,500 in cash in a plastic bag, to be paid out to our porters. We touch down in Timika on the Indonesian part of Papua Island at seven in the morning. The heat is unbearable. Our entire luggage is here, but there's nobody to meet us.

Our guides, Meldy and Poxi, are nowhere to be seen. Because I have met Meldy before, I am sent on a search mission. This is totally unknown territory for me. Men are dressed in nothing but penis guards, ladies have bare breasts. Everybody smells, not just sweaty, but also very differently to what I am familiar with in the west. Most people around us have bones through their noses or ears or at least on necklaces. I am totally sweaty within five minutes. I return to our little, lost group of white people. While we are weighing up our options, Meldy and Poxi calmly present themselves. Their faces look as cool as all the other locals.

We are taken to a different terminal, well, a shed really, where about seventy people are all crammed in to get some respite from the burning sun. Everybody from the red race is examining the faces of the white race and the other way around. Our charter flight to Sugapa will not depart for several hours. We leave our luggage with the manager of the 'terminal building' and go for a last civilised cup of coffee in a local café. Drinking exceptionally good, freshly ground coffee in a metal shed by a busy road and eating dried dates and some dodgy-looking pastries, we realise we left the package with the $7,500 in the taxi. Oops! Pure panic descends upon us. We rush to ask Meldy to phone the taxi guy and ask him to come back immediately. He returns and the package is there! We buy him coffee and cookies and praise the Lord.

Meanwhile, Paul and Denise have made it safely to Taipei. They are booked on a flight to Jakarta for today, which means that, if all goes well, they will be joining us tomorrow afternoon in Sugapa. Then we can all start trekking through the jungle. I know this place is the last chance for any type of contact other than satellite phones. These messages are important for our overall morale, so I make the most of them.

We leave the café to board a Twin Otter plane, which takes us literally off the map. *Bye-bye, civilisation! Once again, for as long as it takes.*

We land on an airstrip, rather a piece of scruffy asphalt with a wrecked plane as a memento. It's built on a hillside so planes can stop by going uphill. Taking off is just a case of running off the cliff and hoping there is enough speed to remain airborne.

An extensive village welcoming committee greets us because today is market day. That means people come on foot from kilometres around to buy and sell goods. I stare all around me in amazement. Not only is the greenery far greener than I have ever seen and the bush an impenetrable net of branches, bushes, trees, and shrubs, but the people are so different and so beautiful. Their smiles and gestures are so genuine, natural, and pure. The people of the Dani and Moni tribes are very aware and very alert, living fully in the now. Their civilisation seems barely to have progressed for thousands of years. Walking through the villages on the trip, we witness life at its most basic. The locals use tools that the British Museum proudly displays as artefacts of the distant past. They live in full connection with nature. They eat what they can hunt and gather. They have not lost their hearts to their minds.

The atmosphere is humid and hot, over 30 degrees Celsius (86 degrees Fahrenheit), and the sky is cloudless. Our plane has been loaded with aid food, and we help to unpack rice, oil, fuel, and, much to my surprise, chips, Coca-Cola and other Western junk food. One guy, apparently an important man, judging by the width of his penis guard, leads our procession to the village. Thanks to the market, the place is a riot of colour. We pass naked people with bows and arrows for hunting. We pass pairs of boys, men, women and girls holding hands as a sign of friendship and commitment. We meet guys with very fluffy mini hats, made of feathers from exotic birds. It is totally fascinating. We stare at them. They stare at us. It's like a double-sided circus.

We pass lots of wooden mountain huts and some brick ones, mostly government buildings. We reach the hotel, a small, partly wooden, partly concrete shack, which is our resting place. It has a normal (bucket-enabled) loo. We sleep either on wooden beds or on the floor. We start to mix as a team. We have two Everest summiteers: Francis from Canada and Song from Korea who is sixty-one and lives in Los Angeles. There's also a wonderful Spaniard, Ramon, and a very chatty Mexican woman, Christina. There's one even madder Polish woman, of course. The team dynamic is interesting, to put it politely.

Christina's first words to me are, 'I don't like girls. They are wusses, and I am strong and great.' *Right, I certainly won't get in your way.*

Song looks strong and, in a very Asian way, determined to get to the top. This is his Seventh Summit. Francis is proud to have done Everest. Ramon is totally chilled out. He observes and just goes with the flow. We get a satellite phone message that Paul and Denise are in the air, en route to Jakarta, so it looks good for all the team to finally get together in one place by tomorrow evening.

We drop our stuff, take our cameras, and explore the market. Infants are carried around on mothers' bellies, backs, or heads or breastfed right there and then. Most males are chewing some orange stuff and spit everywhere with emphasis and colour. I later learn that it is a local mild drug. They are like koalas with eucalyptus, always on a high. They all have something in common, a peace and an amazingly genuine, wide-open smile. They are deeply happy and seem to be free … well, freer than we are. They possess nothing in comparison to what I have brought with me on this trip, let alone what I left back home, in terms of monetary value, but they seem truly happy.

They constantly grin at me. Before they shake my hand, they put their hand on their heart to ensure the most sincere and warmest welcome. I am only the seventeenth white person on this path. The whole trip feels like an eighteenth-century explorer's expedition to an unknown land.

The main path through the village is 150 metres (492 feet) long. On both sides of it are metal shacks selling exactly the same thing: basic, Western products like sweets, crisps, canned fizzy drinks, and very basic clothes and some necessities like soap, cooking oil, and flour. We have dinner of fried rice, tinned meat and fish, and some cabbage. It tastes great. I sleep well until the first cock crows.

Day Two

At eleven thirty, we pick up Paul and Denise from the airstrip. We want to start walking straightaway, but the porters and the division of loads are not ready. So we decide to leave tomorrow. We go for a short walk – we have been told not to lose sight of the hotel because there are not enough police in the village. We walk ten minutes in one direction, turn around, and walk ten minutes in the other, just like goldfish in the bowl. That's enough exercise! We spend the rest of the day swapping life stories and playing cards. The person responsible for the porters is a local albino, who has local features but our colour, or perhaps paler than us, with blonde hair and blue eyes. People respect him for those differences.

For dinner, we have fried rice again with the same tinned fish and meat. *Hmm, it still tastes good, but I'm not sure for how many more days.*

Day Three

I wake up at three, play solitaire and then have breakfast. Finally the whole entourage is ready to move. We were supposed to start two hours ago, but it takes ages with the porters. We witness a last-minute row between Christina and Meldy because Christina wants to carry her own full load. We try to intervene and persuade her that it would be bad for her porter. The custom is that men from the villages are porters, and that ensures safe passage. In the end, we all start with daypacks, and all our stuff is portaged in front of us. The albino, who turns out to be a Catholic priest, gives a special blessing for everybody. It is excruciatingly hot. I am wearing long sleeves, a big hat, and lots of sunscreen. The path winds through fields, more tribal villages, backyards, and lots of greenery. There are very wobbly bridges or no bridges and streams. Sometimes there is no path due to a recent landslide. Lots of pigs are snuffling along the path or bathing in the mud to cool down. Pigs are the ultimate currency here. The more you can raise, the better wife you can obtain. So we should respect these animals. Two of them engage in particularly noisy copulation in the middle of the path, cheered on by the locals because it means they will multiply.

It's up and down, up and down for the whole day. Midway through the day's trek, when I am walking ahead of our group, two serious-looking locals stop me, each holding a machete 50 centimetres (19 inches) long. They indicate to me to sit under a tree. I do so immediately and await my fate. We are in cannibal territory. Paul, Denise, Francis and Ramon join me, and we start eating lunch as an argument rages above our heads. We speculate whether they are arguing about who to eat first: me, the blonde, or Ramon, the better built. The shouting is deafening, but we dare not even take a peep and keep eating. After fifteen minutes, we welcome the sight of Meldy who talks to the shouting party. He asks us to get up and start walking. We do, hearing disappointment in the voices behind us.

'Damn, we lost supper,' they must have thought.

We later learn that they wanted to be porters on the next expedition to earn some money rather than eat us for dinner. I breathe a sigh of relief. We walk for six hours before we reach our wooden shack hotel for the night. I share a room with Christina. We wait four hours for dinner. I'm glad I brought my own sustenance. It's fried rice again!

Before dinner, we hear a woman shouting in labour pains while boys are cheering each other on the football pitch in the background. The woman groans and moans for eternity. I want to help her somehow, but know I can't. We finally hear a baby cry. It's a girl, we are told later. Is this real life or what?

The next day I go to the hut where the birth took place, a bamboo structure with a muddy floor and a fire in the middle. There are dogs inside, other kids, and blood from the previous night still visible. I take some photos after asking if it is okay and show them the pictures on the camera screen. They are happy. Having a girl here is good. There will be more pigs when she is ready to marry.

While reading myself to sleep, I notice a huge, hairy spider on the wooden wall. It is the size of my palm. It has fluorescent yellow eyes. I freeze and scream my lungs out. Nobody comes to our rescue, Christina screams too, but much quieter than me. She tells me this spider is poisonous. That is exactly what I need to hear!

It starts moving. I watch the drama from my sleeping bag. Christina bravely takes a wide-mouthed bottle and a piece of paper, captures it and takes it out. I'm glad I'm the wuss and she is the strong one! So, we have ejected the spider that we could see. But what about the ones we can't see? I prefer not to think about this. I pull the hood of my sleeping bag tightly around my face and put a bandanna over my nose and mouth for good measure so I don't swallow some beast in my sleep.

Day Four

We start the day at eight thirty. I wake up hungry to the loud crowing of roosters. More locals gather around us. I feel like I'm on the set of a *National Geographic* movie. All of it is totally surreal and not quite believable. Today, we leave the villages and set off into the real bush.

What a day! We are only the third expedition to use this route. Some of it is still in the making. Walking through the bush is quite astonishing in many ways. It is physically hard to walk because your shoes get stuck in deep mud. It takes a conscious effort to pluck your legs out for every stride. The path is narrow, foreign, overgrown, and constantly changing. There are several bridgeless rivers to pass and landslides. In some places we have to use machetes to hack the path ahead. I'm sure that what I have to negotiate today is beyond explanation to people back home. It is demanding, scary and tiring. We walk for five and a half hours, up and down, up and down, with an hour for lunch. The nature is so incredible all around me. I'm constantly in awe.

When you first look at the bush, it seems to be an impenetrable wall of green without any order. Only when you start looking more closely do you realise how cleverly organised it is; everything has a purpose and its own place. For thirty minutes we walk in an amazing torrential downpour. The drops are so big and frequent that it provides a good head and shoulder massage, if not a slight beating up. I feel like I have just got out of a shower fully clothed. And that's despite having waterproof everything – nothing is really waterproof here. The muddy marks on my gaiters and trousers travel up beyond knee level today. My light mint green top bears the marks of the last two days. Even though it is warm, we shiver for half an hour while waiting for our tents to be pitched. My stomach feels funny. I run for the hole in the ground. Oh dear, I have severe diarrhoea. We use iodine tablets to purify the drinking water, which obviously does not kill 100 percent of the exotic bacteria. It will be plain boiled rice for me. I take two Imodium tablets for the night. I also notice something wrong around my private parts, which feels like an infection. The little I can see is very red and irritated. The only remedy I have is to wet wipe myself all over and apply the antibiotic cream I brought with me.

Our camp is on the bank of a very lively river, now swollen with rain. The sound of flowing water will lull me to sleep in the evening. I share a tent with Christina. We wait five hours for dinner. And, yes, it is fried rice, and it will be fried rice for the next however many days. There's almost no protein. I wonder who in our team will rebel first.

I am back in my tent in dry clothes, but tired, hungry, cold, sore between my legs and with a bad stomach. Tomorrow, I will put my dirty clothes back on, and we will keep going for four more days of mud baths all the way up to base camp, negotiating 1,700 vertical metres (5,600 feet). I'm so glad I did not go on my own in June. I wouldn't even have had anybody to joke with about the sorry state we are in. Let's just take it day by day! This is hard, but again a beautiful experience.

I dry my walking clothes over the fire in the porters' tent. They are smoked by the morning, but dry. And it gets worse every day. I need to do something to improve my morale. I need to spoil myself. I start chewing on my salmon jerky. Then somebody hands me the plastic box of boiled rice. The warm food is heaven. I finish my feast by chewing on dry mango I brought. What a treat! I reach nirvana and fall asleep exhausted.

Day Five

Today is seven and a half hours of walking. Well, that's if you can call it walking. We are tree trunk walking. We are climbing vertical tree root ladders and swimming through mud. It feels like a full body workout. I often have to tuck my poles away and negotiate through on all fours. Thank God, I have light gloves so I don't hesitate to use my hands to grab anything to help me move forward. The last river before camp is waist deep, and there is no bridge. I cross it fully clothed with a giant smile. We climb 900 vertical metres (2,952 feet) through amazing pristine rain forest. The path is so narrow that it feels like I'm discovering it myself. Several times I'm completely on my own, and it feels totally surreal. I am surrounded by the stillness of trees and bushes, unknown flowers and singing birds. The smell of rich and fertile soil is intoxicating and overpowering. I love those moments when I melt into my surroundings and become part of nature.

It is hard work, and I do it mostly on an empty stomach because my stomach bug from last night is very much alive. Despite four Imodium tablets, I stop every so often to give back some greenish liquid from my backside. Yuck! Song is vomiting not far away. Hey, it can only get better!

I try to sustain myself on energy bars. I open one, and Poxi, our assistant guide and cook, who rarely leaves my side when we walk, comes up to me.

'What are you about to eat?' in sign language.

I show him a Tarzan-like strength posture. He nods.

'One minute', he indicates.

He skilfully disappears into the bush. After five minutes, he comes out with some yellow-green thing looking like the inside of the bark cut out of a tree. He indicates that it is his power bar.

I suggest that we swap. We sit down on a fallen tree trunk and chew. He seems to like my chocolate-flavoured protein power bar. The gooey stuff he gave me tastes sweet. I don't know what it is, but it gets me to camp all right.

The camp is literally set on a swamp. To get out of the tent, you need to step into a puddle up to your ankles and schlep, schlep, schlep wherever you are heading. You pee into one puddle. You take water to drink from the other puddle. The natural cycle is tight out here.

I share with Francis tonight because Christina is fed up with the wussy girl and longs for a Spanish chat with Ramon. I have a serious shot of vodka, which I take with me on every expedition, the last known home remedy against stomach bacteria. I need to get rid of this thing if I am to be strong enough for the rest of the trip. I have a nap before dinner, then eat more fried rice. We have fried rice three times a day. What is left from dinner is served for breakfast. What is left from breakfast we take for lunch. Vodka cures my stomach. Thank you, Grandma, for sharing your wisdom. Now I will be able to walk.

I have a secret. I brought two pairs of boots on the trip. One is Gore-Tex in a rather sorry state by now, and we have two more days to go. I will wear those as far as base camp. The other pair is pristine Scarpas, full leather with a solid sole. I carefully packed them at home along with a pair of smart woolen socks. I will wear them to the summit so my feet will be dry, possibly the only dry piece of equipment I have other than my sleeping bag and down vest, which I have been protecting with a vengeance. I am happy. I'm snuggled up in my sleeping bag and listening to the water squelching beneath me whenever I move.

Day Six

Surprise, surprise we wake up to rain, and we put on wet socks, wet boots, wet pants, and wet shirts. I drink buckets of warm water for breakfast, trying to warm up, but no joy. Francis has a cold. He is sneezing, and he has a runny nose. I won't be sharing a tent with him tonight. I treat him to some cold relief drugs as he doesn't have any medicine or tissues. So we start sharing everything we have: aspirin, coldrex, throat remedies, anything to get him healthy so he does not infect more people.

We need to keep moving constantly to stay vaguely warm. If we stop, we start freezing instantly because we are now at around 3,000 metres (9,842 feet). So we simply don't stop for the whole day, perhaps just for ten minutes for lunch. It is more of the same swamp crossing, smaller or bigger puddles, and more bush. The state of my clothes is beyond recognition. Mud has become the fibre; and the fibre has become the mud. By the end of the trip most of my clothes are beyond rescue and I leave most of them behind.

The sky is cloudy, and the terrain becomes less bushy. We are walking through two-metre tall ancient ferns. I feel like I'm walking through Jurassic Park, with giant dinosaurs lurking only metres away. I try not to make any noise so I don't wake them up. Today feels so much like an eighteenth-century expedition of explorers who have just discovered a new land. In front of me I can see a human caravan carrying carefully divided loads. The human train is spread for miles, but it is easy to spot the colours against the green of plants, the orange of moss, and the angry grey sky.

Suddenly out of nowhere, I hear a scream like a beast being killed. The porters run round frantically. We are told to sit where we are and wait. More screaming and disorganised running continues. After twenty minutes of waiting, I see two porters turning back with no load. I later learn that one of them had a severe attack of malaria and had to be immediately escorted back to the village. All malaria remedy is for the climbers. Yes, did I mention mosquitoes? And leeches? And lizards? And who knows what other exotic bugs? Bedbugs have eaten my back. I can't get them out of my sleeping bag, so I have more bites every day. They itch, swelling up in red lumps. Whenever I scratch, I get a mini infection because everything around me is so dirty. My favourite bugs, though, are those that are self-illuminating at night. I like looking at them and imagine where they are flying to. They light up in different colours as well, and some have various points of their body lit up. Nature again is amazing.

There is one porter woman, who is seven months pregnant and refused to stay at home. Her husband is walking with us. She does not get any concession for the fact that she is pregnant. She needs to carry exactly the same load as everybody else. I try not to look at her as she struggles through. I know she would not give any of us her load. She is very young, too. All the porters walk barefoot with one piece of shirt and trousers on. And I'm complaining about cold feet. *Come on, woman. Toughen up. One more day to base camp.*

I can't believe that none of the other climbers are taking malaria tablets. I only have enough for myself, so I cannot and will not share. I am also stunned by the way the other climbers underestimated this challenge because the mountain is only 4,884 metres (16,023 feet) high. Some of the conversations are staggering. These people, the Everest summiteers included, did not think this through. Some didn't even bring energy bars. Some are traveling too light because it is a tropical mountain. Well, the peak next to our goal is glaciated! Some people don't have any medication; some have no repair kit. Someone gets fed up with the food and stops eating rice. Someone else gets fed up with the physical exercise. Well, she didn't really want to be here in the first place. It's madness. No wonder we finish the trip with serious pneumonia for one person, total exhaustion for another, and a near divorce in the making.

Day Seven

I wake to the sound of very gentle chanting, but with great strength as if through a collective consciousness. I peep out of my tent. The world is silent and still but for the thin smoke drifting weakly up from three tents in front of me. The mist is lifting from the swamp. It's cold because we are now at 3,500 metres (11,500 feet). I crawl out of my tent and follow the sound. I get to the porters' tent, where it looks like they are having a Catholic mass. They invite me in, but make signs of silence and prayer. Today is Sunday. Back at home, I would be in church as well. I look around at the tired and dirty faces and the closed eyes of people who cannot read, but are at an amazing peace with where and how they are. The feeling of concentration and devotion is intense and the chanting almost elevates the tent. The remains of the fire provide much needed warmth. One person leads the tune, and everybody joins in. I start meditating with them. I become the rhythm, the rhyme, and the shared experience.

At eight in the morning, we start our last day to base camp. We have a vertical gain of 1,000 metres (3,280 feet) to make. We are getting fitter in every respect. The sentiment is changing though. We have had enough of wandering and have a strong desire to get to base camp and face the challenge of the rock climb and summit attempt. The fried rice has tired us out. I keep eating but really only because I know I have to. I have lost weight already, another yo-yo to go through when I get back. Today is a taste of what summit day will be like. We have three vertical cliffs to negotiate. They are made of hard, grey rock. There is no protection, and most steps could have been deadly. On the last high pass, where we should have seen our climbing wall, we can only see a mass of grey cloud. We are an hour away. We finally reach base camp and I have a tent for myself, although I am petrified to be in a single tent in this wilderness. But I come to love my time alone at base camp, and all the way back.

This trip has three parts: the six-day mud and jungle struggle to base camp, the rock climb of the summit day, and then the four days of mud and jungle back. The team is not happy and the complaints are mounting. The tents are not pitched ready for us when we come to camp – it's a far cry from Kili. The food is monotonous, and we have to wait for four to five hours for dinner every evening. It rains, somebody snores, the porters smell, and now our stuff smells, blah, blah, blah. And on and on it goes. We support each other, we help each other, but as a team we are fragile. We concentrate on the single goal and have a common vision, getting to the summit, but that is about it. It feels very different from any other expedition I have been on. There is no strong leadership. The guides don't really help us to keep going, and they hardly speak English. I simply accept it. Every day, every step, every hill, cliff, meal and view. I have no complaints.

Poxi is my companion, although we don't really speak at all because his English is nonexistent. We develop a strong relationship though. He is here for me, and he always finds me on the route. He helps me when I get stuck, and he fixes my poles, boots, or whatever. He shares his 'special coconut liquid' because he knows I like it. We automatically assume the roles of a white female and spiritual local, who is not afraid to get close. He is always by my side, possibly in the most subservient way anybody has ever been with me. I don't take advantage of the situation; I appreciate his quiet admiration and service and reciprocate. Poxi is very young, beautiful, and strong, and our lives are in his hands as he cooks for everybody.

I love being here. I am truly myself. By experiencing this extraordinary nature so close-up and through being physically exhausted, I become totally open to what is going on around me. I achieve a state of euphoria, a feeling of oneness with everything that surrounds me. And I am whole and so happy. It feels like being on a different planet. However, deep down, I feel anxious about the rock climb looming ahead. We reach base camp at long last.

Day Eight

I make my tent my kingdom. I take my dry shoes out of their plastic bag. They look pristine, and I put some more water-resistant liquid on them. I put on my dry, warmer trousers, down vest, and dry socks. This feels like heaven. I am warm, and I am at base camp. I am happy. I quietly grin at my cunning 'boots and socks' plan. It worked perfectly. Today is a rest day. At midnight, we will start going up. The other guys wash their things and go for walks, but I sleep, eat a lot, and sleep some more. I review my summit clothes. I will pack my down vest and second rain jacket just in case, plus my harness, helmet, headlamp, my UNICEF T-shirt, energy bars and water.

It is relatively warm for 4,300 metres (14,100 feet). At seven, we have dinner and our last preparatory words. We agree Song should go first, at least at the beginning of the wall, because he is the slowest. We all need to meet by the Tyrolean Traverse anyway because we can only pass it by being together with both guides.

At midnight we form a nine-person train, everybody with a headlamp on. We trot slowly through gravel for an hour. We get to the bottom of the wall, and it is just that, a wall of rock rising into the sky above us. I don't feel fear at this stage. I feel a mobilisation of all my skills, my muscle strength, my ability to handle my equipment on fixed ropes, and my feel for the rock. The first 10 vertical metres (32 feet) is an overhang. *Great, just a little test.*

We start in the cloud. The moisture is dense around us. I bang my head against the overhangs of the rock; it's a good job I have a helmet on. After this close encounter I need to rest a bit because I can hear music in my head and feel slightly dizzy. Climbing at night, even with a head torch, means very limited visibility. You know the path only because a rope is hanging next to you and you are attached to it. Every foot and handhold has to be found, felt, and grasped. I appreciate my climbing lessons. I know what to do in a chimney, and it is a long one. I utilise the foot supports available behind me. I make sure to use my legs first and my arms only in an emergency. I always rest supported by my legs. I make my moves smooth, well paced, and as short as practical so as not to tire my arms too quickly. I appreciate the boots I have with tough, unbendable soles, which give me super grip even though the rock is wet. I so appreciate Troy's advice to take full leather gloves, although they are wet. But thanks to my wool liners, I feel warm. Most of all, the knife-sharp rock doesn't cut my palms, and they don't bleed. Thank you! I adhere to the practice of always being supported in three places so that, at any point in time, you move only one leg or one hand. I am careful, but move forward.

Because I am an inexperienced rock climber and anxious about what I am doing, I watch my every move. After three hours of climbing nonstop, I become very aware of every move of every part of my body. I am aware how much hold my fingers can take and how much tension my thighs can stand. I know to stop when my legs start shaking. I stretch my feet in my boots to avoid cramp. I tell myself that I am doing really well. I so don't want to fall into the abyss below. Suddenly, the insulation of my head torch gives way to the moisture in the air, and I lose even that weak stream of light. *Oh, sugar! I can't see a thing.* I freeze from anxiety.

'Think quickly,' I tell myself. 'The queue below me will start forming fast.'

I try to switch it on and off and on, but nothing. It's gone. I know it is not the battery because I changed it last night. It's pitch black and more than an hour until sunrise, that's if I will be able to see any sun with this dense cloud cover. I take several deep breaths to control the panic attack coming on. *Shit, shit, shit.*

And then I have a flash of inspiration. Eric Weihenmayer, the world-famous blind climber, climbed Carstensz Pyramid, the same route, just two months ago. If he did this and other much more challenging climbs, then so can I. I also remind myself that when I was on Kilimanjaro summit day, I switched off my head torch so I could feel what to do. With this new trust, I start to feel the holds instead of seeing them. I instruct myself: *Nothing changes, woman. You just keep doing as you have done for the last God knows how long.*

Three support points, one limb looking for a hold and up, then another limb looking for a hold, and then up and so on. Just keep going. I tell everybody that my headlamp is dead, but I am okay and start my blind ascent. I want to live, so I am even more aware of every move and every moment. I remember not to tense my muscles because they would get too tired too quickly. After an hour the sunrise begins, and gratitude and hope fills me. I become aware of how cold and wet everything I am wearing is and how short of breath I am from time to time. I am aware of how I am sometimes risking more than I would like to by making a sudden move or a move that is too long because there seems to be no other choice. Step by step, I ascend to a ledge where everybody stops for a pit stop of food, water, and toilet. Poxi finds me and checks up on me. I am fine. We share an energy bar. We have four more rope lengths (around 200 metres or 656 feet) to the summit ridge. I think the worst part is behind me, but what do I know? After my sugar intake, I feel refreshed. Because there is light, although we are still in a thick cloud, I feel more confident about those four ropes ahead. I try not to think how on earth I am going to descend. *No, don't even go there. First get to the top. You can worry about the descent in a couple of hours.*

We change the order of climbers. Ramon and Francis go first. I am third and then everybody else. A hand comes out of nowhere and I hear a voice.

'Grab my hand. That's the best way to get to the level of the ridge.'

I grab the hand and help the person behind me in the same way. We have reached the summit ridge. Again, Poxi checks up on me. I am fine. We walk on unroped for twenty minutes on a steep ridge and reach the famous gap, the Tyrolean Traverse.

We are shocked at what we see, and the air is thick with our expletives. What we can see are four old ropes dangling over a missing piece of rock some 30 metres (98 feet) long and perhaps 50 metres (164 feet) deep, which then goes 1,000 metres (3,280 feet) down on either side. Poxi is going first with additional rope, which will be used to pull those who don't have enough strength to pull themselves. That would be all of us. We wait at one end and take pictures of each other with ashen faces. We need to wait for everybody to go through the same routine. I observe that the ends of the ropes, which we are going to hang from over the gap, are frayed and well worn. One looks really bad. But the others are newer. I examine the anchor of those. It's a rock! What a surprise. No more examinations, please. Ignorance is bliss at times like this.

I am third to go. I need to lower myself enough to be able to clip into the four ropes, but not quite so low that I fall. Meldy helps me. Off I go, head last, legs spread apart, clipped at my stomach to the harness, and backpack down. I clip in my safety, which would probably not help much if something happened, but it makes me feel better. I try to imagine Tarzan and his free-style acrobatics on the lianas. I need to concentrate though and start to push myself on the rope. It's going well until I get to the middle, of course. Now I will have to pull myself slightly uphill because my body weight has tightened the rope. That is why the fifth rope was used. Poxi and the other guys on his side encourage me to pull harder. I am close. Now I need to turn myself around using air and goodwill. It's impossible, but I do it. I cannot remember how because nobody could help me. I end up being too close to the rock though and cannot move. Poxi cannot get to my harness to unclip the four ropes. Apparently, the people on the far end of the traverse laugh loudly. From a distance, I look like a squashed fly on the wall swatted by a news-paper. Cheers, guys! I need to pull myself up above the overhang I am glued to with my hands. I get clear instructions and follow them, but I am tired, scared, and totally sweaty. My apprehension rises. *What exactly do I do now?*

I feel everything tensing up. Is that my limit? No, no, no. After three attempts, I manage to create enough space for Poxi to manoeuvre between the rock and me. I finally get freed from the ropes for the others to take their turn hanging in midair. I sway around on soft, cotton-like legs. *Gee, only one more go on this on the way down!* As we wait for everybody to get across the cold intensifies as there is no sun and we are still in the cloud.

With thirty more minutes to the top, we set off as soon as everyone has crossed the gap. After ten minutes of walking on the edge unroped I am feeling confident… until we get to another gap, perhaps 2 to 3 metres (6 to 9 feet) long. There is a rope, but nobody wants to pull anyone anymore, so I have to clip in, kind of jump, and hope I land on the other side where Francis is currently standing. He gives me his hand in midair. I mean, how much fun can you have in one day? I have no choice. After three deep breaths, I jump and land exactly where I wanted to. My legs are soft again. I hug Francis, and we clear the way as the others make the jump.

After ten minutes we approach a little, really a tiny, gap in the rock, which is three steps wide. Well, that is two steps too many, no? And there is no rope. And then, because I have done many hours of climbing, I am really cold now, I have lost my torchlight, and I have gone through two difficult, technical things, all the fear and nervousness about this day, built up over the last six months, has become concentrated in this very moment. I don't know what to do. I am paralysed. I cannot move. I have Francis in front of me and the others somewhere behind me. I can see what he did, but I don't believe that I can do it. He turns around and talks to me. I cannot hear the words. I am really scared. Paul behind me literally shakes me up, and I start comprehending again. They also seem challenged by what we can see. We look at the missing rock from every angle. After we have talked it through, I stiffen my resolve and execute the agreed strategy and instructions.

'Left leg, a bit to the right, right hand to the left, and right leg closer to your left leg. Good going, Ania. Now move your left leg up ten inches.'

Fuck! How much is ten inches?

I shout back, 'I think in centimetres.'

But all of them are from North America, and there you go. We laugh. So I start moving my leg.

They shout, 'Higher, higher, to the left, higher. Yep, you got it.'

Great! I am on the other side by Francis, who gets another spontaneous hug. We help Denise and Paul and keep going. I lose them somewhere. Fifteen minutes later I can hear Ramon and Francis, 'One short rope, and you are on the top. Step to the right when you are off the rope.' I don't believe them, but it is exactly as they said. I sit down to appreciate the effort I went through and relax all my muscles for now. We cannot see a thing around us. Just like on Kilimanjaro, I see nothing from the top. I am happy though. We pose for pictures. We hug, talk, and spend too much time on the top for my liking. Everybody wants a picture with everybody else. The pictures are poor quality because we are in a thick, grey cloud. Suddenly, it starts snowing, and the temperature drops well below zero. That means the rock is not wet now, but slightly iced and very slippery. The ropes are very hard because they are frozen. We decide to start the descent immediately.

The way down is pure survival for all of us. We get hypothermia, Christina's pneumonia takes hold, and Francis and Ramon get lost taking a shortcut. It's dark because we are in a storm cloud. I get to the same little gap without any ropes and am stuck for movement again. Now I have snow everywhere, and the gap is still too wide for my liking. Christina shouts at me, losing her temper. Fear has frozen me. Poxi is ahead of me, he looks back at my frightened silhouette and very white face. He comes back down several steps and extends his hand. I grab it like my last resort and cross over. We hug. The team sticks together only until after the Tyrolean Traverse.

Our morale dips to unprecedented levels. People are seriously grumpy and unpleasant and shut down any social interaction. We shout at each other, there is less concern for one another and we just want to get the hell out of there. The situation is very potent for accidents. Denise almost divorces Paul a hundred times – she did not want to come here and deal with this shit. Christina is coughing her lungs out with every step. We are freezing and getting more and more tired with every step, or rather rope length of rappelling. I notice with horror that some of the ropes are not anchored at the bottom. Yes, that means that if you lose grip, you would not be secured even being clipped in. I remember what an American guide said to me on hearing I am going with a local company. 'There will be an unfortunate accident on Carstensz. It is just a matter of time.' Because the ropes are hard from being wet and frosted over, we cannot rappel down other than one by one. That takes ages. When you are waiting for the person in front of you to get off the rope, you freeze from lack of movement. With the snow coming down and melting at lower altitudes, we are rappelling through freezing streams or rather waterfalls of vigorously flowing water. It is all over us, splashing everywhere. My boots are wet inside because the water gets in from behind my jacket or above the boots. Everything is wet and cold. My body has lost the ability to keep warm, despite my physical activity, due to the slow progress. My fingers can hardly grab anything because they are totally stiff from the cold. All my blood is focused on my core functions, sustaining my vital organs and brain. I hope so anyway. When I'm preparing to rappel another rope, I am ultra careful handling the figure of eight device in order not to lose it, because that would be a total disaster. Denise has lost hers, and now Paul is using a spare, which makes things even slower.

Moving down, I can see the rock and the route we have climbed up. In some places, I am totally shocked. How on earth did I come up through here without any holds? I will never know. I try, however, to concentrate all my energy on getting back down to the safety of base camp. I can finally see the base of the wall, where we started at one thirty in the morning. I put my feet on the ground. Poxi is behind me. We hug. I immediately start to shudder with cold, exhaustion, happiness, and the knowledge that the most difficult part is over. We have got to the summit and down the wall.

I have another secret, of course. I put down my backpack, undress from the waist up and change all my layers. I put my down vest on top and a dry raincoat. I sit down, eat an energy bar, have a drink of freezing water, and start my plod back to base camp through the gravel path for an hour. I am still shivering from hypothermia. We get to camp at different intervals. We don't check who is in and who is missing but I can see that Paul and Denise are in. I crawl into my tent, change the bottom of my clothes into warm, dry garments, and wrap my sleeping bag around me. Then I start to seriously shiver. There are no warm drinks and no food for another five hours. I can hear Paul and Denise talking to the United States Embassy in a bid to get help, because Denise was hit by a boulder and cannot walk. I don't dare to ask. I know she cannot imagine walking out on the same route we came up. We have four more days of hard work through the mud and bush before we get to Sugapa. They make several calls, but the embassy does not react because nobody is seriously injured. What we don't know is that the embassy contacts our guide's company in Jakarta, confirms that everybody is okay, and never calls back. This causes a bit of international friction on the trip.

I fall asleep until the warmth of the afternoon sun wakes me up. I am swollen beyond imagination. I take a picture of myself and don't recognise my own face. Lack of protein, overnight exhaustion, peripheral oedema and hypothermia have all taken their toll on me. I am seriously hungry. No, I am starving actually. I reach into my summit pouch and start indulging in my prize food, raisins and nuts. I make sure to chew them slowly, one by one, to get the best out of every bite. I don't want to leave my sleeping bag, but the food has arrived. Surprise, surprise, it's rice and very little else because our guides are obviously tired too. I pack a bowl full of warm rice, take hot water with me, and crawl back into my sleeping bag. I eat until I am full and fall fast asleep again. I sleep for thirteen hours straight.

Day Nine

The next morning, we kind of crawl around the camp and wait for a really big breakfast. I would eat anything now really. We all spread our wet clothes from the summit day all over the place to give them a chance to air and dry. We are still wrapped up tightly because the weather has not improved much. We start talking about the descent from the summit. We need to vent our feelings. Poxi and Meldy say that neither of them, on their twenty-one expeditions so far, has ever had such bad weather before. We swap stories of frustration, fear and difficulties, and personal strength and wild satisfaction. We hug and congratulate each other. The smiles appear on our faces because we realise we have reached the summit and returned safely to base camp. We need further motivation however for four days of mud bath. We know what is ahead of us, and some of us are dreading it.

The breakfast is very late, around eleven o'clock, but warm and big indeed. It's the same stuff, fried rice, but it is food. We eat, pack, and leave base camp to get to the site in the middle of the swamp camp. I am slow, but I kind of want to take it all in. At a pass at 4,500 metres (14,800 feet), I look back at the wall I climbed up and down yesterday. It looks magnificent and daunting from here – shiny, sheer and vertical. I can see the tiny gap in the summit ridge, the Tyrolean Traverse, and I am glad it is all behind me. I feel satisfaction and a great sense of accomplishment. I have completed the most technical climb of the Seven Summits and probably in my life. After having negotiated two steep cliffs today, I know that, from now on, it is just a matter of keeping on walking and appreciating where I am because I certainly won't be coming back any time soon.

I stay behind the group. Poxi is with me. We sit down at some point and admire the Zebra Rock, a perfect reflection in a lake of surrounding peaks and forest. We take pictures. I love being in this pristine large space of outstanding natural beauty. It is so wild. I get to camp last. All the tents are occupied but one, which is in the middle a puddle. I look around. Nobody seems interested. I ask for help, but nobody comes out. I move it higher up and tie it back into the ground in a light rain. It starts pouring down, but thankfully I am inside by then. As I am blowing up my sleeping mat, I hear that Paul is injured. They have no first aid kit and he has a serious cut through his arm, right to the bone. He cannot remember how it happened. It looks nasty. When I touch the flesh around the wound, it is hot and red. The infection is raging inside. We examine our options. I propose to pour hot water over it and then make a compress from liquidized iodine tablets and cover with my plaster. If it gets worse I also have antibiotics. We will see. The next morning we repeat the process. Nothing serious develops, but it was close.

We have dinner and prepare for sleep. Before bedtime, the sky clears up and the stars come out in their millions. I stare into the sky and take it as a prize for a hard day. The air is fresh and cool. Life feels good. I dive into my sleeping bag.

Day Ten

We wake up to a very grey sky. We have three more days of walking, and today is a really long day. We need to climb two serious hills. It is cold, gloomy and windy. Ramon has stopped eating, and we are concerned about his strength. Francis walks on his own and gets seriously lost for at least two hours. Christina is quiet because her coughing wears her out quickly. Paul and Denise are not too happy again, together and individually. I walk on my own for most of the day. I am tired but feel good. I am losing weight dramatically because my private supplies of food have run out. This expedition was supposed to be over by now. I had already kind of reconciled myself to the fact that the organisers lied to us, but now not having enough food starts to become a real issue.

After a long tiring day I sleep like a log. I am not swollen any more, indicating that my body has recovered slightly from the summit bid. As we sleep lower every day, we should start feeling better.

Day Eleven

It is Sunday again. I participate in the same holy mass ceremony in the porters' tent at six in the morning. Today is colder than yesterday, and it is raining from the start. Everybody is sniffing loudly. We are discouraged from starting to walk before everything is ready to go. That sets off the porters who are tired and want to get back as soon as possible. But the group gets impatient and leaves the camp too early, which demoralizes the porters further. The day starts with crossing the waist-deep river without a bridge. We make an agreement about the furthest point we will walk to tonight so nobody passes it. But the group in front does not stick to this. I join some of the porters gathered in front of a wooden shack and wait for Denise, Paul, Song, Meldy and Poxi. It is raining again, and all the water is pouring down from the mountain above in swollen streams, making the mud bath even more difficult to negotiate.

The others are clearly way ahead, but unlikely to reach Sugapa by night-fall and probably already walking in darkness, which is just too dangerous and simply irresponsible. When Meldy and Poxi get to where I am, they are absolutely furious because we have only one tent between the six of us. It quickly transpires that we have dry food and the other part of the group has the cooking kit. We have a pack of Ramen noodles between every two people and a couple biscuits. For night shelter, Meldy breaks the padlock on the shed. It is full of barrels of suspicious, asphalt-smelling stuff. We get to a room full of dust and fire smoke. We are supposed to sleep in there. We put our bandannas over our noses and mouths so we can breathe. I adapt to the circumstances and try to sleep. By now the bedbugs have bitten my back so much that I cannot get comfortable in any position. The sweating during the day exacerbates the itching. I have been in a vicious cycle of agony and itching for ten days. Being knocked out by the smoke and lack of oxygen makes me sleep deeper.

Day Twelve

There is no breakfast so we share whatever biscuits were left from the quasi-meal last night and purify water from the river with iodine. We start the last day of our march. In three hours we reach the place where the others stopped the previous night. They had nothing to eat other than grilled corn that the locals gave to them. I present whatever biscuits I have left, and that is greeted with great enthusiasm. I learn that Francis left two hours ago on his own, which is incomprehensible to me. We start the last five hours of walking.

The last bit of the path is seriously uphill, another heartbreak. We reach the top of it and sit down. We are tired, hungry and dirty beyond belief. The sun is very strong now, and we are frying. Today is market day again. A woman with a basket stops and gives us free oranges and bananas. We want to pay, but she won't accept anything. Our giant smiles and sincere thanks are payment enough.

We finally reach the village. My first mission is to find a bucket shower, where I pour water over myself from a barrel. I wash my hair. It feels ecstatic. I put on the only clean change of clothes available and feel blessed. Poxi calls me to one side and gives me a pendant made of a wild boar tooth. He asks for the UNICEF T-shirt I had on the summit. UNICEF is well respected here as they run a school in a nearby village. We exchange other gifts, emails and phone numbers. Somebody has bought Fanta, Coca-Cola and Oreo biscuits, and we are having a feast while waiting for dinner. The celebration of a successful climb that lasts for at least three days has begun.

Day Thirteen

The next day, after a very light breakfast, we go through Sugapa for the last time to the airstrip. As we see and hear the engines roaring toward us, we start jumping up and down with joy. It has been such a challenging experience, physically, emotionally and interpersonally. I remain glued to the small window in the plane as Sugapa shrinks to a little dot. The jungle seen from the air looks impenetrable. We land in Timika and go straight to lunch, a serious overdose of lobster and other exceptional seafood. We stay in a very simple hotel for the night where I stand in the shower and savour the water running down my back and over my starved body. In the evening we have another celebration meal of more exquisite seafood.

When I return to Jakarta my intuition tells me to go to the business centre and withdraw the £10,000 I have put into an Iceland ISA savings account, earning interest for the Antarctica trip, which will go ahead in less than three months in fact. Five days later, Iceland defaults. I like my insight and intuition! I switch on the TV in my hotel room and hear that Lehman Brothers has collapsed and a number of big banks in Europe have been nationalised. I check on the internet to see if my employer still exists. It does! The deepest recession since the Great Depression of the 1930s is on its way. Wow, I cannot quite believe what I am hearing. Panic is on all the TV channels, but I feel numb and unaffected. I switch off the TV and concentrate on organising my trip back to London.

I arrive back to a grey, rainy autumn day. I have a shower and sit down on my sofa with a cup of tea. I look at the Thames and hear familiar sounds of boats and other people's laughter. I am content, quiet and totally at peace with myself. Later that evening I join some Antipodean friends for dinner, something I had arranged before I left. At the end of the evening after a beautiful home-cooked meal of duck, they suggest I cycle home on one of their bikes. Thanks guys – there is no way! I actually fall asleep on the underground on the way home.

On Monday, I send pictures and the following account of my trip:

Dear All, Yes, I had a successful trip to the top of Carstensz Pyramid in Papua and back down again. All in one piece! What we had to endure was, however, beyond any expectation: an ill-prepared expedition, which turned out to be four days longer than expected and only one guide speaking some English, losing porters to malaria, eating mostly fried rice three times a day, crawling through mud for seven to eight hours a day, walking through rivers without bridges, almost cutting our own way through the jungle, sleeping in some dodgy places full of bedbugs, spiders as well as some scary situations with cannibals and machetes and a very technical and challenging rock climb (fifteen hours nonstop) on the summit day.

Additionally, the weather turned on us on the summit from tropical rain to a snowstorm and minus 5 degrees Celsius (23 degrees Fahrenheit), so rappelling down from the summit was pure survival through rain showers in our summer clothing, where any wrong move would have been deadly. The experience was so very profound, deep, and fulfilling that words like remoteness, wilderness, somebody's helpful hand, outstanding natural beauty, being hungry, dirty, and coming back home have a totally new meaning for me. I would like to express my deep gratitude for all your donations to UNICEF. Local villagers know the organization and its good work has meant that I had to leave my summit T-shirt behind because they felt so proud to have it. Your donations kept me going. Thank you.

***

After the expedition I feel permanently tired. My knees are agony when I walk. I take 1,500 milligrams of glucosamine sulphate and have lots of warm, eucalyptus baths while trying to recover. I need to start training for Antarctica by carrying 30 litres (8 gallons) of water on my back very soon. But my hips and knees hurt from being in the cold and damp for days. I use deep heat cream every evening, but I fear my knees will not recover before getting on the plane to Chile. I quickly put on the lost weight. I will need that and more to survive the next trip in Arctic conditions. In fact, I don't care a dot what I eat. I catch myself eating a thick crust pizza one night close to midnight, then a cheesecake for dessert with a scoop of chocolate ice cream.

In the office the atmosphere is gloomy and depressed. We start mass redundancies. People get a phone call and are told to go to a specific office and sign redundancy papers there and then. I see deeply disappointed faces. The rows of desks clear out and we start working in a ghostlike office. I feel for the people around me, but the situation has no hold over me whatsoever. I am happy and full of hope inside. I sing in the office, give a presentation to improve the morale of my team, share stories from my expeditions, and work twelve to fourteen hours every day because my transformation programme is in the user acceptance testing phase.

Being close to death on Carstensz gave me a new perspective. What we do at work is not deadly; our family conflicts are not likely to cause hypothermia, and many of the problems we believe we face are not real difficulties

– it is we who make them insurmountable. If you program your mind to see the positive and the opportunity in life, then even if faced with disappointment along the way, I believe you should always find solutions.

CHAPTER 6

It's worth the wait

January 2009
Antarctica, Mount Vinson – 4,892 metres (16,050 feet)

BOOKING this trip in July 2008, prior to Carstensz, I wonder how Mt. Vinson will challenge me and help me grow. I know how to train for load carrying, I know the techniques for handling the cold, I know the necessary rope work, I know the route, I know how to camp on snow, and I'm so looking forward to being in a place so pristine and so far away that I would never even have considered visiting if it were not for the fact that it is one of the Seven Summits. Everybody says I am mad, with which I wholeheartedly agree.

One friend comments that going to Antarctica is a strange way to make sure I get a white Christmas. With a great degree of curiosity and openness, I anticipate another great lesson in life.

I arrive back from Carstensz in late September 2008, so that leaves only two months to prepare. I am fit, of course, but I still need to shore up the load-carrying strength in my lower and upper back. I know it's not enough time to recover fully after what I went through in Papua. My knees still hurt, despite taking huge doses of glucosamine sulphate and other medications, hot and cold patches, and special baths. Once more, I take up my routine of carrying 30 litres (8 gallons) of water to work and back in my rucksack every other day. My hips hurt, and my collarbones hurt from the load. My body is telling me it is too soon to punish it again, but I feel compelled. I have all the equipment, I know the guides well (Mountain Trip), I know one other person going and I have already paid $30,000 for this in full. I simply can't wait a year.

But most of all, I am so very mentally ready for this challenge, and that is what really counts. After fighting the low temperatures on Mount McKinley (Denali), I adopt the attitude that going to the coldest place on earth would just be ... you know ... cold! As it turns out I don't get especially cold in Antarctica! A great example of how you can use your mind to overcome physical challenges.

When I get the news that Jens from Denali is going on the same trip I am totally ecstatic! I so hope he again shares some of his strength with me by supporting me with his smiles and companionship. I also hope he carries some of my load (yes, I don't mind being a wuss for Jens!). But that is before I see the stunning Swedish blonde with legs up to her armpits that he is sharing this trip with.

Get in your place, woman. At the back of the queue!

He does still help me a bit though. Bless him. And a big thank you to Stina. She turns out to be not only stunning, but also great fun company, and physically and mentally very strong indeed.

Because my transformation program at work is in full swing, to keep up my training, I generally leave home at around five to be fully operational in the office by around seven. Many evenings I walk back after nine. All I am capable of doing when I finally return is have a shower and go straight to bed. Once again, the security guards at the main entrance to my office know my movements to the dot. I keep up my weekend cycling and trek in the Surrey Downs and Sussex. And this being England, of course the weather is not great. For the third time in my life, and during the most significant global economic crisis since the great depression, I have a zero balance in my bank account. I don't fear the future but I take out mortgage protection insurance just in case. It is all happening at once. On top of that, my very long-distance relationship with Troy who I had met on Mt. McKinley doesn't manage to sustain itself and comes to a disappointing end just before the trip.

My mum comes to visit for a week. Walking me to the door one morning, she says 'Who would have known that, after carrying you and caring for you as a little girl, I would be saying farewell to you one day? A strong woman leaving home at five in the morning and in the dark with 35 kilograms (77 pounds) on her back to go to the office, preparing to explore Antarctica. I am scared to be proud of you.'

A Polish girlfriend lives with me for three months while she learns English. This supporting presence means a lot to me. She sees me off to Carstensz, welcomes me back, not judging what she sees, she makes me that first cup of tea on my return, a rare pleasure. She also helps me with domestic stuff when I am out and about.

In November, I go for a practice weekend in Scotland with a boyfriend and Ann and Dan from Aconcagua. We scale several peaks, roll in the snow, eat well, and have tremendous fun. It proves to me that I am strong, psyched up for a challenge, and ready to go.

The Wednesday before I leave, as I am walking back home with my backpack for the last time on a cold rainy December evening, a raw egg flies through the air and hits my jaw just where it connects to the rest of my skull. It hurts badly and tears well up in my eyes. The egg bounces off and breaks at my feet on the pavement. I could not turn around, run or simply speed up my pace even if I wanted to as I have 35 kilograms (77 pounds) on my back. I look ahead at the building where I live, massaging my bruised jaw and feeling thoroughly deflated. The next morning as I chew my breakfast with difficulty, I wonder why somebody would be so unkind.

The last day in the office (Friday, December 12) goes well. I am ready to go by four thirty. I send the following email to my supporters:

> Dear All, Here I go again. It is the sixth peak out of the Seven Summits (the highest peak on every continent), which I am climbing to raise funds for UNICEF. I have completed Kilimanjaro in Africa, Elbrus in Europe, Aconcagua in South America, Mount McKinley in North America, and Carstensz Pyramid in Australasia. This one is Mount Vinson in Antarctica, the coldest place on Earth. It is 4,892 metres (16,050 feet) high. We fly to the ice from the southern tip of Chile on an old Russian duct-taped plane and, from there, still by propeller plane, to base camp. It will be minus 40 degrees (Celsius and Fahrenheit), strong winds, and pretty white. I hope to huddle up with some penguins for additional warmth. As you sit to your Christmas dinners, think of me carrying a backpack (25 kilograms or 55 pounds) and pulling a sled (25 kilograms) and the kids you can help by donating to UNICEF. Please give generously.

The flight from London, via Paris, to Santiago de Chile takes forever. After sleeping the whole way, I land at nine thirty in the morning. The brother of a dear friend from London picks me up, and for the whole day I am looked after like a Polish princess. We go to a luxurious hacienda overlooking the city at the bottom of the Andes, where I had climbed Aconcagua two and a half years earlier. We have a fantastic lunch. Then I sleep on a hammock by the swimming pool until dessert, lemon sorbet with some berries, is served. It is as if all my giving on Aconcagua is flowing back to me. For the first time in my life I just graciously receive without feeling guilty that other people want me to feel good.

On the plane to Punta Arenas, because it is so close to the South Pole, with the right weather you can see the curvature of the Earth as you come in to land. I get lucky. It is fantastic to see the sexy curve of our home as if from space. It is wonderfully rounded. Although it is close to midnight, the spectacular sunset unveils right in front of my eyes due to the polar day. A feeling of joy fills my heart. Earth … home … peace.

Heidi, one of the Mountain Trip guides, picks me up. I check into a hotel room and crash. The next morning we have the most serious equipment check I have experienced to date, signifying we are going where normal people don't go. I have everything of the right quality, which shows I have accumulated a lot of knowledge over the last few years. In the afternoon we visit the penguins.

The team is very international – for the first time I have two Japanese guys on my team. Greg (an Australian on our trip) immediately calls them Sushi and Sashimi for ease of memory … they seem to like their new names, judging by their snorts of laughter on first hearing it!

The following morning, we all have a briefing with the Antarctic Logistics Enterprise (ALE), the only commercial company that operates flights to Antarctica under a special contract with all the Antarctic treaty countries. The briefing is conducted in a very condescending, arrogant manner. We are shown horrendous frostbites, and made to feel stupid and reckless. We are shown the facilities at Patriot Hills. The weather forecast is bad so we are on standby every twelve hours.

After three days of waiting and after having visited every museum, café and shop in a very small town (even the cemetery got a visit), we have clearance and are summoned to the airport. Everybody gears up. The check-in process is cursory. We have passports, but nobody looks at them, and nobody checks the bags even though we are carrying a lot of very dangerous gear indeed. We do not have any boarding cards. It is as if we are to disappear into an unknown land and people do not want to leave any trace of our existence.

After six gruelling hours in the airport, wearing our serious winter gear, and after we have polished off the entire stocks of two small bars and the ice cream stand, the flight is called off due to the weather at Patriot Hills. Utterly heart-broken, we check back into the hotel. I need to start sharing the cost with somebody, and that's how I get to know Greg, who turns out to be a dream room and tent mate. My time with him on this trip involves a lot of serious two-way therapy for each other. Greg climbed Everest two years ago and remains my main information source for my next trip.

We go back to waiting mode – it ends up being nine more days of waiting! It is worth noting that, until this trip, I was the most impatient person you could meet. I would hurry up the coffee machine in the office. I would have seven or eight chat or internet sites running in parallel so as not to lose time. I would read four books at the same time. I could cook, iron, read and talk over the phone simultaneously in order to have more time for something else. Wait for a bus? No, I would rather walk. Wait for somebody to propose to me? No, I would propose, sort out all his problems, and be ready for the next adventure. While I was once refurbishing my flat, I started mending both bathrooms at the same time and ended up not being able to wash at home for a week. Or there was the time when I so wanted to fix the new ceiling lamp I had bought that very day that I could not wait for my boyfriend to come round and give me a hand. So there I was, balancing on a chair with my mountaineering head torch on, manipulating 240V wires while Nigel ate his supper by candlelight nearby. I even once inserted a life-to-do list in a Valentine's Day card, setting out an impossible deadline. When booking things, I would plan seven hundred years in advance, right down to the smallest detail, and based on a vision of the future that was far ahead of anyone else's imaginings. I would make outrageous demands on my colleagues to do the impossible and deliver before the expected date on projects at work. I would usually be miles ahead of the entire team and obviously losing people on the way to implementation, as I would be operating in a 'three weeks from now' frame of mind while everybody else was still on today. Patience was never my strong point, to put it mildly!

What a wonderful way to learn to let go of anything and everything. Twelve days of having no control whatsoever over your fate is a long time. Finally, life is generous enough to teach me patience. Thank you.

Two more days pass with the team on standby every morning. We are called back into the ALE office. The satellite weather reading is dreadful for at least thirty-six hours. By now we know every single penguin in this small city, where even the main newspaper is called *El Penguino*. Some of us sigh, some shout, some pull out and go back home, some drink more vodka ... certainly the Russian team. People are frustrated and exhausted from the wait. Our team decides to have a quick trip to the famous *Torres de Paine* in Patagonia. We hop on a minibus, drive for seven hours, share a bunk in an eight-man room of a youth hostel (I'm the only girl), get up at two thirty in the morning, jog for five hours to the lake at the bottom of the Torres in trainers, and return in time for breakfast. At ten o'clock, the minibus picks us up and we drive seven hours back to Punta. Although crazy, it is a welcome break in the waiting game.

Christmas is approaching quickly. We make plans. There are only two restaurants open in the whole town on Christmas Eve. We are in a Catholic country, so everybody has to go with the flow of no turkey and the main celebration being on the twenty-fourth. We basically book one restaurant for ourselves, and I have yet another Christmas away from my family, with almost total strangers, eating ceviche and enchiladas instead of the traditional Polish twelve-dish vegetarian dinner. But I would rather be here, fully alive, than in Poland.

I go solo to a midnight mass. It is an exhilarating experience because the traditions are very alive in Punta. There is an authentic Holy Family with three kings, shepherds, angels the whole lot. The mass is like an amazingly orchestrated live nativity scene full of the incense and wonderful singing. People in the audience are dressed up ceremonially, except me of course, as if they were paying homage to the real newborn baby Jesus. The solemn atmosphere seems to elevate the roof of the Gothic-style church. I walk back through a ghost town while everybody is inside eating supper. I meet a black cat and make a wide circle so as not to cross his path.

Back in the hotel, Greg and I organize a movie night and day. We bring popcorn, chocolate, lots of beer and wine, and more. We rent *Seven Years in Tibet*, *Long Way North*, *Perfume*, and many other classics. We watch over twenty long films while waiting for the weather to clear. On Christmas Day, we go to Shackleton's Bar. Oh, yes, everybody on the trip is reading some form of a story about that trip. How on earth did those people, who had none of today's high-performance equipment, survive a whole winter on the ice and still not eat their dogs? Respect! We are frequent guests at the La Luna café, where the owner's handmade ice creams are the best I have ever eaten. As a result we all put on serious fat, just like the local seals preparing for a long, cold winter. We all try to stay fit. Greg and I walk for miles every day along the beaches. We also rent bikes and cover every path in the area.

Those twelve long days of waiting, however frustrating, are a true blessing to me. I could finally fully recover from my previous expedition. My knees and hips heal with the moderate exercise, but remain strong. I eat well and regain my full strength. I am physically ready.

The planned nineteen-day schedule was supposed to be:

Stop 1: Paris

Stop 2: Santiago de Chile
Stop 3: Punta Arenas
Stop 4: Patriot Hills
Stop 5: Vinson base camp
Stop 6: Low camp
Stop 7: High camp
Stop 8: Summit and back

However, by the end of day twelve of the expedition, we are still only at the third stop. I have taken three weeks off work for this trip. I know I could still make it back on time in the unlikely event that all goes to plan. I decide to worry about holidays, work, boss, project, and all the potential consequences, after a successful summit.

We remain in good spirits and never get bored: we organize an intercontinental ping-pong tournament, play cards, share books and swap stories. We get to know each other very well. We have a saying, 'What goes on the mountain stays on the mountain.' On the second day in Punta, somebody says, 'I will get all of your screwed-up stories from you because we all have one. Otherwise, we would not be here.'

These 'stories' are varied. One of us is dealing with seventeen years of married misery, having gone through a torturous divorce process over three years ago; still hating the former significant other to the bone, and laying all the blame on the other party for what happened. One of us is in a serious midlife crisis, where the only goal after coming off the trip is to buy a Porsche... the dealer is ready and waiting with the right colour. Another is buying a business across the Atlantic. There is a serious affair with a psychopathic boss to consider, and a long drawn out farewell to a beloved partner who died on an expedition ten years earlier and is still too present to forget. There is a decision about what to do with life going forward from a business perspective. There is a power wife waiting back home and who still has a full grip on the hubby who is seriously out of his comfort zone on the ice. And finally there is an amazing youth, full of anticipation, hope, mischief and fun. That is just some of the team and their life baggage.

Day One

We finally board the *Illushyn*, a Russian bomber plane with a glass floor in the cockpit so you can see exactly where the bombs would fall. It is a four and a half hour flight. Instead of snacks, we get earplugs because it is not insulated. We have to shout to each other and it reeks of aviation fuel. Overall, it is seriously dilapidated and in urgent need of repair. The rather improvised toilet has a large sign saying, 'It's not as long as you think.' Landing on hard ice on rubber wheels is an art. The Russian pilots manage to do it just perfectly, as they skilfully place the aircraft on the runway that stretches for miles. We have to change into full winter gear on the plane. The moment the loading gate opens at the tail of the plane, we are exposed to a new type of cold – the bitter, penetrating, don't-have-any-part-of-your-body-uncovered polar type of cold. You can feel it everywhere, even through thick layers of woollen gloves and hats. Now it hits home precisely why it is only possible to land safely in this place if the weather conditions are exactly right.

Everything in Patriot Hills is run with military precision. From setting up tents to removing human waste, everything is perfectly planned, packaged, and executed to the dot. Everybody is under the command of the camp manager, a lady who lost two fingers to frostbite and is in her third season out here. The staff come back here year after year, and I can see why. The place is just totally amazing. With a beautiful strong sun like today, everything sparkles and shines like we are walking on diamonds, not snow and ice. The sculptures on the horizon are stunning, ever-changing. Being here is like stripping everything back to real life. Anything we have here is just essentials. There is no conspicuous consumption, no artificial comforts, improvements or distractions. Human contact is deep, straight to the point and without politics and hidden agendas. This place is totally uninhibited.

Today it is comfortable because there is no wind. It dawns on us that the people gathered in the tent have been stranded out here in dreadful stormy conditions, waiting for the lifesaving plane to arrive, while we were eating, drinking and being merry in the warmth of Chile. And we were complaining!

After dinner we set up our tents because we do not know when the weather at Vinson base camp, our next stop, will be good enough for us to take our next plane. We familiarise ourselves with the setup. Most of all, we learn how to walk on blue ice. It's very dangerous and can lead to serious accidents. So be careful! We learn how to use the Antarctic toilets with very special features for ladies (a bucket) and gents (a barrel with a pipe) for number one and a wooden box with a toilet seat for number two. We get used to using sanitizers after any activity to avoid spreading bugs between ourselves and strive to leave no trace of our presence on the ice. I love the idea of sustainable mountaineering. It reminds me that I am only a guest here.

Day Two

One night has passed. The place is beautiful. I often walk out of the kitchen tent and just stand there to gaze out at the white horizon. I am totally hypnotized, although, in essence, I am looking at nothingness. The clarity around me creates clarity within me. I will take it home and retain it for months to come. This is like a real Christmas with everything white and covered with snow. I roll in it. We build things out of it. We love it.

One day has passed playing cards, talking, walking, and sorting out the food for the mountain. I'm reading an amazing book by Ayn Rand, *Atlas Shrugged*. The book has over a thousand pages, so it's ideal for here. In a couple days my book is cut into several parts with a pocketknife and is read simultaneously by four to five people while we wait out a vicious snow storm. For now, our spirits are high because we are finally here. And being here is just amazing. There are no colours, no visible plant or animal life, no smells, and no noise apart from the wind. If it were not for the camp, it would feel like we were on a different planet. The air is so amazingly clean that we can see for miles. The snow here is very dry. In fact, we are on the largest desert on earth, where it rarely snows. It is so dry that I get a nosebleed every morning.

Day Three

I get up around six, at least I think it is. I have no clue any more what time zone my body is in. We are in the polar day and it never gets dark. The sun just makes a little circle above our heads every twenty-four hours. When it gets really cold (-40 degrees Celsius and Fahrenheit) a halo effect is formed around the sun, giving it a holy aura.

Because I get up first, I help to pack 200 eggs for our group. I crack open fifteen eggs, put the contents into a Ziploc bag, mix it with some flour, milk powder and water, and chuck it out of the window to deep-freeze. These are used later to make scrambled eggs, pancakes or omelettes. Bill, our lead guide and co-owner of Mountain Trip, has hurt his knee, and it needs icing. It's easy. We just grab some ice from in front of the tent, put it in a bag, and he is fixed.

The weather at base camp is clearing so we can fly. Landing is pretty bumpy and we are lucky that our Twin Otter doesn't nosedive into the powder snow. The pilots are Canadian and just wear T-shirts under their down jackets. I can see the summit of Mount Vinson for the first time. It looks far away, but reasonably achievable, which cheers me up immensely. We start setting up a camp for our group. I gather snow for water and dig in the mess tent structure. Everybody arrives and we soon have dinner.

The cold here is something else. For two hours this camp is in the shadow of the mountain. Standing outside even for fifteen minutes can give you frostbite. The freezing cold is so penetrating that we have strict instructions on when we can leave the camp to move up, when we can leave our tents, and when we just need to stay inside in sleeping bags to make sure we don't weaken ourselves and our immune systems. One of our team has a chest infection. I supply him with eucalyptus sweets and tissues but he is getting worse every day. I am secretly relieved that I am not sharing a tent with him.

Today, we try to cure the team member in deep midlife crisis. He is totally adorable but cannot see it himself. Stina and I are hard at work to boost his self-esteem. We make a lot of progress. By the end of the trip, he is well on the way to getting married, having kids, and forgetting about the Porsche!

We also try to explain to the henpecked hubby-to-be that he needs a bit of his own identity, preferably lots, but today is his fiancée's birthday and he is sad he is not there for her. He gets lots of group hugs.

In another group there is a Korean national hero who lost all his fingers on both hands and several toes to frostbite, yet still climbs. He is determined to do the Seven Summits and will probably be the first ever fingerless person to achieve that. So, I know a blind climber and a no-grip climber, and I think I have it tough. I feel humbled.

There is another Polish lady – a media celebrity – on the mountain at the same time as me. For Christmas Eve she came to our hotel where we spoke Polish and wished each other *Wesołych Świat* in our mother tongue. She misses her toddler daughter terribly, and I try to cheer her up a bit.

Day Four

We wake up to tremendous weather and decide to move up a camp. We pack our load onto sleds and in backpacks, and set off for a six-hour walk, winding gently upwards. Walking here is different than on any ground I have ever been on. The wind shapes and freezes the snow into hard waves, and one has to step over them. The sled gets stuck, so there's constant stopping and starting. It is amazingly hot. In fact, I am only wearing a single layer, which is simply unheard of. Partway up we break into a sort of run. There are seracs and ice falls on the path, and we don't want to be hit. We pass a couple of emergency caches, which proves to all of us that this place really can be very dangerous when the weather turns ugly, as we are soon to discover.

We reach low camp where I change my sweaty top instantly, change my triple boots to down booties, and get going with the tent setup. We build snow walls around the tents to protect us in case a storm hits. We familiarise ourselves with the pee hole and the poo loo. Everybody is using a wag bag system out here, and we will be taking it all the way back to Chile. Thank God that everything freezes in less than a minute! Today we have pizza for dinner. Don't you just love those guys from Mountain Trip? This is followed by ice cream. Well, that is debatable pleasure out here, but I have lots of it until I'm in serious need of hot water to defrost my stomach.

I smuggle a hot water bottle out with me to warm up my sleeping bag and snuggle up. Greg and I read and swap more stories. We review all the love and hate relationships in our lives and try to understand each other's views. Greg helps me to un-attract myself from the guy I am blindly attracted to at that moment. After a last pee, we decide to go to bed. Well, we have actually been in our respective sleeping bags all the time, but now we close our eyes and start snoring.

For me, this expedition is all about gaining confidence in being totally self-sufficient on a mountain in difficult conditions. Everest will demand that of me. So I am trying to do everything as if I am out there already. The 1,200 metres (3,936 feet) of fixed lines here will represent the Lhotse Face for me. The little edge at the top will be the knife edge at 8,800 metres (28,870 feet). The little pyramid 100 metres (328 feet) before the summit will be the Hillary step in my mind.

We compare notes with Greg regarding Everest. I know quite a lot already. He shows me his video and I almost cry when I hear his laboured breathing through the oxygen mask on the summit day. It seems terribly hard work and everybody looks totally dead when they come down.

Mt. Everest, for 99.9 percent of the Polish population, is a mountain that is simply not climbable. Only our top-notch Himalayists like Wanda Rutkiewicz,[3] Jerzy Kukuczka, or Anna Czerwinska[4] have succeeded. Most people, including most mountaineers, don't view it as attainable. At least I grew up with this notion. Maybe the ingrained Polish national inferiority complex has created that mind-set. For Greg, however, it was totally different. His uncle climbed it with a friend. They were too late to descend from the summit so they had to bivouac without oxygen by the rock off the South Summit (approximately 8,700 metres or 27,800 feet). His uncle lost two fingers and a couple toes, but he did it. At the time, it was the highest unplanned bivouac on Everest. Greg used to sit on his uncle's lap and listen to the story over and over again. His mind was programmed through those tales into believing he could do it himself. So, unlike me, he never had a barrier in his mind in the first place.

Over the ensuing months I still have to deal with that mental barrier and a lot of fear.

---

[3] The first Polish and European and the world's third woman to reach the top

[4] The first and, to date, only Polish woman to complete all Seven Summits

Day Five

Today is a rest day. We are itching to go up. Most of the other groups, the Germans and Russians, are going to cache for high camp. We drag Bill out of the guides' tent and demand that we move. He sends us back to our tents with our tails between our legs. The uprising is over in three short minutes.

We go for short walks instead to keep in practice. We also set up the ropes to practise what awaits us tomorrow. Everybody joins in even though we have all done it before. Nobody is too proud or too bored. This refresher could save our fingers or even our lives.

The meals here are short events because of the cold. When we are all in the kitchen or the mess tent, it is nice and warm. We can even unzip our jackets, but the minute that there are only two or three of us, we start to freeze, and we have to retreat to our sleeping bags and the shelter of our tents. And that is where a thousand-page book is a real lifesaver. And it is such a good book that we all devour it and spend time swapping our thoughts on it.

Day Six

Finally we are on the move. The plan is to carry the cache up a sixty-five to eighty-degree steep slope for 1,200 metres (3,937 feet) and then return to low camp. As one does on New Year's Eve, I suppose? We do it individually. I love that concept because it further tests one's self-sufficiency on the mountain, which I will need for Everest. It takes us six and a half hard hours to get to the top. It is the same well-known routine from Denali. I shout, 'Anchor!'. I manipulate the safety carabiner and ascender. I shout, 'Clear!' I take twenty-five steps. I shout, 'Anchor!' I manipulate the safety carabiner and ascender. I shout, 'Clear!' ...... I catch up with the first person I need to pass, who is too slow for my pace. I have never done this before.

I ask, 'Can I please pass around?'

He says, 'Not here. Wait until the next anchor.'

I respect his fear as I have my own reservations as well. We get to the anchor and I step over the rope to be in a better position. I switch my safety carabiner first above the anchor and then the jummar above the carabiner.

We both rest for a minute or two. I will pass more people both coming up and going down this slope. In time, it becomes second nature.

In the middle of this slog Bill orders a twenty-minute rest stop. After which I have great difficulty putting my pack back on and getting upright because the pack is so bloody heavy and the slope so steep. At the top of the slope we put on more clothes and sit down for another twenty minutes to make sure our bodies start producing more red blood cells, because we are now 900 metres (2,952 feet) higher. The strongest rope (not mine, of course) takes some stuff and moves it straight to high camp, which is an additional hour's ascent. The rest of us descend. Again, each person goes separately.

Back at low camp I have a treat, Chilean chocolate from my goody bag, which I share with Greg. I groan in pleasure. I love dark chocolate, and it turns out that he does too. I worked hard today, but I feel fine and don't have any serious muscle pains. This confirms that I did enough training. Again, like on Cartensz Pyramid, people have underestimated this mountain. Most didn't spend much time training because it is only 4,892 metres (16,050 feet) high. I am particularly glad I invested the time in pack carrying.

We have dinner and wish each other 'Happy New Year!' over a steaming cup of hot chocolate. We embrace and go around to everybody, not just saying 'Happy blah, blah, blah,' but speaking from our hearts. Meanwhile, the Russian contingent has set up a Christmas tree (sort of) and they are getting highly intoxicated in traditional Russian style. We are all fast asleep well before midnight.

Day Seven

Our team takes a rest day. It is better to acclimatize here where it is warmer rather than at high camp. We are amazed that the Russians decide to move camp today after their hard party last night. Perhaps all that vodka keeps them warm. Or perhaps it is the legendary Russian soul. Whichever it is, I am glad I am not part of that team. It is not advisable to drink alcohol in cold conditions because it dehydrates you even more. The warmth that the liquid creates evaporates very quickly, leaving you feeling even colder. The German group moves up as well. It will turn out that they do not take enough food with them though.

Today's topic is 'your screwed-up story yet again,' and there is a new litany of topics to work on. From toxic siblings, ever-controlling mothers, excessive drinking, Swedish-style sex nightclubs[5] through to sadistic teachers. This is topped off with some serious talk about business development and career change, which some of us are considering. Because we have an executive coach with us, we touch upon all sorts of behaviours, break it all down, and put it all back together again.

By now I know I won't be back in the office on time. I reconcile it within myself. I made a choice and I take full responsibility for it.

Every day we measure the temperature inside and outside the tents. It was -17 degrees Celsius (1 degree Fahrenheit) last night inside the tent. It seems unbelievable that we are all okay after having breathed such extremely cold air for ten hours of sleep.

Day Eight

We are moving camp. When we last did this exact route two days ago, we had two-thirds of the load and nice weather. Now it is windier, and my pack is closer to 33 kilograms (72 pounds). Although we know what to expect of the day and are apparently doing it much quicker, it feels a lot more difficult. I can distinctly feel my shoulders hurting. To me, we seem to have dropped to a snail's pace, but Bill ensures us that we are doing better than two days ago and he is quite proud of us. Looking back, I think it was a motivational technique, but at the time it meant a lot to all of us.

Patiently, step by step, again passing other people going up, I finally get to the top of the slope. The wind is bad now and we need to wrap up. As soon as I stop I start freezing. Bill looks at me and asks if a bit of shelter would help so I can put on my puffy pants and down jacket. He pulls out a piece of Gore-Tex that looks just like a giant condom and pulls it over me and my rucksack. Out of the wind I am able to function once again. I change my gear and put on my face mask, goggles, and summit down mitts with hand

---

[5] In one Swedish nightclub, there is apparently a wall with holes just big enough for a male implement to come through. Ladies wanting some pleasure line up against the wall, and the intercourse happens there and then between total strangers.

warmers in each. I do it quickly, knowing the others are suffering in these conditions.

After I get out of the condom, which turns out to be simply a bivi-bag, I see that Ken is struggling with his crampons and pants. I kneel in front of him, take off my gloves and help him sort his gear out. Somebody else is helping Michtaka, and others are attending to themselves. It is times like these when your character is thoroughly tested. If you are not honest with yourself, your guides and your team with respect to any problem you are having, you risk serious frostbite and, potentially, death. You have to be truthful, with full responsibility and integrity for yourself. If you tell even the smallest lie, it will end up affecting you and your team. It could cost you dearly.

We all re-gear. The other two ropes have left fifteen minutes ago and are probably reaching camp by now, setting up their tents. Bill divides the rest of us into groups with compatible walking speeds. We continue our plodding, roped up and traversing up a steep slope. It takes us exactly an hour and a half to get to camp. The route is so deceptive. You reach a little peak thinking, 'This is it!' When you finally get to the top of it, you see another one. It's really quite disheartening. We are walking in snow that gets stuck to the bottom of our crampons, so after every fifteen to twenty steps, we need to bang the ice axe against the metal of the crampons to shake off the snow and ensure the crampon teeth are gripping securely. At some point my crampon gets loose for some reason. I need to stop the whole rope. Again, stopping in this wind is the last thing you want to do, but if you don't, you might lose a vital piece of equipment that will prevent you from continuing. As I fix my fittings, having taken my mitts off, the rest of the team tries to stay warm. Most people appreciate the small stop to catch their breath. My hands have stiffened up from the cold, and I am trying to get them warm again. Hand warmers are the best invention in the world – my hands slowly start to feel alive again in my mitts. We keep plodding against the wind, which is getting worse with every minute. Snow blows it into our fragile figures and we bend forward even more. It would not be possible to breathe in without a face mask. When I take it off for a second, the needles of snow and ice painfully force their way into my nostrils and my closed mouth. I cannot imagine not having goggles either.

We reach camp and the storm is in full force by now. These are the most extreme conditions I have ever been in. The storms on Aconcagua and Denali were kids play in comparison. The other groups had decided to go for the summit today and are coming back as we approach camp. They look frozen solid and very grumpy. But they have all summitted, though in awful conditions. I congratulate them and they tell us in detail what awaits us. That, however, will not happen for another thirty-six hours. From now on it is a case of pure survival for us.

Whoever has their tent up is already in it. I crawl into mine. Greg is there, shivering in his down suit and sleeping bag. I organise my stuff, blow up one pad, and blow up my feather bed, another best invention (Swiss). Michtaka visits us as he doesn't have a tent yet and needs to hide. We snuggle up together, three of us in the two sleeping bags. We get a bit of hot water each to warm up. I get my super chocolate out, and everybody takes giant bites. From his pocket, Michtaka produces a green tea-flavoured Kit Kat chocolate snack bar. *Oh, my God! It is so good, but why can't you buy it in Europe? Perhaps a marketing opportunity!*

After a while Michtaka leaves the tent to start pitching his own. Greg is bitterly cold so I start massaging him. Well, it's more like beating him up to make an impact on his body through the double thickness of an expedition-rated sleeping bag and an Everest-rated down suit. He screams and yells (maybe with delight), but it is good exercise. It warms me up as well, so we continue with the friendly beating rounds. It's also good for increased blood circulation. Heidi, the guide, comes in with dry soups, hot water and food. We select our feast of rehydrated chicken with Ramen noodles. It is the ultimate of service for our guides to walk around in this cruel wind and hand out goodies. I am deeply happy to have gone with Mountain Trip. Thank you, guys.

The wind is so strong that we are advised not to leave our tents, even for the toilet. And it is so loud that we can hardly hear each other, even when we are right next to one another. We eat our food, put in earplugs, and bury ourselves in sleeping bags. It was a hard day and we need to rest. We hope that by the time we wake up the weather will have cleared and we will be good to attempt the summit. Well, we hoped in vain.

Day Nine

I wake up not knowing what time it is. It really doesn't matter though because, judging by the conditions outside, we are not going anywhere. Our tent is full of snowdrift, and I cannot see even a bit of Greg. He is so wrapped up in his sleeping bag. I take advantage and pee using my funnel and square Nalgene bottle. I bury the pee bottle back in my sleeping bag because it is crucial that all liquids stay liquid. I take a frozen wet wipe and attend to my face. I have to blow on the tissue so it defrosts and does not scratch my skin. I take another frozen sheet and wipe my body. My period is finally over so I can sort everything out. I gather all the solid rubbish in one bag for removal later on. I celebrate getting to high camp by changing my underwear. It feels so clean!

It is a waiting game. Our tent is all frosted up, and we basically have snow falling inside as well as gathered in the corners of the tent. Everything that is not inside a sleeping bag is frozen solid. The scream of the wind persists. Everything is moving. If we were not inside the tents they would fly away. I take a couple of short videos with my camera, presenting the inside of our tent and the deafening noise. I listen back to it and cannot recognize my own voice. Finally, breakfast arrives at two and we eat a portion of porridge each. We all need to get out of our tents and reinforce the structures because the wind has weakened the anchors of the tents. We dress up like we're going out into ... well, an Antarctic blizzard.... and crawl out.

Everybody is at work. Moving at altitude is beneficial because it aids acclimatisation and prevents heart attack. One of Greg's friends died on the mountain making a very sudden movement after lying down for a day. We cut blocks of hard snow with a snow saw and build hip-high walls around our little homes. We recheck the anchors and try to dig out our crampons and ice axes, which were left outside and are now buried somewhere safely away from the tents. I take advantage of being outside and have a pee. Or to be more precise, I pull my pants down literally in front of everybody (not that anyone cares), because the location of the pee-hole is very exposed. The wind bites my butt severely and I lose feeling almost straight away. Instead of creating a puddle, the stream is spread into frozen mist instantly ahead of me. I go to the toilet, but then cannot locate my wag bag. After searching for two minutes I find it buried under a heap of snow. The toilet is behind a snow wall, so there's a little more privacy and less wind. Relieved, I use hand sanitizer to clean up and get back to work. After about two hours of hard work, battling against the wind and snow, we are all exhausted, but the job is done.

We go back to our tents and dinner is served. It's more rehydrated chicken and noodles. It does not matter that the water is lukewarm by the time it gets to us, because the food tastes just fantastic. Our salts are replaced and we feel warmer. I know I am rapidly losing weight again. We go back into our sleeping bags, and for the rest of the evening Greg and I talk. He used to work in the anti-terrorist police force and tells me the story of when he had to shoot a person (a baddie), the only death he is responsible for. I tell him about life in Communist Poland, how I left in 1996 with one bag on the bus for England, about my life in Russia and Romania, my complicated family stories, and more. Our tales mix and go on forever. The wind outside ravages the empty, icy space, and we feel 'safe' under two pieces of thin material, storytelling. All that's missing is a log fire and a good glass of wine. We have food up here for ten more days, including the emergency cache, so I have no concerns about dying from starvation at least.

During the night we both wake up time after time trying to find a more comfortable position or to cover our ears with one more layer so the noise is not so loud. Without the sun, which is behind the summit at night and hidden by the storm clouds, the temperature inside the tent drops down to below -25 degrees Celsius (-13 degrees Fahrenheit). Not even for a moment do I take off my fleece gloves during the night. I have a hat to sleep in and an eye mask that warms up my face and covers my eyes. My buff covers my mouth so really the only bits of me sticking out are the opening of my nostrils. And I love it! I am focused, living life to the full, caring for myself, and totally aware of every bit of myself.

Day Ten

We wake up at around nine thirty the next morning, and I find myself in a corner of the tent with Greg almost on top of me. Now I know why one side felt warmer! I feel very well. Breakfast arrives. The wind has subsided, which could be good news. Martyna, the other Polish lady, comes to our tent looking for food and water because their supplies have finished. They are packing up camp and going down. They lost one tent last night, torn up by the wind, and had to regroup. The Russian group is going down as well. Everybody says they will wait for us at base camp or Patriot Hills. Our fifteen-person team becomes the only living organism for miles around in the harshest environment on earth. It is totally amazing that there are perhaps, at most, only two to three hundred people at any one time on the whole continent. When the scientific expeditions go on their week-long discovery missions, they take supplies for one month, just in case!

Bill asks us to prepare for the summit bid. We do it reluctantly because the weather is still dodgy. He suggests we go for a walk for one to two hours, 'and let's see'. We rebel. Nobody wants to waste energy unnecessarily. He insists, and we follow. One team member stays at camp as he has a headache. I have a slight headache myself. One hour into the walk I realize I have forgotten my UNICEF T-shirt to show in my summit photo for my supporters. I cannot turn everybody around now so I will have to Photoshop something in.

The wind abates, and a beautiful day starts around two o'clock. It is rather warm (-15 degrees Celsius or 5 degrees Fahrenheit) considering. The pace is so slow that we don't get too hot. Because we are so close to the South Pole, the concentration of oxygen is less than at the same altitude at the equator, so, in effect, this mountain is well over 5,000 metres (16,500 feet) high. We plod on for seven hours on a gently raising plateau. I cannot eat or drink anything. My headache is weird. It disorients me (classic altitude sickness), but I don't feel sick. Again we pass emergency caches. To our astonishment we can see the trail of the people who went for the summit two days ago and even last year, despite the many storms that have passed. It does not snow here really. The marks left on the ice are left here for a very long time. That is why we cannot pee on the snow, even when walking between camps. It all goes into bottles and then designated pee-holes.

We stop in front of a steep slope leading up to the summit ridge. We leave our backpacks and only take cameras, power bars, and the smallest container of water each. I still haven't eaten anything. I feel slightly dizzy but cannot imagine eating now. We start plodding up the slope. This is the most dangerous place on the whole mountain – there should be fixed ropes here, but there are none. If somebody slides the whole rope would almost certainly slide with him. It is exceptionally steep. We get puffed out after every ten steps. My goggles are fogged up and freeze. The pace is slow, which suits me. The sun keeps me going. After an hour we reach the summit ridge. We all know it is around forty more minutes. I think I will feel the same on top of Hillary Step on Everest. Only then would I consider telling myself that I might actually have a chance, which would be after more than twenty hours of being in the death zone.

Guys from previous ropes have improvised fixed lines to ease the climbing. The ridge is rocky so it's a little tricky. I can see how my technique has improved and my fear has diminished since Denali two and a half years ago. But I am not complacent or overconfident in any way. We all go solo from now on. It is exposed on one side, but I am all right, totally focused on every step.

Walking back from the summit, Heidi asks me how I feel.

'I'm okay,' I say.

She advises, 'There is that edge ahead of you, so make sure that if you fall you go left.'

Yes, that would be only a 1,000-metre (3,280-feet) fall, while on the right it would be more like 2,000 and a long slide back to high camp. I come to the edge. I imagine myself being on Everest with exposure on each side being 7,000 metres (22,965 feet) and 8,000 metres (26,246 feet) respectively. I fix my gaze on the other side, a little pyramid. I make sure I have a strong grip on my ice axe in my right hand and set off. The snow crunches loudly with every step. I am ready for anything to happen. I count my steps.

I congratulate myself after fifty slow and well-measured steps. Now I'm onto the pyramid. Again, I try to climb it rather than traverse around. At the

Cone of Kilimanjaro – the highest free-standing volcano in the world.

Freezing in a snow blizzard on top of Africa with zero visibility.

Sweaty, dirty but happy on the way down.
I naively think "high altitude mountaineering isn't so bad".

View of the route from the barrels – Elbrus base camp.

My team negotiating steep iced slope to the saddle.

On top of Elbrus. I look and feel amazingly amateurish.
Photo by Paul Fejtek

The full beauty of Aconcagua revealed at sunset. Photo by David Pitson

Weakened by serious indigestion, hiding from a sand storm on route to base camp – Plaza the Mulas. Photo by Dan Parry

The Penitentes – a snow stalagmite forest sculptured by sand and wind.
Photo by Dan Parry

Seven vulnerable tents at Berlin camp. Photo by Dan Parry

Flat summit of Aconcagua where I dance and eat energy bars, ecstatic at having passed my high altitude test. Photo by Dan Parry

Just before flying to the ice of Mt. McKinley with my overwhelming 35kg (5.5 stone) pack.

Practising winter climbing skills at upper base camp. Photo by Jens Trolle

Rest before the head wall. I grab the 'safe anchor' of Jens' knee.

On the ridge to high camp. Exposed like never before,
I cry through emotional exhaustion.

Hard at work. Reinforcing ice walls at high camp.

Playing Egyptian rat screw at a high altitude casino
with a handmade deck of cards.

Breathtaking view from high camp.

Dramatic decision making on the summit ridge. The wind is picking up.

Autobahn, a one way street to Denali pass. No speed limit if you fall. Photo by Jens Trolle

After a testing climb, I stand on top of Denali at a quarter to midnight. Photo by Jens Trolle

The Moni and Dani cannibal tribes live in wooden huts set in lush greenery.

Men from the Dani tribe. The wider the bamboo the higher the status.

Girls go topless in Papua.

Dinner time. Not sure what is more tempting –
the worm or the plate. Photo by Paul Fejtek

Magnificent view of the challenge at hand – Carstensz summit wall.

Beyond fear. Hanging off frail ropes
over Tyrolean Traverse.
Photo by Paul Fejtek

In a cloud, on top of
Catstensz Pyramid the
weather turns on us
in an instant.

Back from the summit, with symptoms of hypothermia and serious peripheral oedema, I fail to recognize myself.

Seriously slimmed, dirty beyond imagination and extremely happy after completing the most technical climb of my life.

We land on rubber wheels on the blue ice of Antarctica in an old Russian bomber plane.

Carrying a load to high camp on
a steep slope with a giant smile.
Photo by Greg Linsdell.

With a throbbing headache,
severe anaemia (that I am not yet aware
of) and climbing purely on will power,
I stand on top of Mt. Vinson.

Thirty six hour storm at high camp. I experience a new type of cold.
Photo by Greg Linsdell.

Antarctica at its best – white, blue and black.

Pure joy of being out there. Photo by Vivian Rigney

With Migma at Snow Lion Lodge. She is illiterate, but runs her own lodge, is educating children in London, and every summer cooks in a restaurant in France.

With our premiere, high-altitude Sherpa team at Everest base camp.

A good omen – a halo forms around the sun during our *puja* ceremony.
Photo by Scott Woolums

A body being taken off the mountain.

Crossing a ladder over a bottomless crevasse – it was fun!

So-called mouth of the Ice Fall. Going down, we rappel a long stretch.

Dinner in camp two – cold, dark and far away from home.

An unhelpful jet stream. With high winds on Lhotse face,
we decide to turn back. Photo by Scott Woolums

Room with a view – camp three at its best.

My team mates on Geneva Spore.
Every move is an effort on this
almost vertical soft rock.
Photo by Bill Allen

South Col – Camp four.

With blue rucksack, scaling the famous granite wall of Hillary Step.
Photo by Bill Allen

An hour's contemplation on the top, trying to take it all in.

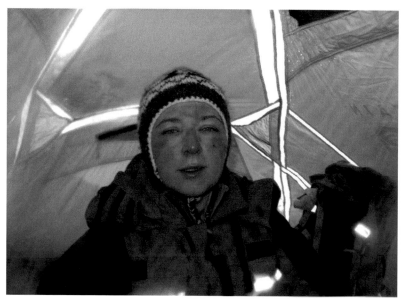

Beaten up, I celebrate the successful summit in silence.
Photo by Vivian Rigney

View from the top of the world.

At the opening ceremony of the Peace School 29 April 2011.
Arupokhari, Nepal.

top of the pyramid I can see others celebrating 100 metres (328 feet) in front of me. I keep going, focused, and with a smile. People wave to me.

Yippee! Summit number six is in my reach.

We all pose for photos. Bill asks me how my head is.

I reply, 'It feels empty. I haven't eaten anything today other than breakfast.'

He produces some Clif Shot Bloks and squeezes three out for me. I swallow all of them and instantly perk up. They have lots of natural caffeine.

The weather is gorgeous. Bill says it has been the best summit day for him ever on Mount Vinson. I take a summit panorama video and we start the descent. We rope up again for the steepest bit, which we zigzag down vigorously. I can feel blisters forming on my heels, but I don't care. We get back to our packs, drink, change clothes and, once again solo, all descend to high camp. I love going down and I move fast. So by the time Greg gets to the tent I have wet-wiped myself, changed my clothes, attended to my giant blisters with Second Skin, and partially packed. I am quivering with joy in my sleeping bag. Dinner is rehydrated chicken and noodles again and it tastes even better than on the previous nights. We swap tales of today because Greg and I were on different ropes. Thoroughly tired but deeply content, we fall asleep.

Day Eleven

In the morning, there is a moderate wind.

Bill orders, 'Let's get the hell out of here.'

We are packing as the wind gathers momentum. Some guys are struggling so we help each other dismantling tents as we want to have a coordinated exit. We almost run down to the top of the fixed ropes. I am on a rope with the oldest member of the expedition in front of Vivian (my future tent mate on Everest) and I. Behind me, I have Ken with his bad chest and Bill. It is pure torture. We are roped up for safety in these conditions, so we need to keep to the pace of the slowest person, who is two positions ahead of me. The packs are very heavy as we are taking the whole camp down in one go. The wind is merciless – any exposed skin will be frozen in seconds. I count the anchors. I count the ropes. I try to remember how long we still have to go and where the slope angle will change and shelter us a bit. The only good thing about it is that the wind is blowing into our backs rather than our faces. I am so grateful for that. However, that poses the challenge of staying vertical because we're on a fifty-degree slope facing downwards. We all have one arm wrapped around the rope and safety carabiner clipped in, and we dig our heels strongly into hard snow. Suddenly, the first person on my rope falls facedown. We need to stop. It takes a long time for him to gather himself up and get going. Then Vivian in front of me loses his hat (which is why I have one that ties below the chin). I offer my spare but he is ok with his hood – he ends up with a frostnip on his ear. I notice my crampon isn't holding properly onto my boot anymore. Again, we all have to stop as I sort myself out. If I hadn't had hand warmers in my mitts, I am not sure whether I could type these very words now. Nobody wants to take even a minute's rest. We all want to be off the ropes and at low camp level where there seems to be no wind. Although it might only be a deception, it is a welcome thought for now.

We have been going three hours solid. Patiently and slowly, we get to the bottom. I can feel that one of my blister plasters has moved and my sock is irritating the exposed skin. I have forty minutes of flat walk to low camp. I can do this. We unrope, and I switch to my fifth downhill gear. I always wonder where I get the accumulated energy from to run back home. I get to camp and take off my enormous boots. Oops, we are dealing here with several blisters in strange places on each foot and a nasty-looking right toenail, kind of purple. I put my feet into the snow to cool them down. That helps or maybe just freezes the pain. Whichever it is, I feel better. I put on more Second Skin and change my sock combination. Other team members start arriving. The weather is much better here, and we decide to stop for lunch. The enchiladas are served. We all have at least three each, and with renewed energy start digging out our sleds and equipment. We rig up, and Greg offers to take all of our gear on his sled. I agree eagerly for now, not realizing what agony it will cause me on the way down to base camp.

We start our descent roped up. I am last on the rope. What a mistake! And I thought I was getting it easy. As I attempt to stop the sled banging against Greg's legs in front of me, the difference in our weights is just too much for me. It is 60 kilograms (132 pounds) of me against 90 kilograms

(198 pounds) of Greg plus at least 30 kilograms (66 pounds) on the sled. I cannot stop it, nor slow its momentum or inertia. Each step is agony as I dig my heels deeper into my boots and blisters and I struggle to manage the disobedient sled, but it has a mind of its own. And I feel bad that I am letting Greg down because it regularly bangs against his calves. I remember the pain of the last stretch of the Denali glacier with a final uphill slog, but never anticipated a heartbreak hill going down. I am being proven so wrong yet again. After an hour of this painful experience I am relieved to catch a glimpse of base camp around an hour's walk away.

At camp I instantly change into my down booties to stop the pain. I am tearful and just don't want to move any more. The tents are pitched and reinforced, and dinner is served. I then visit my friends Ramon, who I was on Carstensz Pyramid with, and Martyna, the other Polish lady. We congratulate each other and share a biscuit or two. There are no flights back to Patriot Hills today because of the weather. It is amazing to note that there is no navigation used here (difficult magnetic situation). Everything is based on visual assessment of the conditions. Because the contrast is so low with everything being white, the conditions must at the very least be 'good' before flying is considered.

Three bottles of bubbly appear at dinner, a gift from ALE. We can all relax. I drink more than usual and it goes nicely to my muscles instead of my head, making my blister agony a distant past. Slightly incapacitated, I crawl back into my tent and apparently snore throughout the night.

Day Twelve

We wake up to wonderful weather, at least for up here, but are told the flights won't be operating that day, but perhaps at night. We patiently spend another day waiting. We play rugby, roll in the snow, read more and operate a high-altitude casino, where cards, roulette and bottle are played. To our surprise we discover that litres of wine have been cached up here for our safe return from the summit. That is great news, except that all of it is at exactly room temperature, which is -10 degrees Celsius (14 degrees Fahrenheit) at midday. We defrost the wine, keeping cartons of it in our down jackets and rotating. Whatever becomes liquid is quickly poured into cups and immediately polished off so it doesn't freeze again. I enjoy some Spanish red wine that's still almost frozen solid – my first ever wine lolly pop!

Scott, who will join up with Mountain Trip to lead an Everest expedition in 2010, talks to us about Everest. At least five people are interested in going in 2010. Ken is keen to book now. Good job there is no credit card machine out here. Miraculously, his chest has cleared a little, and at least he can breathe without a struggle. Back home it takes him a good five weeks to get rid of it completely.

I again spend some time with Ramon, who is going to Everest this season, and Martyna, who is delighted that she will soon see her baby again. There was a report on Polish TV about the storm we had two days ago. I dare not to think what my mum is going through. I will call her from Patriot Hills. We draw straws for who goes on what plane and get ready to leave at three in the morning.

Day Thirteen

As I tiptoe out of the tent so as not to wake Greg, it is unbelievably cold without the sun, and I quickly close all my zips and Velcros. As we listen to the plane approaching we all move constantly to stay relatively warm. The plane lands and I am finally climbing up the little ladder to warmth. Such a relief!

As we fly out, I am glued to the window and feel regret in a sense that this adventure is ending. I have enjoyed being so exposed to the elements and sharing the joy with others. I have calmed down enormously and reached much deeper into myself. It has been a great form of meditation.

At Patriot Hills I help with preparing breakfast in the kitchen tent. What bliss to be able to sit down at a table and have a gas stove and lots of hot water. Even the toilet is delightful after days of aiming into the wag bag. When the rest of the team arrives, we devour defrosted hot buttered buns. 'Oh, my God!' we all groan in pleasure. I never knew that bread and butter could taste so good. We take so many things for granted at home. I will cherish this taste for many months.

We listen to the Korean meteorite scientific research mission. They found a 6-kilogram (13.2 pounds) meteorite, and it has been a good season.

All of the Koreans are as thin as my finger. Their faces are frostbitten, but they are floating from joy and satisfaction.

We organize an international card playing tournament, read, walk and exchange addresses. There is a Norwegian expedition two tables down, who just beat the Guinness record of travelling light to the South Pole. They look ragged and exhausted, but again with giant smiles because they have lived life to the fullest for the last ten days. We take many pictures of all of us, then eat dinner and drink more wine. There are no flights back to Chile today or overnight. Perhaps there will be one tomorrow. I call my mum on the satellite phone and tell her I am okay, but stuck a bit while waiting for a plane. My mother interprets the message as, 'Oh, my God! My little daughter is stuck on the Antarctic, cold and far from home, and there is no way out.' Her husband calls the Polish consulate in Chile, somebody else wakes up Bill's family in the middle of the night in the United States, the consulate gives my family the contact details of ALE, they call ALE who find me on a passenger list waiting at Patriot Hills for transport back to Chile with an unknown return date. This diminishes my mother's confidence even further. So my dilemma is this. Is it better to be in touch with people or just tell them when I am back safely at home? God knows.

I also send an SMS via satellite to ask Nigel to tell my boss that I am obviously stuck on the ice and don't have a return date. My boss sends the message around the bank so everybody is aware. He attaches the link to the blog, waiting for any news on our return. I get some fantastic emails on my return because of that. And it is great to know that people are actually following the story throughout and are not totally ignorant of what I am doing.

So we have another long night ahead of us on the ice. The four of us play cards, and drink whiskey and wine. We finish all the Pringles, all the M&Ms, and any other junk food we can find to offset the alcohol. We are shivering around the table because there are only four of us in a big tent and the stoves are switched off. But we keep playing, drinking and laughing. It is light throughout the night. At seven in the morning, a lady comes in to start making breakfast, so we stumble back to our respective tents.

Day Fourteen

I wake up at five … in the afternoon! Just in time for pre-dinner snacks. The kitchen tent is packed. We have more arrivals from the South Pole, another Guinness-breaking record of some kind by a Canadian expedition. Everybody is sharing stories again. We are told to pack everything and get ready as a plane is coming and we will be taking off at six thirty in the morning. We gather, tentless, in the mess tent, and await our fate. I am reading the last chapters of my book. We spend another sleepless night on the ice.

Day Fifteen

We watch the landing of a giant plane – it is an operation of considerable finesse. The safety precautions are amazing. The runway has to be swept clear of snow to make sure the plane has enough blue ice. The blue is deep and astonishing. The Prince of Monaco is on this plane and plans to ski to the South Pole. We meet him briefly and carefully walk toward the plane's belly, which swallows us up in its dark interior. I am almost the last to board, so I get the side seat by the toilet barrels. We are all too tired to care. There are bodies sleeping everywhere after takeoff. The smell of petrol makes me nauseous and sleepy so I take up position on some container. Curled in a foetal position, I sleep through most of the flight. We change back into light clothes during the flight as it is still summer in Punta Arenas.

When the door opens after landing, all sorts of noise, smells and colours hit me. I move toward the bus mechanically, but realize I am having a similar out-of-body experience as I had after Denali. I need to take it slowly. There is no passport control again and it is back to the hotel. Greg leaves me for ninety minutes. I pour hot water into the bath and play with the bubbles for twenty minutes like a five year old. I am having my first shower/bath in over two weeks. As I wash my hair, I take pleasure in every movement and savour this simple overlooked activity. I hit the town to get some presents. We all agree to meet for a celebratory dinner at six o'clock because most of us are knackered and want to go to bed early. Most will be catching first flights out as well.

Refreshed, we meet at the Puerto Vieho restaurant, which serves fresh lamb or octopus off the log fire and the best ever salsa sauce you can imagine. We eat an enormous meal each and drink more wine than seems possible. We decide to go to La Luna for the best ice cream in the world for the last time. We all have enormous portions of all flavours and more dessert wine. It is well past one in the morning. We hug each other for a long time while trying to preserve the existence of this outstanding team, which completed its mission. Most of us will keep in touch.

Day Sixteen

I fly back to London via Santiago de Chile and Paris. I exit Heathrow wearing just lightweight pants and a T-shirt in mid-January – I actually feel very warm. I talk at length to my mum on the ride home. Back home, I have a eucalyptus bath and attend to my blisters. The right toenail will go because blood has gathered underneath. I try to put my office shoes on but it's impossible. I will go in flip-flops tomorrow morning.

***

At nine o'clock on Monday morning, January 12, I am back at work, leading a daily stand-up meeting for over ten people. They look at me as if I am a different person from the one who left the office four weeks ago. And I suppose I am. I send the following email.

Dear All, I have come back from Antarctica in one piece and with all my extremities still attached and intact. It has been an adventure indeed. It was the worst season from a weather perspective in five years! Endurance, cold, patience, and surviving in a very unforgiving but beautiful environment were the main themes. To start with, it takes seven flights to get to the Big Ice (over twenty-five hours of pure flying). I waited in a small Chilean penguin city with twelve strangers around the Christmas table trying to remain focused, fit and sane for twelve days. The flight on an old cargo Russian Illuyshin plane was scary and exciting. It could barely hold itself together, and the noise is so great that everybody is given earplugs rather than snacks for the four and a half hour flight.

Then we waited at Patriot Hills for two days for the Twin Otter flight to the Mt. Vinson base camp. From there, we pulled sledges and carried loads in beautiful weather for a day on the lower glacier. After a good rest, we took a load and stored it close to high camp. That involved negotiating 1.2 kilometres (yes, kilometres) (just under a mile) of fixed ropes on a very steep slope with up to 30 kilograms (66 pounds) in the backpack. After a rest, we moved to high camp where we discovered a new type of cold, totally unimaginable until experienced, piercing to the bone. And we still had an outside toilet to use. All waste, including human waste, is flown off the ice to preserve the pristine environment. The air was dry so morning nosebleeds were a normal occurrence. We got caught in a snowstorm at high camp for thirty-six hours with winds up to 100 miles per hour so we needed to build ice walls to reinforce tents.

We started the summit day in marginal weather, knowing we might turn around at anytime, but this was our lucky day, as the weather cleared. After nine hours I reached the summit and felt relieved, happy and very nauseous. Due to the difference in barometric pressure around the South Pole, for the first time in my life I could not eat due to altitude sickness, which meant I made the summit day purely on willpower, a litre of water, and my own storage of energy. The descent was most challenging physically because we got caught in high winds going down the fixed lines. One member of our expedition got frostnip on his ear! We finally reached Chile on Friday, January 9, instead of December 29, at eleven thirty in the morning. That first hot bath felt ecstatic! Then we hit the town.

I loved every minute of it! I met amazing people! I have accomplished what 250 people endeavour a year. I have been on the moon, where there is no life, no smells, no colours, and no night. Thank you for all your donations. They meant a lot to me. Enjoy the pictures.

My experience on Mount Vinson has helped me to defend myself against the forces in life that corrupt our characters. Money, power and love corrupt people. With time we become very skilful, socially-accepted liars. Very rarely are we honest, even with our friends, when the truth may hurt. The notion of political correctness is where it all starts. And in business it is acceptable to 'be economical' with the truth.

Antarctica is such an unforgiving environment. Survival on the mountain means letting go of your pride, being totally true to yourself, understanding your ailments, knowing when the cold is too much and being brave enough to stop your team and ask for help. There is no room for untruths or even white lies in this environment. I believe my time on Vinson has taught me greater personal integrity: not the integrity that requires recognition from others, but the integrity of understanding fully one's own thoughts and emotions and whether or not they match up with one's own values.

PART THREE

The taste of freedom

CHAPTER 7

Over my dead body!

'OVER my dead body,' is my mother's response in January 2009 when I tell her that, having climbed six mountains, I have decided to press on and complete the Seven Summits. I plan to climb Mt. Everest in the spring of 2010. She just cannot imagine her daughter living and climbing in the death zone for several days. Neither could I at that point.

After returning from the top of the world, people would ask me, 'What was the most difficult moment on Mt. Everest?'

I would reply, 'The most difficult moment was to make the decision to attempt it fifteen months before I went.'

I am aware that the rigour, routine, discipline and pain of preparation I am going to put myself through would be unbelievably hard to sustain and accept willingly. Combining training six days a week with a full-time job, writing a book and raising money would be a challenge in itself. I don't want to compromise my social life either. Basically, I want it all. I know that on Everest I will do everything to succeed, but must also fully accept, without regret, whatever happens.

January, fifteen months to go

It is January 20, 2009. I returned from Antarctica a week ago, and feel very tired. I just cannot imagine that I will be climbing Mt. Everest next. The thought of it paralyses me into inaction. Physically, I feel like a little puppy licking its wounds and my blisters are omnipresent. As with all my recent adventures, my colleagues know I have started the process of healing and recovery. I can sleep twelve hours a day and still feel like sleeping some more. I am not sure what is going on. Vinson was not too bad in terms of the physical challenge. Yes, it was rather cold, but, thanks to excellent equipment, I did not freeze on any of the days. I decide to take a month off any physical activity. I don't even stretch, and I eat copiously, anything I want and whenever I want.

After a month, even after putting on 3 kilograms (6 pounds), I am still as tired as before. I take an iron store level test and the results are bad. My iron level is fifteen on a scale of thirteen to 150. It all becomes clear now. I buy molasses, beetroots, dandelion, wheat germ oil capsules, and more. Being a vegetarian, it will not be easy for me to bump up my iron level just like that. I juice stuff, mainly spinach and carrot, every morning and hope all will be well. Knowing the cause of my tiredness cheers me up, but also worries me no end. Is fourteen months really long enough to build up my reserves so I can live and climb in the death zone for several days?

February, fourteen months to go

Work is totally mad. The biggest transformation programme in operations in this bank is going live, and I am the global lead for it. I work three consecutive weekends without a break. One night, I just grab three hours of sleep in my sleeping bag on a mat in the shower room. We, the project team, take taxis home on a daily basis after ten or twelve at night. One weekend the team is in the office straight through, after spending two nights at our desks. I am so glad I am not training and worrying about Everest right now. I give 150 percent to the job. At the end of it, it is a great success.

March, thirteen months to go

I start my training with a personal trainer, David from Pure Sports Medicine. I get a heart monitor and try to cycle hard as per the programme. I do not even complete the first round. I could not breathe with my heart rate at 175 for thirty seconds. After thirty minutes of fighting, I give up. I don't do sprinting! I am all about endurance and long distance. My whole body aches after yesterday's strength day and today's cycling, and I have four more days until rest day. I have a big salad for supper and a handful of dried berries to cheer myself up.

I am in the middle of week two of my training programme. I am still tired, I sleep more than I ever used to, and I just cannot find a comfortable position. The training programme is more than I can handle for now, but I know that my body will reluctantly adapt to it. Soon, I hope. I have a call from the medical centre about my iron level retest. It has significantly declined over the last two months from fifteen to nine. And I need the iron to perform, train and live. I am not sure what to do next. My doctor insists I change my diet and go back to meat. How does one do that after so many years without?

I buy a piece of meat. It is lying on the kitchen worktop while I look up meat dishes on the internet. After cooking it I sit at the table. I glare at the meat on my plate; it glares back at me. I try to eat half of it because my guts are not used to digesting concentrated protein in this form. I will finish it tomorrow. My stomach is uncomfortable during the night with its unfamiliar content. I need to introduce meat slowly. I also get a prescription to take 200 milligrams of iron in tablets every day (the daily norm is 14 milligrams). I buy two types: alkaline and sulphate. I have no idea which one will be easier for me to absorb. The next blood test is on June 1. I am very anxious.

April, twelve months to go

Well, what a walk and what an Easter! There's certainly lots of penance involved! The South Downs Way with 100 miles of rolling chalk hills, escarpments, and open land in four days. A piece of cake?

I set off at seven o'clock from Winchester on Good Friday. I have lunch in Exton and get to South Harting on my knees. It rains almost the whole afternoon, and I walk through 43 kilometres (27 miles) of mud. The next two days are really rest days because the distance is only 32 kilometres (20 miles). I am snoring by seven o'clock at night.

On Saturday, I start at eight in the morning. There is no convenient pub for lunch so I get all the way to Amberley by four and collapse on the steps of the Black Horse pub where I consume a giant lamb shank and two pints of

Guinness (for the iron content, of course). It rains again. I tuck into another huge meal for supper at seven and again am snoring by eight.

On Easter Sunday, I'm not sure how, but I start at seven with pain in my legs from the outset. I have lunch exactly halfway and then get to Clayton for the night. Thank God, the last 3.2 kilometres (2 miles) to get to the Jack and Jill Inn are downhill. I feel exhausted. I can hardly move my legs and arms. My feet and tendons hurt. I am in pieces.

On Monday, as I wake up, my training partner decides to quit. Poor lad, he survived but with endurance as a swear word for the rest of his life. Sixteen months later, however, he does his first triathlon, and he is in training for an Iron Man. I told you this stuff is contagious!

So I set off for the last 48 kilometres (30 miles) on my own. Midmorning, a stranger literally scrapes me off a rock. (We date for a while after this encounter.) He keeps me going until Alfriston. I consume a whole salmon and two smaller fish in an instant and at least three pints of water because it is baking hot.

Finally arriving at the Eastbourne station, I kneel to buy my ticket, talking to the machine with deep emotion and promising myself never to have silly ideas like that again. But on the train back to London the amnesia of pain and effort is already kicking in, I am eyeballing the North Downs Way, 257 kilometres (160 miles), for the May long weekend. I get to my flat around nine o'clock, only to find the lift does not work and there is no hot water. Wonderful!

I have to go to the physiotherapist because my ankles have swollen up like hell.

'Hmm. Why did you choose to walk over 32 kilometres (20 miles) every day with a heavy backpack without enough preparation?'

The tendon on the top of my left shin is not doing well and needs lots of ice.

I do a financial plan for the year and reveal a gaping hole in my expedition budget. I don't yet know how I can fill it.

I start the second set of four weeks of training. I feel rested after last week, which was a lower load week. I see David again and he commends me for my good progress. I am not sure if this is a placebo effect, but I feel much stronger.

Thursdays are my new Mondays. It's the worst day of the week because the training is: cycle hard, which involves getting my heart rate up to 170 beats per minute, three times for five minutes. That is hard. I managed today to almost do it, and I feel well. I eat meat, lamb mainly, every day this week for lunch.

One Sunday I go walking with several friends of mine who are going up Kilimanjaro in a couple weeks. (Yes, they are indeed more of my victims.) As we gather for dinner in a local country pub, they are delighted that I order meat and wine.

'Finally something (that is, Everest) has corrupted you,' they say.

I have become a normal person, not some grass-eating bore. Nice. One can always count on one's friends to tell you the truth.

May, eleven months to go

Training is in full swing, and the blues and greens of early summer help me. Nature is waking up, and I start feeling much stronger, too. As the days get longer and it gets light at five thirty in the morning, it is easier to get going. One Sunday in Essex, after four hours of walking, the skies break loose and I am totally drenched. I reach a pub in a rather sorry state. Although the pub is still closed, the owner takes pity on me and gives me two free cups of coffee to properly warm me up. Then it is a long taxi ride home. I have a hot bath and a nap, then go to the cinema.

I am changing roles at work. I will be working in the collateral management department. It is a mission impossible type of job, but I feel ready for the challenge of new faces, new function, new processes and new location.

In mid-May I celebrate my birthday in a restaurant. Reluctantly, I have yet another steak, my iron fix, which I almost finish. It has been a wonderful evening. I walk back home after midnight. It is warm and I am thinking that in a year's time I will be waiting at Mt. Everest base camp for a summit weather window. The next day I get up at six and am on the North Downs Way at eight twenty, ready to walk for eight hours with 10 kilograms (22 pounds) on my back.

From May 19 I am keenly monitoring activity on Everest as the weather window has just opened up there for summit bids. I know three people there and am anxious for them. I check blogs every hour on their respective summit days. It is agony when I read, '07.45 a.m. Everest time, no news yet, sorry.' Then, one by one, all of the guys I know summit and get back down in good health. I scream out every time, my colleagues in the office are convinced I am losing it. Well, I lost it a while ago. The best news is that the guides and Sherpa team who I am going to be climbing with next year all make it up in good time, good condition, and good spirits. Hurray!

During one of my lunchtime fitness tests, David measures me up and reports I have put on 1.6 kilograms (3.5 pounds). Great!?!. My waistline is a centimetre smaller, and my hipline is a centimetre smaller than two months ago. David says that all is good because I have lost unhelpful fat tissue and replaced it with muscle mass, which is three times as heavy. Then we get to my chest line and he proudly reports that I have lost a centimetre there as well. I say: 'But David, my chest line was supposed to go the other way!' He says, 'Sorry, I cannot help you with that'. We laugh.

Next we embark on the pinch test, which measures the proportion of fat and muscle mass in millimetres. It has changed by three millimetres (0.1 inch) in the right direction. In the gym he almost kills me in a series of tests. I have a super bike ride and knock twenty-eight seconds off my previous result, which is great considering I haven't done much cycling. I can do eighteen full, slow, and low push-ups and collapse on my face. I can hold a squat against the wall for over forty seconds. I manage to hold a plank for over two minutes. David is happy with my progress, which is fantastic news. So now there is just the iron blood test, which I need to pass with flying colours, and then there will be hope!

One Friday evening I get on the commuter train down to Kent to start walking at six on Saturday morning. I am in my trekking gear with my rucksack full of water, and I am eating supper. People are watching me with great interest as I consume two giant Cornish pasties and an XXL Snickers bar. Let's consider. Each pasty is around 1,000 calories. During forty-five minutes of fast walking, one loses around 280 to 300 calories. I will be walking for over twenty-five hours during the next three days. I could have eaten more pasties and shocked them even more. *Damn, an opportunity lost.*

During the weekend I eat enormous meals five times a day. I am not a cheap date anymore!

By now, I have done eight weeks of structured training, and I feel so much stronger than in March. I cannot comprehend how I climbed all those other mountains. I have trained hard for each one of them, but what I used to do is nothing compared with the torture now. It is all a step change.

My mum visits during a low effort week, and I spare her the details of my days. I just leave home at five thirty every day in all sorts of outfits and come crawling home. Her cooking props me up for the evening. We have yet another serious 'over my dead body' conversation. She has brought press cuttings from Poland with a recent series of deadly accidents in the Himalayas. *Thanks, Ma!*

After hours of negotiation, feeling as if I am losing the battle, I say, 'Mum, I have decided to go, and I will. Nothing can persuade me otherwise. You can either support me in the effort or limit my chances through negative thoughts and worrying. I would like you to help me and support me.'

She is crying on the sofa, I leave her to digest the hard choice at hand.

I have started cycling seriously. One day I cycle with friends to the Henry Moore sculpture park north of London. After five hours in the saddle (thank God for my padded shorts), and a massive lunch at a pub, I cycle back while most of them decide to take the train. Back at home I calculate that I biked over 104 kilometres (65 miles), just like that, in full sun without sunblock. And I pay for that. The whole of my right side has been fried, and I actually have sunstroke and fever in the evening. Hence, the next two days are rest days. And 'ouch' this, 'ouch' that days.

June, ten months to go

The world revolves around training, although I am dating the guy who scraped me off a rock on the South Downs Way. He actually walks with me, 32 kilometres (20 miles) at a time, at a good fast pace. Work is going great, and I have been to the cinema, concerts and theatres. I still have a life! I have yet to manage to do the full training routine three weeks in a row, though. For now, it is beyond me, for example, the cross-training day, which involves dying on three consecutive machines in a gym, or the cycle hard day. I wonder who this is designed for. After some sessions I am so red in the face from the effort that people in the gym offer to call an ambulance. I train twenty-four hours a week.

I am anxious about the results of my third blood test which are due soon. I meet up with a professional nutritionist because I need to figure out how to eat 6,000 calories every day for five to six weeks above 5,000 metres (16,404 feet). I prepare the trial menus and experiment with them on training days. This is actually quite good fun, although I have been accused of eating sawdust mixed with bird droppings. I have learnt a lot about how to combine different types of food for maximum nutritional value with minimum digestive effort.

Finally, I get a call from my doctor who tells me that my iron level has increased to seventeen over the last two months. It seems slow but I am delighted. I am definitely on the right track. *Yippee!*

I go to Surrey to finish off the North Downs Way, and walk for six hours. I have a standoff with about twenty-five bulls and have to jump a barbed wire fence. Of course, I have a red backpack. In the evening I am invited to a recovery dinner where I consume a quarter of a cow (revenge), almost raw, and half a bottle of red wine!

I love Mondays, the rest days. They are marvellous. I get up at seven – what a luxury! All I need to do is to go to work, eat well and go to bed early. I usually get on the bus in front of the house and sit down. I sometimes race old women for a seat and push them away at the last minute. (Just kidding!). For lunch, I take the lift down one floor to the cafeteria to the annoyance of everybody in the lift. I stand on the escalators on the tube instead of walking up, I take the lift up to my flat, and I indulge in doing nothing. I know what it means to have a rest day now.

Mid-June, I go to Poland to celebrate my dad's sixty-fifth birthday and do nothing but eat and party for three days. Such a break feels absolutely gorgeous after two and a half months of rigour. I have another 'over my dead body' conversation with my mum, who has changed her tone slightly to, 'But you will be careful.' We are making progress. I hear from my sister that some inheritance money will be paid into my account later this year. This will be just in time to pay the deposit for the trip.

On my return, I walk 40 kilometres (25 miles) with a friend on the North Downs Way. There is no pain! What a difference from Easter. I like my new strength. I buy myself a city cycling mask to wear during exercise, to see how it would feel to have a proxy oxygen mask on and keep up a high level of physical exertion. There are several things I am glad to be discovering at sea level.

1. Breathing with a mask is not an effortless, subconscious thing. You actually have to think about it and make sure you do breathe in and out.
2. Because the air is warmer inside the mask than outside, your nose runs, and you have to swallow it because you will not be wiping your nose at 8,000 metres (26,246 feet).
3. It gets really sweaty, wet and yucky. Up there, I will have it on for three consecutive days and nights nonstop.
4. You cannot see your feet fully or rather the ground before you, which is psychologically difficult, especially above 8,000 metres (26,246 feet).

When I get my period this month, I cannot move for four hours. Nobody talks about this topic, and it is so vital in female mountaineering. Altitude totally screws up your hormonal balance. So girls, expect it. Above a certain altitude you should not take the pill to regulate it either. You could die. I am trying to get used to the pain of cramps and still be able to do something physical, however with dismal effect this time round. I need to stop drinking the tiny amount of alcohol and coffee I still allow myself and increase my intake of soya products.

July, nine months to go

I visit my grandparents in Poland – a three-day eating extravaganza again. They will be praying for me during my expedition. After training with my cycling mask on, I become very interested in the efficiency of oxygen exchange in my body on a cellular level and have signed up for continuous breathing sessions with a wonderful coach, Jane. Wow! It's a totally new awareness level for me. I am almost levitating. This will be so useful in the death zone.

I have my second fitness assessment session. David is happy with me again. The body composition has improved. I lost more fat from my waist, and the muscle mass is building up nicely. I have managed to double almost all of my initial results for strength exercises. I am told I could have done even better because my heart rate did not reach the maximum of 182 (I am not sure). I am delighted that the hard work is paying off.

I have a full physiotherapy MOT[6]. I have most of my vertebrae turned and tendons squashed and muscles tortured. After an hour I feel as if a bus has run over me. Of course, it is all for the better. I am much more relaxed now because I know I have made significant progress. I still have eight months to go and my enthusiasm is as strong as ever!

I do ninety minutes of biking at full speed through London at eleven o'clock at night. Not very sensible, but I like biking through the streets and red lights when nobody is around. I like having the city, my training ground, to myself.

I walk four hours with 15 litres (4 gallons) of water in my backpack. My shoulders can feel it, but nothing major. But the weak left ankle tendon does not like the load at all. I do some self-mending, but it feels like I will need physiotherapy again. And I am so looking forward to tomorrow, a rest day. *Yes. Yes. Yes!*

I love the tradition of the Proms, a festival of classical music concerts throughout the summer in London. After getting home at a quarter to midnight after a Prom, I get up at five thirty and naïvely think that a bike ride of 130 kilometres (80 miles), London to Brighton, would last six to seven hours. It takes us ten. Madness! My arse is sore! Biking in the hills is quite different to city cycling. The ride is a lifetime dream of my fifty-nine year old friend, and I really just go along as a support crew. Everybody tells me

---

[6] Certificate of roadworthiness given by Ministry of Transport

beforehand that the Devil's Dike at the end is a killer. I tell myself that I can push my bike up that hill. It's a practice ride for me, not a race. But when the hill appears in front of me, beautifully covered in summer grass, flowers, and forest, I put the bike into the lowest possible gear and pedal up it, panting from the effort. I take in the breathtaking view from the top. I can see the sea. We jump with joy, lie in the tall grass for a while, and then press on.

On the train ride back I appreciate the softness of the seat on the train, and bless myself for making a simple sandwich in the morning and packing the heavenly dark chocolate. Back at home, I feel very content after a hot muscle soak bath and a snack. I have lived another day of my life to the fullest.

Later in the month my training morale hits rock bottom. I am wracked with muscle pain for three days running after my last physio session and a deep tissue massage, which was supposed to help. I am sure it is helping, but it is certainly taking its time. Two vertebrae are not rotating in my neck. It's a constant painful reminder. I am totally de-motivated. Thank God it is a lower load week, and I will be seeing my trainer on Friday. Perhaps he can enthuse me with some passion for some more physical pain. I stick to my training schedule, but it is such a chore this week. My trainer tells me that people who train as much have to expect pain – as simple as that. It is normal.

I am not happy. He prescribes a restful weekend. I go to the sauna to help my muscles relax and recover through increased blood flow. Wonderful.

August, eight months to go

I walk the Thames path with my boyfriend. The day is beautiful, warm and sunny. We finish off the stroll of 28 kilometres (18 miles) with a meal at an Indian restaurant and snore in perfect harmony at eight o'clock. My right hip is aching, but all feels good.

As per my schedule, today is a rest day. I feel good, and my lower back is not aching anymore. Tomorrow, Rosy, the physiotherapist, will fix my neck, and I will be back on track. I feel strong and ready for three more weeks of heavy routine before going on a trip to the Alps!

I am devastated in a sense. Rosy has identified that my pelvis has been misaligned and my right leg is 2 centimetres (0.75 inch) shorter than the left.

That has been the case for probably the past three weeks. After an hour I am aligned back to the centre, but it takes up to a week of hobbling to get my muscles back in gear. In the meantime I still train, but less than my schedule demands.

After skipping a training session altogether on Friday, having another massage, a sauna and a good sleep, I feel better. During my biking in the morning, I analyze my injuries and put them in priority order for attention. The most serious one, but on the mend, is the tendon in my left ankle. Next is the right wrist, also on the mend. Then there's the pelvis. I think that is just a small accident and a one-off because my posture is normally fantastic. That just leaves my neck and shoulder pain. They're good friends. They'll be with me everywhere I go, and it will be painful if I need to carry anything above 15 kilograms (33 pounds). So I am great. Really!

I have visitors, Greg, my tent mate from Antarctica, and his girlfriend and more are staying with me. I watch his Everest videos once again. I don't cry this time as I did in Antarctica. Now it looks very difficult but not impossible any more. I am shifting my mind-set, which is exactly what I need, a great turnaround from nine months ago. I get a fantastic present of sheepskin boots for base camp. I will get to love them dearly on the mountain.

I get back from the Alps full of renewed energy. I had an amazing training holiday, with twelve days of sun. We do an average of 700 to 800 vertical metres (2,296 to 2,624 feet) up and down every day. My body performs exceptionally well. There's no pain and no complaints. I am well trained. I carry a 17-kilogram backpack, and all is great. My left ankle tendon has finally healed and does not give me any grief. My right wrist is almost there. It does squeak a couple times when the going gets tough, but nothing serious. The raw energy bars, chocolate and electrolytes work great for me. So I am preparing the list of my favourite snacks to take to Everest. It is hot, and we need to drink 5 to 6 litres (1.3 to 1.5 gallons) of water every day. We sweat copiously. The recovery time for my muscles is very good, and I do not need much sleep to recuperate and be ready for more. Great results!

We celebrate our completion of the Tour de Mt. Blanc with a Champagne dinner in Chamonix, and we are so roudy that the restaurant owner has to isolate our table from the rest of the guests. On the last morning we do a

1,500-metre (4,921-feet) ascent in three hours, which is a very good time. On the Everest summit push I will be climbing 1,000 metres (3,280 feet), and it will take me up to twelve hours. That seems incomprehensible to me now – to move so slowly for such a long time. Then I will have to get back down! Back in Chamonix we pluck up the courage to paraglide in tandem, which provides a new perspective on the steep tracks we were ascending and the overhanging cliffs we admired.

September, seven months to go

I had my third fitness test this morning. And I managed, despite the fatigue after the recent trip, to beat every single test but the push-ups. My trainer is very happy with me. We agree that my body composition is perfect and I don't need to put on any more weight or lose any more fat. Wow! What a statement that is. Basically, I am close to reaching my highest physical potential, so I now need to just keep it up and prepare for the next training-test experience, the high altitude of the Ecuadorian volcanoes. And I have three days of rest ahead of me. Life is good! I savour every moment of it. I do nothing physically demanding and eat well. I go to the sauna, enjoy wonderful weather, and keep writing my book. Bliss.

My boyfriend from South Downs Way, North Downs Way, Thames Path, and Alpine holiday has dumped me. Apparently I am too alive, too happy, too funny, too active, too accepting, too busy, and too crazy, and that is just half the story. I walk slowly back home from the corner of the street where he communicated this to me. Thankfully his decision does not seem to be affecting me greatly; I feel in perfect emotional balance. Also, deep down, I know we are not for each other, at least not this time round.

It's the first day of my new training routine. I thought I was strong, but after just one set of exercises I feel dead. The next day's muscle pain confirms that I have to keep going. I have a minor head cold and cannot exercise outside. I consume mountains of garlic and lemon.

I have reviewed my equipment list, and I will have to start doing some serious shopping soon.

During one of my intense yoga sessions, I believe I see divinity. I connect for the first time with the unexpendable source of energy or pure existence. I feel so at peace. After thirty-six years of going to the Catholic Church every Sunday, I don't feel that need anymore. I realise that spirituality has nothing to do with religion. If I am open, I can cross that line anytime, anywhere. I love my new level of awareness.

I had a fantastic biking practice yesterday and today. The weather is beautiful, and the streets are empty. Richmond Park is my favourite new training ground, a fantastically vast amount of greenery in London. The deer walk around it lazily. In the evening I see Almodovar's film, *Broken Embraces* at the cinema. What a treat!

I have helped another lady over fifty to get to the top of Kili. I am so proud of her. She has just booked her flight ticket to come with me to Everest base camp. This stuff is highly addictive, so watch out!

Now it is Wednesdays that are, by far, the worst day of the week with the new interval training routine. This is only the second time I managed to go through it all:

- Three sets of 1,000-metre (3,280-feet) rowing with two minutes rest in between
- Three sets of biking 2,000 metres (6,561 feet) at level nine (should be twelve really) and, in between, four minutes of biking on level five (should be eight)
- Ten minutes on a cross-trainer at level twelve.

My work on breathing coordination has helped me. I have a wonderful body massage as a prize and drag my feet home to crash.

I spend a weekend with my family in Poland. It is my Christmas visit because I will be training in Ecuador in late December. It is a familiar routine: lots of meetings, very little sleep, and an incredible amount of food. It is such a relief that my family has finally come to terms with my going to Everest. I feel accepted and supported. It brings me great peace of mind. I need everybody on my side.

October, six months to go

Oh my God, I only have six months left. The fear or, rather, real anxiety is kicking in. I need to somehow deal with it creatively. This week is a lower load week. I have a review with David, and I am messing up only on one exercise, which is very encouraging feedback. I also do my yoga and connected breathing sessions. After seven months, I have finally figured out how to regulate my breathing when I exercise intensively and I can strain myself physically more than I ever thought possible.

I fall off my bike in Battersea Park one morning and get a swollen and bleeding knee and pain in my right wrist. The whole experience is pretty humiliating because I have not fallen off a bike in thirty years. Well, perhaps I needed a lesson. My confidence level is getting too high. After a forty-five-minute nap at home, I go out again to play in a squash tournament because I signed up for it months earlier. Silly me! I play three games, but cannot run well because of my knee. Playing also irritates my wrist more, of course. Will I ever learn?

Mondays have become part of the weekend by now. I am so conscious that Monday is a rest day, and I don't need to do anything other than ten hours in the office. Today, however, my injured arm clicks wrongly and the pain is intense. My physio tells me take 400 milligrams of ibuprofen until the pain and swelling go away. I am disappointed because this week is supposed to be intensive training week. I am unable to progress much because of the bike accident. What's more, my left shin muscle has totally seized up and I cannot walk. It's probably a result of shock after my accident, playing squash, and walking with too much weight on. Deep heat and lots of shin love will be required.

After stopping the ibuprofen, I have a fever. My body is visibly fighting the injuries, so I can't train much. At least my knee and wrist are healing and the shin feels much better, but my shoulder is still a problem. I am unable to go through my full routine this morning in the gym although the rest of the week is not too bad . I do the high-intensity days, but on Friday my friends say I look tired. I reflect on what I have been putting myself through. Three days a week I am in the gym for seven am. I exercise and stretch for a full hour, have a shower, dry my hair, and run to work where I am at my desk by eight fifteen, with most colleagues coming in after me. The other three days a week, I exercise outside. Rain, heat or wind, it doesn't matter. I keep going.

One Friday morning, straight after my gym session and before I even have a chance to grab breakfast, I am called into my boss's office. By the way he closes the door behind me I know he has some news. He says he has decided that I don't fit into the structure anymore. I need to find a new position, but, of course, the company is very supportive of me. I need to transition my duties to this and that guy, let's say, in a month. *If I lose my job now, I am not sure I can go to Everest in the spring!* It is a total shock to me because he has been pretty disengaged for the last two months, but that, of course, might have been part of the strategy.

Four hours later I have a meeting with another managing director, the head of the middle office who has a shaky proposal for me.

Over the weekend I have a wonderful walk with three ladies on the South Downs. We wander for four hours in absolutely stunning scenery of red, yellow, green, blue, and the white (chalk cliffs). Two of those friends are coming with me to Everest base camp. The walk is a bit too slow for me, but really great fun. The conversations cannot be repeated in public! In the evening I thoroughly massage all my previously aching parts to avoid cramps and muscle seizures.

I am thinking of the Ecuador bonanza for Christmas, eight mountains in nineteen days. Hmm, even to me that sounds mad. Wonderful. I like mad.

I travel east of Manchester to PHD, specialists in down products for expeditions, to order my down suits, summit mitts and a light sleeping bag. I am so looking forward to that visit. With my imaginary eyes, I see myself rolling in down as if in hot snow. What a treat. Customer care there is fabulous and very personalised, so I order the design I think will work best for me. I get a chance to dip my arms into a giant bag of down and feel the difference between the 800 and 900 types. And what a difference it is.

November, five months to go

I start working in my new role at the bank today. The job is enormous, and I need to recruit at least ten people, train them up, and execute on projects. In six weeks, I am going away for three weeks. In five months, I am going away for two months. This is a hell of a schedule, but I was not born for the easy. I plunge in.

Time starts passing faster, or perhaps I have finally allowed it to move in my head. Up until now, I was holding on to every day for dear life. I did not want the months to go past because I feared not being ready in time. Recently, my mind switched up a gear, and I beam with excitement. I do a 40 kilometre (25 miles) walk with a 15-kilogram pack along the Thames Path with my ex-boyfriend. I still like his fast pace. The weather is gorgeous, the last warm day of autumn it seems. When we arrive at Windsor, the castle is fantastically set against the red sky of the sunset, definitely a camera moment.

I plan to start the fund-raising campaign in a serious way before Christmas, and preparations and interviews take up a lot of my time now. With Everest I decide to support The Sarswati Foundation – a local NGO from Nepal – and help them build a school for 400 children in a deprived village. How much more can I pack into my life at the moment? I'm not sure, but bring it on! Yesterday, I walked for five hours with a 17-kilogram (37.5 pounds) pack in Greenwich. It is lovely and warm. I test all my new clothing, and I like every bit of it so far. Again, I shop around for gear.

I beat my personal best in cycling: 72 kilometres (45 miles) in less than three hours, on a kind of girly shopping bike! And I can still walk! It's a good week of training. I have not missed a session, although my lungs feel congested. The high-intensity day is tiring.

I have done the bulk of my shopping for the trip now, but still have bits and pieces left. It takes forty-five days for the down goodies to be delivered, so I'm glad I did it this side of Christmas. The days are passing at the speed of light now that I have unleashed time. With less than five months left, I start feeling more and more ready for the challenge and don't mind the weeks sprinting in front of me. They are so full anyway.

Training remains on track. I bike for ninety minutes after nine o'clock one night. It is amazing how much I enjoy that now. I put on my helmet, go into my zone, and just pedal on. The cars grind the fallen, colourful leaves into the asphalt and create a beautiful carpet.

I manage to retain a social life. Tonight, I am going to a dinner to celebrate the ninetieth birthday of Mr. Kaczorowski, who is to Poles like Mandela is to South Africa. He was the Polish president in asylum for a half-century. I have to pack a backpack in order to be able to train in the morning, work during the day, and go to the party in the evening. I simply collapse once I get back home, but am so happy.

I spend two days at home due to a chest complaint. I need to get rid of a bad cough before I fly to Ecuador to train at high altitude. I don't remember when I last spent two days at home. The illness stays with me for ten days, and I spend two more weekends at home to make sure it is over. At one point I have to go to the doctor and beg for antibiotics because nothing is helping. I am not feeling any better with medicine from the chemist and my overdoses of garlic and lemon. I probably make things worse by excelling during my retest session with David, which leaves my lungs puffing for three days. That's another lesson in life. Don't sprint for 4 kilometres (over 2 miles) when you have a chest infection.

December, four months to go

In the first week of December I start exercising lightly. I feel much better. Perhaps an extended break like this was needed to recover from my ailment. At home I make great progress with my book and shopping for Everest.

I go to a gastroenterologist because I'm getting increasingly bloated. After some tests, he decides I have an overgrowth of yeast in my body (*Candidiasis*). In fact, it is seven times the norm. Great. I get a very strict diet and some amazingly awful powder to drink as a solution twice a day. I start Bikram Yoga sessions... that is ninety minutes of extreme stretching in 70 degrees Celsius (158 Fahrenheit). It's a fantastic feeling though. I do my intense day with no problems.

Finally the day of departure comes and I am off to Ecuador. *Yippeeee!*

What a trip! Great walking, cheap food and good company. Eight Brits and one Pole. Fantastic landscapes and mountains, or rather volcanoes, wild lakes, indigenous customs and people, and lots of healthy exercise. For the first week, all is great. I climb everything I am supposed to climb and more. I feel strong, fast, fit and furious. I easily acclimatise to the altitude of 5,000 metres (16,404 feet). Waking up in the middle of the night in the second week, though, to attempt the 4,690 metres (15,387 feet) ascent of Cayambe, I get a strong muscle spasm in my lower back. Despite excruciating pain, I make it through the first four hours of climbing into the night, but then have to turn around because my footing is not safe anymore. After a dramatic descent, when I am in tears from the pain, I have to go to a local physio who applies strong drugs, injections, and electric shocks. I then rejoin the group and attempt Cotopaxi at 5,897 metres (19,346 feet). I am first on the summit with lots of energy, time, and strength to spare. I hope that, with a full recovery, I am set for the highest peak, Chimborazo at 6,310 metres (20,703 feet).

The night starts well. Three hours into the hike I am still confident. Unfortunately, by around 5,500 metres (18,044 feet) I no longer feel properly myself, as if parts of my body do not belong to me. My head is not clear, my footing is not right, my tongue has a life of its own, and my fingers and toes are all puffed up. Suspecting severe altitude sickness, I decide to turn around with a heavy heart. The descent is slow. The lead guide diagnoses me with cerebral oedema, although he says females don't have brains. We decide on an immediate descent from 5,000 metres (16,404 feet) to the local village. He gives me enough steroids to treat a horse. I end up on a local bus, lying trembling on the floor in a giant down jacket. After getting to around 3,000 metres (9,842 feet), the symptoms subside. A big meal and a good nap leave me feeling as good as new.

With that richness of experience and now knowing how it feels and how easy it is to make a mistake in the grip of summit fever, I am even more ready to face Everest. And I cannot wait. What I need to seriously consider is if my altitude sickness was an accident, or does it mean that my body does not want to be at altitude anymore? I will not know until I try again. This is a concern. I contact Peter Hackett, the world-famous high altitude doctor. We exchange several emails, and he says, 'Don't worry. Just go. If you got it once, it does not mean that you will get it again.' I decide to believe him and not ask for a second opinion. I really like this one.

January, three months to go

After resting well in Baños, a spa town in Ecuador, and a weekend back at home, I launch back into my training routine. My trainer says I am very strong. I have built up more lean muscle mass and am in top form. That is good to hear. London is snowed in so I do not cycle but do everything else. It's cold, dark, and horrible, but that doesn't bother me at all. What bothers me is that I only have eleven weeks left to go, and anxiety is setting in, though I feel increasingly ready. Steve from the Ecuador team has said that he will simply live by my schedule and support me in training, shopping, and anything else I need to do to complete my preparation. I accept the offer, and we become one.

It's the worst week for me in a long time. My back has locked in three places along my spine, and I am in agony for two days until I meet Jay, my new magic physiotherapist while Rosy is on maternity leave, who unblocks everything. I crawl out of the medical centre on all fours. I allow myself to feel sorry for myself for about five minutes and then straightaway do 64 kilometres (40 miles) on my bike that weekend and seven hours hiking with 15 kilograms (33 pounds) on my back. I go to the seaside to rejuvenate and train with Steve.

I just don't know where the time is going anymore. My work is amazingly intense. I have recruited almost ten people by now, three are already on board, and the rest will be joining just before I go or during my absence. A bit cheeky I guess, but at the end of the day I might not come back at all. Nobody seems to mind though and appreciate working with somebody crazy enough to attempt Mt. Everest. I have a good week of training.

I have a sudden, huge panic attack about the idea of going to 8,848 metres (29,028 feet), which subsides after talking to my tent-and-rope-mate-to-be from New York, Vivian, over Skype at one in the morning. Steve is still keeping his promise to train with me for the big E challenge. He is visibly losing weight. Having him as company has transformed all my lonely days into a lot of fun, although I am still knackered every night. Mondays are still the best days of the week. My spine has locked again, but much less than last week, which means we are getting to the root cause of the issue at last.

I am doing lots of interviews, and people are asking me to authorise the text they want to publish. At the beginning it irritates me that I don't have input into the article, but I give up after a while when I realise that trying to control the media is a lost cause. I am giving two lectures in March to raise money. I spend my nights preparing material. I have also committed to running a weekend workshop at the end of February on personal development in my new venture. I write long shopping lists for Steve for the weekends, because I am struggling to cope with the pace of events. The crew at Ellis Brigham know him well by now. I so appreciate that unconditional support. Thank you!

February, two months to go

I have another good week. I am feeling ever stronger, and am stretching a lot. I have discovered a proper road bike. It is an amazing thing. It is really embarrassing to say that I am learning to cycle properly at the age of thirty-six, and I just love it. I am averaging 21 kilometres per hour cycling (13.5 miles) on 96- to 112-kilometres (60- to 70-miles) runs mostly through town, after which I can still walk and don't fall asleep in the cinema. Now that the numbers of weeks left before the trip are in single digits, the whole thing has started to become very real. I am doing lots of visualisation. I can see myself saying, 'This is only halfway. Just keep going.' When the training gets tough, I imagine myself in front of the Hilary Step and make myself complete the routine: the bike, the swim, the walk, the row, the weights, and the stretches as if I am facing the last few metres to the summit.

My spine has locked up again. Jay comes to my rescue. I have started seeing a Chinese acupuncture specialist. He puts me into a trance of some sort with dozens of needles stuck in me. His massage involves rubbing my back with a vacuum cup, leaving black marks under the skin from burst blood vessels. I am also eating some God-knows-what herbs because he feels some accumulated dampness in my body. I will believe in anything at this stage. I need to feel good, and after every session with him I do. He gives me special plasters – heat pads, full of chilli oil. Those pads feel wonderful on my back and shoulders.

I am planning my good luck party. My mum is coming over to cook Polish dishes for over forty guests in my flat. Several other people from Poland are coming as well.

March, one month to go

I make an executive decision to stop all training, apart from little walks here and there and a bit of cycling. It feels amazing to be able to stay in bed until seven, albeit using the time to write or correct articles and presentations. I am also closely in touch with Subhash, the founder of The Sarswati Foundation for which I am raising money.

It is still very cold outside, and I wrap myself up well as I don't want to pick up any colds or bugs. I keep the acupuncture going to improve my Chi energy and boost my immune system. On the canal on the way to my tube station, the little ducklings and some other sweet newborn chicks are getting noisier by the day. Spring is close, which gives me hope.

My public speaking events go really well. I have received a lot of great feedback.

The good luck party, with balloons, flowers, lots of homemade Polish food, a cake in the shape of Everest from Steve, and lots of booze (not for me though), goes exceptionally well. People are reporting that I have a very wholesome mix of friends from all walks of life. All the farewell hugs feel very different. I am really saying good-bye to everybody, just in case. I want them to keep going at it, even if I don't come back. Life is so much fun. We clear up a bit at four in the morning, and my four guests take over the living room floor for the rest of the night.

I take my mum to Victoria International Coach Station because she refuses to fly, telling me 'It's far too dangerous'. We rock in a full embrace for a long while. She does not want to let go. Finally, I peel her tiny arms off my muscular body. I see pure fear in her tear-filled eyes. I wipe her cheeks with care, squeeze her hand, and say, 'Be brave'.

CHAPTER 8

The hen party

O H, my God! I am leaving for Nepal in ten days. I am getting extremely anxious now. No, let's be honest. I am simply scared. I have all my bags packed neatly, waiting in my living room. Eight weeks of life in the most extreme conditions are stuffed into five duffel bags. At work, I am handing over all my projects to Rob, who will be looking after the team and my work. Thank you! Work was so good about my leaving. I walk around three buildings shaking lots of hands and getting several bear hugs. We have two farewell lunches. My colleagues challenge me to a 6,000-calorie lunch and joke that they hope to avoid a head count freeze over the next two months. I love it.

The phone rings. It's my dad with a suspiciously crackling voice. He asks me to sit down. He says he has been emergency evacuated from his ship and is in a hospital in Klaipeda with a heart condition. He passed out and is having some checks done today. He says, 'I am old and slowly wearing out. I am getting out of order.' We chuckle a bit. My throat dries up and tightens. I can taste bitterness, and my eyes water. Steve is preparing lunch in the background. Hearing my father's dear voice coming from a small plastic box with this terrible news is heartbreaking. I don't know what to say. My thoughts are racing, calculating if I would have time to go and see him before I go to Nepal.

He says, 'Ania, you just keep going as if nothing had happened. Go and climb your mountain. Just come back safely. If I die, please spread my ashes over the Baltic Sea. Remember, life goes on.'

I mumble some words, and we exchange best wishes. We hang up after a long silence. Nothing more can be said. I don't know if I will ever hear my dad again. I sit on a chair for a while, ponder, and feel the tears rolling down my cheeks.

What a wise man. Thank you for a great lesson.

For my last four days, Easter weekend, I go to East Anglia with Steve. I do lots of walking along the beach, with no backpack at last. I also eat and sleep a lot. I connect with the spring world waking up from winter. The weather is great. I talk to little buds of flowers, saying my farewells. During yet another idyllic walk, I get an email from Mountain Trip. Heidi, a guide who got our team up Mt. Vinson in Antarctica and was supposed to fly with us to Everest, died tragically in an avalanche in Colorado. They cannot retrieve her body, and her beloved dog is refusing to leave the scene. I pass the message on to other members of the Vinson expedition. We are shocked. The condolences flow for days as if we have all lost a family member. One of her carabiners will hang on the top of the world in two months, giving us a feeling of reconciliation. Now I am shaking and crying in the middle of a half-empty beach. I look far off into the calm sea and try to see Heidi's soul as it connects with her beloved man, who she lost over eleven years ago in an avalanche on a different mountain. I feel calmness engulf me as Steve's arms wrap around me while he finishes reading the message.

It is hard to pull myself together that day. I need a lot of space. I do not speak much. She had always been extremely safe and strong.

Day One

On Easter Monday, we see *Alice in Wonderland* at the IMAX cinema in 3D. What a great introduction to the world of wonder I will be immersing myself in for the next sixty days. It is a film about me—moderately mad. I constantly talk to animals and flowers, I touch leaves, and I hug trees. Leaving the world of civilisation, investment banking, and the rushing around is like falling through a rabbit hole. Today, everything is for the last time. It's the last wake-up call in my bed, last cuddle, last Moroccan tea, last cinema, last salad, last comfy shower, last smell of London, last kiss, last chat with my mum, and last latte.

At the last moment, Steve asks me to pack eleven envelopes. Eight are numbered and to be opened every week. There are two for my birthday, which falls in May. One has 'when the going gets tough' on the front. I pack them in a plastic Ziploc bag not realising how much they will mean to me on Everest.

At the airport, departing is much more difficult this time. I am sure it's because I am leaving Steve behind, my best friend who has supported me through all the training during the last quarter, who spends the last days with me, and who I know could have gone with me and had a go, except we had met too late. My mum suggests getting a deal for him on lastminute.com, but unfortunately that doesn't quite work for Mt. Everest. Bless her. On the other hand, it is good to feel this strongly about somebody. In fact, the thought of the welcome back hug in the airport will keep me going, hopefully to the top and back.

I board the plane for the seventh time in my Seven Summits challenge on my own. Well, not exactly. I have four ladies, my good friends, with me. They're all over fifty. It's totally hilarious. They are escorting me to base camp. I divide my overweight bags between them and avoid extra charges. Steve calls it my hen party. I don't know if he really means it yet. Having the trekking group with me totally diverts my attention from the above base camp part of the trip. And oh, boy! We have so much fun!

The flight to New Delhi is great. As usual, I sleep most of the journey.

Day Two

We are seriously delayed in Delhi, and after much confusion over the correct gate, we go through the gate labelled Kabul and board our plane for Kathmandu. When we get to the Yak and Yeti hotel I have only ninety minutes to repack my bags because we are sending the load up to Lukla and base camp. Great, my first surprise! After a frantic sort through my gear in my hotel room, I wave goodbye to my four bags that I will see in fifteen days or so. It's time to meet the rest of the climbing team and eat something. Here they are again, Vivian and Bill (from Antarctica), Paul and Denise (from Elbrus, Denali and Carstensz), Cindy, Joana and Scott; everybody is in great shape and high spirits. We chat about our previous adventures until very late. Everybody is looking strong, prepared and focused on what is ahead.

Day Three

I have the last interview for the Nepalese press in the morning, and then I am leaving the world behind me. I retire to my room and meditate. I need to deal with all the news from before the trip. My dad is weak, but doing okay. I need to come to terms with the fact that, from now on, it is just me and Everest. I have not had a stomach upset yet and have been here for two days. I'm doing well. Whenever travelling in Third World countries, I subject myself to very strict rules: drinking only bottled or treated water, not even brushing my teeth with tap water, no meat, ice cream, ice, salads or milk. I only eat cooked or fried food to avoid any stomach issues, especially before a trip like this.

I feel my head is not in the right place so I meditate long into the night and regain peace. I am looking forward to getting up tomorrow morning at five thirty and going onwards and upwards. I am not thinking beyond base camp at the moment. Let's just get there first.

Scott, the expedition leader, later known as 'the Dude' after we got indoctrinated by *The Big Lebowski*, goes to the ministry of tourism and gets our expedition permit, a little piece of paper worth $75,000!

Day Four

We get to the airport, the dilapidated domestic part of it, for six thirty, only to wait for six hours on various sofas, in the airport café and buses. I watch the local people. Old couples in traditional gowns are holding hands, and little girls are running around chatting to everybody. They all seem to be so free. It's an amazing contrast to Heathrow's stiff security announcements. 'Don't use the trolleys for fun. Keep your children with you at all times. Only one bag allowed onboard. No liquids even if it's baby milk. Keep your luggage on a leash, or it will be destroyed. Don't smile. Don't think. Don't live.'

Everything here is disorganised and slow, but from now on, everything is on Nepali time or mountain time, and nobody minds. We land late in

Lukla, ranked as one of the most dangerous airports in the world … safely. The runway ends with a big concrete wall, and the asphalt is approximately 412 metres (1,351 feet) long. It looks like a little sausage from the air. Sir Edmund Hillary built it as part of his hospital project over forty years ago.

Nepal is a wonderful country. Anything is possible here. It has never been a colony. Everything here is homemade or grown. There is no concept of local planning. No street is straight. The flag is two red triangles with a white sun and moon, and it has its own time zone, fifteen minutes ahead of India. And until the tragic royal massacre over a decade ago, it was a peaceful Buddhist kingdom. Kathmandu is a very hectic and pretty dirty city, where the traffic is crazy, the streets smell of rotting sewage, and there are lots of beggars everywhere, aged one to a hundred. Walking around is an adventure in itself. Tourists wear masks so as not to get lung infections. At this time of year the thick smog prohibits seeing the views of the Himalayas. Such a shame.

In Lukla we have a quick lunch, which we chew carefully because there might be small stones in the rice. Breaking a tooth here would not be fun. We start walking, three hours of gentle undulation, and finish in the dark. We pass over our first high bridge. Good job it is dark as the sound of the river ravaging below is somewhat menacing. We have our first blessing, yellow strings to hang around our necks for good luck from a lama. We also get *katas*, off-white shawls for good luck and a safe expedition. There is still mobile reception here, so I text away. We have dinner and crash at eight.

Day Five

Our team has naturally divided into the A Team (the climbers) and the B Team (the trekkers).

We get up early to walk in the shade and relative cool of the morning. The air is heavy with moisture. I don't have a worry in the world. I am finally here, walking up to say hello to Mr. Everest, my new teacher of life. I feel a sense of solitude. It's just me and nature. As instructed, we always pass the praying stones, *stupas*, wheels, or poles on the right-hand side. We exchange greetings, 'Namaste' with everyone we pass on the paths. We want the spirits of this country and those snow-capped peaks on our side. I like the spiritual

Buddhist character of the trip, the smell of sandalwood incense in the villages, and the soulful eyes of the lamas and the Sherpa. The *stupas* are my favourite symbol here, with the eyes of the Buddha penetrating to the deepest corners of your soul. They check up on us time after time. Nothing can be hidden. And they give the impression that they are following you as you walk. The whole picture is made of just two or three simple lines, but the meaning is profound. I don't mind this otherworldly scrutiny. I have nothing to hide.

The porters stoically earn their living in a rather brutal way. They sometimes carry over 100 kilograms (220 pounds) at a time, bringing loads to locations over 5,000 metres (16,404 feet) up. The locals are poor but seem so happy. Life happens on the streets in front of the houses. Sometimes, kids run alongside and shake our hands. I think of Steve. I cannot remember what he looks like and I don't have a picture. I remember the touch, smell and strong arms around my shoulders, but not the face.

We stop for the evening in Phokding (pronounced 'Fuckding') in a small, dirty, solar-powered lodge. I use wet wipes to wash off the dirt of the path and tiredness. I have an afternoon snack and a nap. Naps are a great mountaineering tradition. We play hearts before dinner. At eight o'clock, eyes start rolling, and we retire to the snoring quarters. The rooms are tiny and amazingly simple, not unlike prison cells. My room buddy, Vivian, and I are doing great.

Day Six

It is a big day. We walk for six hours through villages on a dusty path. We enter the national park area and go through multiple police checkpoints. The Maoist army, who basically force a ransom from the owners of the lodges, tea houses, and sometimes from trekkers, usually man the checkpoints. I arrive first at one of them and am stopped at gunpoint. I say politely, 'I will wait here for my mates.' The other six arrive; nothing happens, but for a second my heart is in my mouth. There is a massive hill at the end of the day, just when you are tired and want to sit down. No, nothing is easy here. But the beauty more than compensates. I have two walking poles, my daypack, and a hill. Right, left, right, left, right, left. I go into a trance, even Steve is gone from my head, the world does not exist. There's only my steps, my muscles, the sweat running down my back, my forehead and my arms. The hill takes two to three more hours. The rhododendrons are in full bloom and the yaks' bells are ringing melodically. On the way I have a brief exchange with Vivian.

'I have been training for this for twelve months'.

'Sod your twelve months, woman. I have been waiting for this for thirteen years!'

We finally arrive in Namche Bazaar, the trekkers' mecca of the Khumbu Valley. A town carved out of the rock; streets follow the ancient agri-terraces. We stay in a lodge that belongs to one of our Sherpa. Thuktun, the son, goes to school thanks to the money raised by the clients of Scott and Mountain Trip. There are five more kids for whom expeditions like this enable a better future.

At the end of the trip, we meet Thuktun in Kathmandu, where he gets special permission from his school to have lunch with his benefactors or, rather, a bunch of skinny, dirty climbers exhausted from a successful climb. We take him shopping with $100, a huge amount of money in his hand all at once. He will have to consult his dad on what to do with it. He's an intelligent, thoughtful, skinny and warm kid in too-big trousers, too-big shirt, and too-big glasses. He says he wants to study science but his father cannot afford it. To put a child through a college costs $1,200 a year in Nepal. A teacher's salary for a year is $1,500.

We get news today that a whole plane of high-ranked Polish officials, both civilian and army, died in an air accident in Russia on April 10. It's another shock, difficult to absorb at the outset. Ninety-six people have died en route to commemorate the seventieth anniversary of the Katyn massacre.

Day Seven

We go on an acclimatization walk to 3,880 metres (12,729 feet) to the Mt. Everest View hotel, where Japanese tourists are flown in by helicopter, where oxygen is pumped into the rooms, and where a night costs $100. This compares to the $3.50 a night that we pay. We set off at eight in the morning. On arrival at the hotel, Everest presents itself to us with a bit of cloud hanging to the left of its top, as if it is too shy to be seen naked. I can, however, clearly see the last 700 vertical metres (2,296 feet) I will be attempting in six weeks or so. It looks distant, incredibly steep, windy and totally unclimbable, but kind of cool and inviting.

I have had a pulsating headache for the last twelve hours, but surprisingly it improves at higher altitude. For medicine, I have a big lunch, topped off with an apple pie with custard. Then I take a two-hour nap, and the headache is no more.

Overall the team is doing great, apart from one who has picked up a nasty bug and is in bed. I have a shower for $4, apply body lotion, and feel as fresh as a new baby. Every day I take our itinerary out of my bag and, with great pleasure, cross off another day. It's still a long way to get to halfway. The party is on big time. We beat the crap out of each other in silly card games. Linda, one of my hen party escorts, is trying to educate the 'unworldly' Americans in proper English and make them sensitive to local culture. After a while, she gives up, but it made for a lot of laughs. She is a very special girl who keeps the group amused with her English humour.

Day Eight

My left nostril is dry and bleeding in the morning as we walk up windy, dusty paths above 3,500 metres (11,482 feet), so I cover my mouth with a buff to protect my airways. We are going through river valleys, so we go up and down constantly. To climb 500 metres (1,640 feet), we need to do 1000 metres (3,280 feet) of vertical gain and then lose 500 metres (1,640 feet). We have started to come across yaks on our path, long-haired bovine creatures that live at high elevation in the Himalayas. The rule is that walkers must step aside and let the procession through. These beasts of burdens raise clouds of dust as they are urged on by their human leaders, and their bells play wonderful enchanting songs. I sometimes like to sit above the path and listen to the yak train approaching. Unlike other animals, they spend the winter here, and the locals use them to plough the fields, to transport heavy loads, and as dinner. To thrive at high altitude, yaks have larger lungs and heart than cattle found at lower altitudes, as well as a greater capacity for transporting oxygen through their blood. As a result they don't thrive well at lower altitude.

We pass over several high, wobbly bridges, which is good fun. The weather is kind to us. I hug the sun. To my surprise I am still in trekking sneakers without any ankle support. They are comfy and light. I am saving my legs for later when I will need all the strength I can muster.

We get to Debuche in perfect time for a snack, a nap and a good game of hearts. Our expedition leader, Scott, has developed a bad chest infection. I go into a big monastery on the way to listen to the prayers, where the smell of incense is overwhelming. I know deep down that my head is not in the right place. I am increasingly conscious of the altitude gains, and what is waiting above base camp. I am becoming apprehensive about continuing the climb. I fear the cerebral oedema from Ecuador was not an accident. Will I be able to continue above 5,500 metres (18,044 feet)? I dare not say it out loud. I am not quite ready to face the Khumbu Icefall.

As Vivian and I exit the monastery we see Bill, our other leader, incapacitated from a stomach infection by the wall of the holy place. We approach him, but with his face bathed in sweat he implores us to, 'Just leave me here. You go on ahead. I need to stay here for a while and get better.' He retches vigorously. We check his water levels and press on. He eventually reaches our destination two hours behind everybody else.

After dinner, a German lady is carried into the lodge common room with very severe altitude sickness. Her oxygen saturation is 52 percent, which is close to dying. Luckily, American doctors are with us tonight. She is injected with very strong steroids, given some fluid, then put into a Gammow bag (oxygen tent) for the night. In the morning a helicopter evacuates her to safety. She has been in a semi coma the whole time, so does not yet realise how lucky she is to be alive.

Our evening ritual is to check everybody's oxygen saturation level of which I keep a log of the results. After seeing the German woman almost dead tonight I don't need to remind anybody to take their oxygen test ever again.

Today, we have our first proper sighting of Mt. Everest from one of the lookout points. It looks big and daunting! I bow deeply in a respectful Namaste greeting, hoping it will accept me as a guest.

Day Nine

Today we are trekking up to 4,350 metres (14,271 feet). The walking is easy through very deprived villages. On the way we stop for our first official *puja* ceremony (a form of honour and worship) with a lama. We walk into his house where he gives us a blessing, tea, and more *katas* (blessed shawls). He looks like he might have tuberculosis because he is spitting heavy phlegm into a fibre tissue. He chants for us with great intensity. We feel very special, uplifted, elevated and full of energy after the brief session. We also visit a 300-year-old monastery, which is mysterious, cold and dim. I am rudely awaken from my feelings of bliss when I bang my head on the door so hard that I see stars. Meanwhile, Scott's chest infection is getting worse. He hardly moves and he breathes with effort. It is a concern because we are only going higher at this stage. The air is drier every day, and the path is dustier.

We arrive at the wonderful Snow Lion Lodge at Dingboche, where we stay for three nights to get accustomed to the altitude. I love being here. Migma, the lady who runs the lodge, is just like a mother to us all. She has a little bakery where we indulge in cheesecakes, chocolate cakes, apple pies and cookies, and she does all sorts of teas and tremendous coffee (so I am told, because I don't drink coffee on a mountain). My roommate Vivian is very chatty and has a great sense of Irish humour. In a deep voice and with his oh-so-sexy Irish accent, he motivates me with, 'Get your arse in gear, woman. We are going to check up on the yaks.'

I have bedbug bites on my neck and calves. Because I am allergic to them after Carstensz, they develop into ugly, amazingly itchy blisters full of puss. I take some antihistamine tablets that make me sleepy. My bug friends will be with me until the frost of over 4,000 metres (13,123 feet) finally finishes them off. I will have over thirty bites by then.

Day Ten

Today is a do-nothing day. I just move around a little, eat and be merry. Unfortunately, against my better judgement, I wander up a 5,000-metre (16,404-feet) hill in very windy conditions on my own without water. The views are good but I pay for this 'I-am-so-strong' folly with a cold and a small chest infection overnight.

In the afternoon I have a revealing conversation with my most long-standing climbing buddies from the group, Paul and Denise. They say that I have changed a lot over the years. In a sense they don't recognize me anymore: I don't laugh at the same jokes that I used to; I don't react in the same way to the stories they tell; and I seem more distant with a constant smile. I am critiqued, and the overall assessment is not too great in their eyes. The two other team members are more on my side. We explore the psychological aspects of self and relationship awareness. I find it difficult to explain myself in this confrontation: I am on an internal journey; I am not sure where it is leading me, but I definitely want to get there. Paul and Denise cannot understand that a transformation like this is possible in a person. There has been no single trigger in my life to make me this new Ania (i.e. nobody close to me has died, left me, and I haven't had any head injury to induce it). I thank them for their assessment, and we agree to disagree. I am happy that two people who have known me through similar circumstances for several years and mountains have noticed the transformation that my extreme adventures have brought.

In a burner in the common room, yak dung is burnt in an attempt to keep the wooden room above freezing, at least for the duration of our supper. The burner stands in the middle. A kid of no more than perhaps eleven years old sets up the fire. The dung smells like dung, which is what we end up smelling like. The smoke is thick and we cough like an orchestra before the fire gets going properly. The food is tremendous here, and we eat enormous portions. A typical day's menu would be:

- Breakfast: A big bowl of egg fried potatoes at around seven thirty
- Snack: A pancake around eleven o'clock
- Lunch: Sherpa stew, a thick veggie soup you can stand your spoon up in, with around two loaves of bread around one o'clock
- Snack: Apple pie with tea around three thirty
- Dinner: Dal Bhat, a traditional Nepali staple food consisting of lentil soup and cooked or steamed rice at six thirty

As a result, I have only lost 2 kilograms (4 pounds) so far. After three days at Migma's, I am back to my pre-trip weight. Great news!

Day Eleven

I am sick as a dog and spend the whole day in my sleeping bag trying to employ self-healing sessions. I ask the others to supply me with mountains of food every three to four hours. I only go to the loo from time to time. I am sad and disappointed that I was so stupid to do that lone walk, but what can you do? One needs to accept one's stupidity. Julia has severe food poisoning and has not eaten for three days. She is losing anything she eats both ways. In the evening I talk to the guides about Plan B if she and I are unable to walk with the rest of the group tomorrow. Of course, it's possible to organize anything here. The only thing to seriously consider will be our morale if we have to stay here on our own another day. Let's see in the morning. Scott's chest infection is getting better.

Day Twelve

I don't really want to go today, and am dragging my feet to even get out of bed. There is a nagging feeling. I am not sure if it is anxiety about continuing to ascend or the illness I am dealing with. No, deep down, I know we are three days away from base camp and I am getting scared again. I feel weak as the six o'clock start time approaches, but, encouraged by Bill, I go up a small hill to see if I can breathe at all while walking up. I am stable, but walk really slowly. Vivian encourages me. 'Come on, you wuss! Pack your arse, and let's go!' I pack my bag and will try to get to 4,950 metres (16,240 feet), even if I am last.

I am really slow, but manage to get to the next lodge before the B Team. I am surprised by my strength. I have a power nap straight away and once again go to bed at seven thirty, having swallowed a couple aspirins.

The views today are absolutely spectacular. We are completely out of the villages and into the area where even the locals don't stay for the winter. It's pure wilderness, what I like the most. Walking through outstanding natural beauty, seeing the porters pass me almost barefoot and with unbelievable loads fixes my head. Now I want to get to base camp and touch my mountain. I am ready. Tomorrow, we are going above 5,000 metres (16,404 feet).

Passing through the Everest cemetery where over 200 climbers lie sobers us up. None of them wanted or planned to stay here. I wander around the little stone graves in silence... Nothing is calling me to stay. It will all be good.

Day Thirteen

Today's hike is a very short in distance, 5,000 metres (16,404 feet), but it takes three and a half hours because I am still recovering from my illness. Everybody has recovered from stomach, chest and other ailments. We are pressing on like a well-oiled machine. We stop at Gorek Shep at 5,150 metres (16,896 feet), three hours away from our final destination. Tomorrow, the first part of the expedition will be complete.

I see Everest base camp for the first time today, a very distant city of yellow tents. I am apprehensive at first, but then, absorbing the beauty of the several 6,000-metre (19,685-feet) peaks surrounding it and seeing the moraine of the Khumbu Glacier I will be walking up in several days, I tune in. I can relate to it all. I warm to my home for the next five weeks. I am close now.

Day Fourteen

We arrive at base camp for lunch, which is served in a comfortable mess tent with tables, chairs and a lighting system, all solar-powered. In fact, our team doesn't use a generator at all on this trip, which again is a great way to do things in such pristine conditions. It is so exciting to be here, sorting out my bags and climbing gear into smaller packs. Everybody is in great shape and good health, apart from Iza's tooth. She goes down one day earlier. We have the first view of the Khumbu Icefall, 900 vertical metres (2,952 feet) of moving ice. Yes, it looks impossible to climb through. Let's not worry about that now though. We have three days of acclimatisation, good food and small walks to get used to the altitude before we ascend. We need to move through the icefall efficiently because it is the most dangerous section of the climb on the south side of the mountain, and we will go through it six times.

We see two big avalanches this afternoon, but both a safe distance away. I try to warm up some water for a shower in the sun, but it does not quite work so I am going to bed for the fifth day in a row without washing. Nice. Thankfully I have a single tent. Our oxygen saturation levels are above 90 percent, which is really good. Spirits are high.

The dinner is just amazing. We have starters and then proper oven-baked pizza and chocolate pudding. All is just exquisite for this elevation. Yum! Everybody scoffs down huge portions. We always have seconds, and Vivian usually finishes off my potatoes. We play music from iPods and share stories. We laugh long into the night.

Day Fifteen

I have a terrible night. I struggle to breathe. I cannot really sleep because my nasal fluids are building up and flooding down my throat. I end up sitting up for most of the night feeling sorry for myself and sniffing quietly. I fear that, while a good blow of my nose would make me feel a bit better, it might set off an avalanche.

Today is a shoot-me-anybody-please day for me. I have tonsillitis for the first time in about thirty-two years. Even though I have no fever, my throat is swollen, and I cannot swallow anything. Everyone else is in ice climbing training, and I am shuffling between the kitchen tent (hot water and honey) and my sleeping bag. I am told I look sick. Cheers, guys! My joints ache as well. My heart is racing at 150 a minute. My oxygen saturation levels fall to the lowest levels of under 80 percent. Clearly, I am fighting an infection. This is not good. Bill is not feeling great either, so we both go to the Everest ER tent.

I get enough amoxicillin for a horse and am told to keep warm. Easier said than done! By the evening my throat feels as if I have swallowed a handful of razor blades. I am on fire. I take my first sleeping pill ever in order to relieve my suffering during the night and have some rest.

Day Sixteen

I am marginally better, so I again just stagger out of my tent for meals while everybody around the camp avoids me like some disease. I am sorting out my food for the higher camps after ice climbing training in the morning. Every portion is carefully selected, packed and marked. Many vital decisions are to be made. Then I bathe in the sun, sorting my gear in front of the tent. I feel nervous about being sick and leaving the base camp for higher up in a couple days. I ask the mountain if I am ready and if everything will be okay. I have severe diarrhoea from being stressed, the new type of food, the antibiotics, or the altitude. You choose. Suddenly, a wonderful, colourful butterfly flutters around and sits on my sizable mountaineering shoes. I ask my magic question, and it responds with a delicate movement of its wings. All will be good. He stays with me for a long while. I admire the frail creature that has flown so high to calm me down.

I suddenly remember that Steve gave me cards to read, one for each week. I open the first two immediately and start crying like a baby. They are full of shared memories, support and unconditional love. They are funny, too, but I crawl back in my sleeping bag, curl up in the foetal position and cry myself to sleep.

I wake up and call him from the satellite phone. This is significant. I have never communicated with anybody from a mountain before. This is my lesson in relating: relating to myself, my illness, my pains, my mates, my mountain and my Steve.

It is a sad day. The trekking ladies are leaving the camp and going back to civilisation. I give them a letter to post to Steve. They don't even give me a single hug because I occupy the farthest corner of the mess tent to stop my bugs from spreading. I'm very antisocial. I feel sentenced. I watch them leave through the opening of the tent, their figures receding until they become one with the rocky background. The remaining team members look at each other with understanding. Now the real work starts. The hen party is over.

Enjoying vulnerability

April – May 2010
Asia, Mount Everest –
8,848 metres (29,029 feet)

Day One

WE officially meet all our high-altitude Sherpa and the kitchen staff today. We are pleased to learn that four of them are lamas. Trying to remember all their names proves impossible. There is Tarke Sherpa, Pasang Gombu Sherpa, Sange Sherpa, Mindu Chin Sherpa, Temba Sherpa, Dawangchhu Sherpa, Penba Chhater Sherpa, Pem Chhiri Sherpa, Pasan Terdi Sherpa, Sohen Chhissing Sherpa, and Dakusang Sherpa. Short, bulky men, made of pure muscle – these people make expeditions like mine succeed. If not for them, we simply wouldn't stand a chance. For example, our expedition needs 109 oxygen bottles strategically placed on route. Every bottle weighs 3.5 kilograms (7.7 pounds). Then there is our food, group tents, ropes, emergency equipment, solar panels, kitchen gear, and so much more.

A different and very special group of Sherpas, the Khumbu Doctors, maintain the ladders, ropes and route via the Icefall. Again, without that help, we would be there for months, meandering through almost impenetrable ice blocks.

Today is also our expedition's *puja* day. Without that special Buddhist blessing ceremony, neither we nor the Sherpas would go above base camp.

We have been waiting for it for a while because the little notebook of Buddhist wisdom told our Sidhar and main lama - Dawa that April 21 is the day.

Puja is an amazingly complicated ritual. It involves chanting, serious prayer, and then lots of whisky, wine, beer, food and throwing rice, ash, and flour at each other as well as into the thin air. A special altar has been constructed. Some fantastically intricate holy butter sculptures have been created. All of our equipment – the spikes of our crampons and ice axes, helmets, harnesses and carabiners – has been holy buttered, too. We spend the whole morning at the altar. I like the chanting a lot. The weather is warm and sunny. Suddenly, there is a spectacular avalanche in the distance and a halo surrounds the sun. Almighty nature mesmerises us all by displaying its relentless strength and beauty. I am not sure which of the phenomena to admire more.

Apparently it is a very unusual season weather-wise. It is very warm and people anticipate the first summits will be as early as May 5–6. According to our plan we will just be coming back from the second rotation then, so will certainly miss that window. Our target date is May 16, my birthday.

After lunch we pack our equipment for the higher camps. The mood has visibly shifted. Most of us are tense and quiet. The day has come. I feel much better. At least I can walk again, but I'm still not yet 100 percent. My heart rate is a respectable 73 beats per minute, and my oxygen saturation is up to 83 percent. There is hope.

After dinner we get closer to our premier Sherpa team and watch *Wild Hogs* DVD.

Day Two

We wander one-third of the way up the Khumbu Icefall just as a little trial. We set off before seven. I must say, as strange as it sounds, I like it. In fact, I love it, and I do not feel in danger at all. The 1,000-metre (3,280-feet) deep living mass of ice shifts constantly and unpredictably, and we are like tiny ants snaking through it without leaving a footprint. To me, it is all a snow and ice adventure park, where you have to pull yourself up, swing yourself across, cross ladders over dark and bottomless crevasses, and clamber up ice steps half as tall as you. And we do all that in darkness at more than 5,300 metres (17,388 feet), scrambling breathlessly for five to six hours nonstop. When we hit the camp after our little trial at around eleven, our snoring is so loud that we almost cause an avalanche.

I open my third card from Steve. It makes me laugh. It's about a camel, which is trying to pronounce our unique Polish vowel sounds. Its mouth is half open and looks like it is in some weird, severe seizure.

Tonight, we start our first rotation. We need to get to camp one and then to camp two at around 6,500 metres (21,325 feet) and acclimatise. We are aiming to stay up there for five nights straight. I have terrible diarrhoea brought on by the sheer anxiety and stress of starting the serious part of the expedition so soon. I am still on a handful of antibiotics and feel a bit weak. I cannot believe I am here and actually doing it. It's as if all the preparation and build-up for the trip has been happening to somebody else. I am not really sure if it is me any longer. I watch this crazy woman in love with the mountain, who just happens to be called Ania, preparing for a very short night in a cold, single tent. She wears the stuff she will be walking in tomorrow in order not to waste a moment of precious sleep. And then, donk! She falls into the deep, healthy ocean of sleep.

Day Three

I wake up at two forty-five on autopilot. I get out of my tent, go to the loo and get to the breakfast table at three fifteen. I am first there. Serki, the chef, serves porridge and toast with fried eggs. I eat and drink in silence for a while before the tiny rays of the other climbers' head torches bob on the wall of the mess tent. We leave base camp at four. Leaving the camp, we always walk around the *puja* altar three times to ensure our safety. Dawa burns incense, and we all throw rice into the air as an offering. We walk out of the camp in silence. Only the crunch of hard snow and ice under our heavy boots breaks the night.

Walking up through the full 1,000-metre (3,280-feet) of the icefall for six hours is physically very challenging but magical. I hardly stop because I am weak and always catching up with the others. Stopping also seems too risky because we need to get through the area as quickly as possible.

'Climb efficiently, take small steps, use your legs, and clip in this way,' I hear the mantra of our guides.

The pulls, swings, ladder crossing and climbing we have to execute are beyond any imagination and gym preparation. How naïve 'Are you ready?' seems. You cannot be ready for any of this. You have to plunge in and live it.

Again, it is like being in a frozen wonderland. The different types of ice surrounding us, towering above us and being left behind us as we climb higher through the icefall, are stunning. I touch every bit I can with compassion and admiration. I caress the edges of giant ice blocks softened by the sun. I follow the thin nylon rope up and up and up. The early morning view from the top of the icefall is absolutely breathtaking. I am almost eye to eye with the top of Pumori, a 7,000-metre (22,965-feet) peak. I sit down for a while with a giant smile on my face. I have a snack, drink some water and move on. I love being here, away from the hustle and bustle of base camp. The almost flat walk through a giant crevasse field from the end of the danger zone, as we call the icefall, to camp one normally takes an hour. My body, worn out by the tonsillitis and the demanding six-hour climb, needs two hours to crawl through. Once again it doesn't seem like me dragging my body along the fixed ropes. I'm not there. Bill stays behind me the whole time. On reaching the tent, where Vivian is snoring in comfort, I collapse. I crawl out only for supper and the toilet, or more precisely the plastic wag bag in the middle of the camp. We have to carry it back down with us after the first rotation. Good job it is frozen for the most part. Taking care of your own waste ... what a great way of accepting full responsibility for oneself!

Day Four

Camp one is a very basic site because we are only staying here for two nights throughout the whole expedition. We will just have an emergency tent here after tomorrow. Today is an acclimatisation day. In the morning I get my monthly prize for being a woman... yes, exactly as per plan. We are camping on snow, I am sharing with a bloke, we use wag bags for a toilet in the middle of the camp, at night it's a pee-bottle, I am at 6,300 metres (20,669 feet), and I am still taking a handful of antibiotics three times a day. What a great way to spend a holiday! I spend most of the day in my sleeping bag fighting off stomach cramps. After lunch we walk, with me actually crawling, halfway up to camp two, just for fun. For the night I take half a Diamox to help me sleep better and recover. We are moving to camp two tomorrow.

Day Five

We pack our bags in the morning and start marching at eight thirty after porridge. I have another symptom of altitude sickness, which is total indigestion. Whatever I eat runs through. And I am going 200 metres (656 feet) higher. The path is easy, but with all my ailments I am well behind the group and arrive forty minutes later than the first crowd. I reach the tent and collapse on Vivian. We take comfort in our camaraderie. His Irish sense of humour keeps me alive. We tease each other and laugh so loudly that people outside walk away, thinking a bit of privacy would be in order. He is trying to sit in a net seat and cannot fit his fat Irish arse in it. I am supporting the chair from behind, but it won't hold. We are in hysterics.

The surroundings of camp two are totally out of this world. We can clearly see the Lhotse Face, well over 1,000 vertical metres (3,280 feet) of blue ice, our next challenge: a couple of small ants on the mountain turn out to be a Sherpa team fixing ropes up to the Yellow Band. The ground in the camp itself is like a rock fall within an ice sculpture park. I take a bagful of Imodium for the night. I need to start retaining food.

Day Six

I am sleeping at my personal highest, 6,500 metres (21,325 feet). Being here and feeling good is very important to all of us. We will be here eleven nights all together, weather permitting, and it is crucial to acclimatise. We are not planning to spend a night at camp three, other than on the way to the summit. I give up the antibiotics without finishing the full course. Other than being a bit puffed up in my face in the mornings, I feel well. My appetite is poor, but I force myself to gorge at every meal. Up here we need to eat 6,000 calories a day to keep alive and deal with the conditions. It is so cold here that when the sun sets we need to wear down suits even for dinner in the mess tent. Our team has bonded together tremendously by now. The kindness and care from our Sherpa team and guides is very reassuring.

I take off my boots in the tent. Vivian almost throws me out over the smell. I forgot to wash my woollen socks, and 100 percent sheep yarn combined with a day of being in the boots is deadly. Vivian says I should not blame the poor sheep for the stink. It's really not my feet. Yeah, right!

Our guides are totally supportive. There is a special depth of honesty, integrity, peace and absence of fear in their eyes. No question or inquiry fazes Bill. He is fully aware of what is happening around him, and his intuition is tuned into picking up the smallest signals from the surrounding environment. He's a walking statement of, 'I have always done and always will do all that I can, and I give 100 percent in everything I do.'

Day Seven

Today we go for an acclimatisation walk to the bottom of the Lhotse Face. It is difficult for me again, and I am way behind the team. I need an emergency toilet stop in the middle of an open, flat space. Great! Now everybody has seen my white arse. We rest at 6,700 metres (21,981 feet), breathing heavily and gasping for air at every step. A buff covers my mouth and nose to prevent any lung infection, as that would be the end of my ascent. We will not be using oxygen until the summit bid and camp three, which is at least twenty days away. I feel better and sleep better. There is hope.

Day Eight

We are packing up to descend through the night to base camp for well-deserved rest and recovery. I am so looking forward to my own tent, the bucket shower, face cream, good food (our cook is a master chef), and simply being able to walk to the toilet without losing my breath. Comfort is all relative. To those sitting in the comfort of their homes, base camp would seem unendurable. For us coming down from camp two on Everest, it is luxury.

Scott, our leader, says the first rotation has gone well and everybody is doing great. In my view, I am doing terribly. I am slow and always last to every stop. I struggle inside with this reality. Perhaps I'm just being tired, but

I start picking up on the mistakes of the others and try to use it to boost my own confidence. I know this approach won't take me to the top. I need to fix my head again because nobody here can give me the strength to continue. It has to come from within.

Day Nine

We are ready to leave camp at five. Again, we need to be through the icefall before ten. We almost run down. I am feeling much stronger now. With every metre lower, my body is less and less stressed. What took us three days to climb up, we descend in six hours. At the end of the walk I am famished and feel spaced out. I haven't planned my snacks and water intake very well. We all walk like zombies, hungry, exhausted, brain dead and sleep-deprived. Walking through the icefall requires amazing mental concentration as well as pure physical effort. You need to make sure you are secure. You need to make sure that your feet are well placed for every step. You need to pay attention to what is going on around you and where your teammates are, determine if you need to get help or help others, and be aware of what the ice is doing and be prepared to react. God knows how, actually.

When I get to my tent, all I can do is to take off my crampons, boots and harness and crawl to the dining tent for two eggs and a pancake snack. I tuck in to a generous portion, drink a litre of water, take a bucket shower and crash. For lunch somebody has to actually come to my tent and shake my leg because I am so out of it. My body is going, 'Oh, my Lord! So much oxygen. Quick! Sleep, eat, sleep, eat before she takes me up again!'

I open Steve's card number four. I get to the sentence, 'I hope all is well.' I run out of the tent, shouting in my head, 'No, nothing is okay. The walking is so fucking difficult.' I am confused and am suffering. I am not sure how to get better and refocus my head.

I call Steve and share all my anxiety, my period, my tonsils, the tiredness, and so forth. I am having a good old moan. I don't feel tired, I am not sure what is wrong. I want somebody to give me a choice whether or not to keep going. I don't want it to feel like an obligation. I don't need to continue, it's a choice. Every day I choose to be here. He rationalises all my ailments for me in several sentences and says, 'I believe you can do it.' Then we get disconnected as the satellite turns. Looking at the big, heavy satellite phone, I say aloud, 'Yeah, you smart arse, sitting comfortably inside watching the telly. That's easy for you to say!' But this has nothing to do with Steve, it is my fractious state of mind. I meditate the whole afternoon. I hear the glacier cracking under my tent in a reassuring murmur. Two avalanches crash down. It's dark. Dinner is called and I join everybody for food and a movie, *Ocean's Eleven*.

Day Ten

Today is a catch-up day for laundry etc. Washing in ice-cold water for five minutes turns my hands into ice blocks. I need to stop and warm myself up. The washing is not really clean, but at least it is soaked in a biodegradable soap and smells nice.

We have a trekker group visiting so the climbers move to the cooking tent with the Sherpa. I love observing that underground of activities. It is as if there are two totally separate worlds operating in base camp in complete harmony: the expedition members alongside the intense world of Sherpa activities that is totally impenetrable for a Western person. As most of the Sherpa speak only a couple words of English, we just exchange smiles and simple pleasantries. But what a fantastic observation ground! They are so kind to each other, genuinely caring for each other, but also gently mock each other. Their laughter comes right from the bottom of their bellies, and they smile with every cell of their bodies. Sherpa have structural differences in their heart and lungs. They are totally adapted to living at higher altitudes. They can run up and down three camps at a time, some in white tennis shoes without crampons. They carry 25 to 50 kilograms (55 to 110 pounds) on their backs or foreheads. The sad thing is that more and more of them are choosing to move to Kathmandu to have easier lives than at altitude, and they are in danger of losing that genetic design for the mountains. I wonder what Everest expeditions will do in fifty years. Maybe they'll just take special air transport or a cable car.

We are relaxing. My skin is so dry that whole flakes fall off. I apply cream twice a day, but am sure it will not recover until I come off this beautiful mountain. I am preparing psychologically for the second rotation, which will take me to camp three for lunch. We will spend five consecutive nights at 6,500 metres (21,325 feet). I just hope I will feel better than the first time round. It is all in the hands of the Mighty Mr. Everest, who rules here without exception.

Day Eleven

It's the last rest day. I go for a walk around base camp to look for inspiration for our eight- to nine-hour climb of 1,200 metres (3,937 feet) straight up to camp two overnight. I listen to streams, yak bells and incomprehensible Sherpa conversations. It will be such a hard night and day. At least I am fully healthy, or so it seems anyway. We are trying on oxygen masks for size today. We all look like aliens in them. We have a good laugh, but everything is getting increasingly serious.

Day Twelve

We leave base camp at four o'clock. Destination: camp two. The climb through the Khumbu Icefall is great. I am still surprised where I get the stamina from to endure those ice faces, ladders, and the intense concentration required to do it as safely and efficiently as possible. It drains my internal resources, but as I planned my snacks and water intake better this time, all is good. I love it again. Nature never fails me! It takes me in, I disappear and just follow my instincts and intuition for every next move. It is wonderful to switch off the rational mind. I feel a deep sense of connection and feel I relate to everything in a new way. I belong here.

There is a collapse of the route, but it has been fixed ahead of our arrival. I climb the icefall ninety minutes quicker than the first time, much to my surprise. I manage to halve my time to camp one as well. A helicopter hovers on the line of the top of the icefall. It's a new, lighter model. They will apparently try to touch down in camp one and two this season. Time goes fast, and it's soon ten o'clock. The snow-covered walls around the flat-bottomed route to camp two create a bowl where the solar radiation hits us hard. It's like being in a microwave. The heat is evaporating any strength left in us with unforgiving force. The pace of the walk is snail-like. Vivian comments later that I was so slow that he thought the glacier would overtake me at some point. My legs do not want to move and my steps become micro-sized because I am unable to take a full stride. I almost tiptoe my way up. It takes me two hours longer than during the first rotation. I can't believe it. I am swaying in a semiconscious state by the end of it. A Sherpa helps to carry my pack for the last twenty minutes. When we walk, the power of the sun bakes us. When we stop, it is freezing. I have never experienced anything like that in my life. Sunstroke and dehydration are our enemy. Thankfully it's not a challenging climb, but just right, left, right, left, right, left.

This is a pretty intense day. It turns out to be an eleven-hour slog rather than the planned eight. You never know with this mountain. I have a single tent this time, which is a relief to be honest. I immensely enjoy the secret communion I have with Vivian on this trip, but I need the space to just be. I sleep, eat, and sleep some more. My stomach is used to the altitude, I retain food and I don't hurt anywhere. Wonderful.

Day Thirteen

There is a snowstorm overnight with around 30 centimetres (1 foot) of fresh powder snow and strong winds. I am kept awake for most of the night, gasping for air in my new, single-walled tent. I have to keep banging the walls of the tent so the feeble structure won't collapse on me under the heavy snow. After unzipping my tent in the morning I have to move masses of drifting snow just to be able to crawl out. After breakfast we go for a hike, the familiar route from the first rotation up to the base of the Lhotse Face. Scott calls it a little hike. The weather turns on us from a sunny morning to winds and snow within ten minutes, so after a short break we decide to hurry back to camp two and have a late lunch. The afternoon is spent exchanging jokes, playing cards and drinking hectolitres of tea.

Day Fourteen

Thankfully I sleep better, as I need all the sleep I can get. Today is a rest-well day. Tomorrow morning we will leave at five in the morning for lunch at camp three. For most of us it will be our personal highest, 7,200 metres

(23,622 feet). We will climb without oxygen, spend about an hour there, and come back down. This will complete the goal for our second rotation. My muscle mass built up over the last fourteen months is starting to disappear, although I feel strong. During the first rotation I got over my Ecuadorian oedema at an emotional level, but there is still a little voice in the back of my mind – I cannot be sure. Wish me luck!

Day Fifteen

We did it … and in good time, too. It takes us five long hours to climb to camp three without oxygen. I am not sure if I could have made two more steps, but that's fine for this rotation. I am last from the group. Lhotse Face shows a human face today and has been kind to us with the weather, although we start in rather marginal cloud. The steps in the blue ice are covered with powder after the recent snowfall, which makes our struggle easier. The first 30 metres (98 feet) are simply vertical, and it is amazing to climb through it with a thin rope, ascender, and ice axe for safety. We are totally exposed to free falling if the rope does not hold. I feel as if I am moving like a well-trained ice squirrel and never lose my balance. It feels good to be so close to the ice. Coming down from camp three, after lunch, takes three long hours of rappelling. I enjoy it. It's slightly painful, especially on the steeper bits. The rope marks my white jacket forever. It's like a war wound that will remind me of this day forever.

On reaching camp two I zonk out immediately, trying to prevent my muscles shaking from exhaustion. I wrap up in my sleeping bag and down suit and miss out on the soup. Damn! The mission of the second rotation has been fulfilled. We are sufficiently acclimatised to be able to make our summit bid. Now we need to get back to base camp safely, have a good rest, and watch the weather for the upper parts of the mountain. Our Sherpa team is currently distributing oxygen bottles and team equipment on the route to camp four. Very exciting!

I am amazed to witness what is going on in my body when it is exposed to extreme altitude for so long. Not only does my stomach need time to adjust, but there is no nail or hair growth at all. I have periodical peripheral oedema. Bodily fluid gathers in my face, fingers and toes to the degree that I look obese. I cannot sleep flat, my favourite position at sea level, but need to be propped up to half sitting. All movements are slow. After today's eight-hour hike I shiver for an hour trying to calm my massacred body. I love every part of it though, and am grateful for every drop of sweat that my twelve months of training required, because my muscles are fantastically strong. I sometimes get the impression again that I am not even there. My muscles are trained to perform. Through intuition at a cellular level and being connected to the mountain, my muscles seem to know exactly what to do and how to support and protect the rest of me. When resting, I drift into a different level of consciousness without thoughts. It is an amazing space where I float until somebody calls my name. Dinner is ready.

Day Sixteen

Today is another coach potato day. Although there is lots of idle time here and the others are impatient, I am relaxed. After all I am here on holiday. I enjoy every moment of inactivity because I know that my body is busily producing more red blood cells and acclimatising me to the altitude. The stress of the recent climbs has been tremendous. Tomorrow at five we are going back down to base camp. Good food and silly movies await.

In front of my tent I examine the route up to camp four in the full sun and suddenly realize how much more effort will be required to reach the top of this mountain and get back down safely. It dawns on me that what I have done so far is absolutely miniscule in comparison with the slow, sustained physical exhaustion I will force my body through within the next two weeks. Higher up, not only will I be expending energy climbing, but my body will be eating itself to a state of shutdown for all but its core processes on the final summit push. I remind myself that everybody who has climbed this mountain has told me that the only time when you can really start thinking that you have made it is when you are on the top of the Hillary Step, twenty minutes away from the summit. The year of training and the four weeks here means nothing. It can go any way any time.

For dinner at seven o'clock, I inhale a mountain of very oily fried potatoes and some canned tuna, and I am sound asleep by seven thirty.

Day Seventeen

We negotiate our way safely back to base camp via the icefall once again. On the way down it is warm and snowing. The snowflakes are very big, wet and heavy. They are so heavy that I could hear them falling, yet another secret of nature. I feel wanted by the mountain. I excel in climbing down. I love the humming of my body, fully balanced on one leg or dangling on one hand and not hurting. I am fast and efficient going down. I am first in the team going down and am on my own for quite a while. The blue of the ice combined with the white of the falling snow is soothing to the soul. Part of the icefall has collapsed, and the ice doctors have changed the route. Walking down, I feel much stronger than the first time round. It's a naïve feeling because, after hitting base camp, a five-minute bucket shower and a bite to eat, I pass out in the tent. I relish the silence of solitude.

I open card number five. It is written in very broken, incorrect, ungrammatical Polish. It makes me giggle hard. I feel happy and reconnect with myself.

I go to the toilet and find I am bleeding, but this time from the back. Something isn't right and I am scared. I go to the Everest hospital, a large white tent.

'You have haemorrhoids,' the doctor announces after a finger inspection.

The doctor tells me it is normal here and asks if I have a nappy because they sometimes bleed severely. And dampness would not be good for the down suit. Well, I must say that nappies are not on my high-altitude mountaineering equipment list. I have never heard about anything like this from anybody. This is just fantastic news. I get a special steroid cream and advice. The best cure is no constipation, avoid the cold and bathe frequently in warm water. But of course, that would be a doddle at 5,300 metres (17,388 feet) without a bowl and in a tent. And tomorrow morning we plan to walk for six hours down to the villages.

I have a nightmare afternoon where I cannot find a painless position for myself: lying, sitting, or squatting. Nothing works. I can feel very concentrated pain up my backside. I take boiling water in a bottle to my tent and use a sponge to do hot compresses every five minutes. That feels better, but still doesn't cure anything. I have a bad night with periodic crying lulling me to sleep. I tell Bill what is going on.

Day Eighteen to Twenty-two

On our first rest day we walk for six hours, but most of it is downhill. Every single step provides me with a painful reminder of yesterday's discovery. By the end of the walk I am exhausted from the constant discomfort. I walk like a wide-legged cowboy to avoid any more friction.

I don't do much at Dingboche for two full days, hoping to heal and put some weight back on. I call Steve. I tell him what I have now. He pauses meaningfully and asks if my haemorrhoids are dangling down (sweet!). No, they are not. It's simply an exposed two-centimetre-long vein, which bleeds every so often. Tears roll down my cheeks. I need some strength from somewhere to deal with that, too. He has no advice. Later that day I receive a satellite text message asking how my new little friends are doing. I laugh. With my mind's eye, I salute my new little friends. I need to start liking them. We are a team now!

Our landlady here is amazing. She fattens us up with freshly baked chocolate cakes and generous portions five times a day. Today is the first sunny day in about five, and we can feel optimism flooding back.

On the mountain, the first deaths have been reported on the north and the south sides as summit fever begins. Our target summit push is now May 17 if the forecast holds.

Day Twenty-three

We walk halfway back to base camp and stop in Lobuche. I take a shower, my first in over a week. The warm water strongly caresses what is left of my body. I indulge in the running water and lose myself in the pleasure of the moment.

Day Twenty-four

We are back at base camp. The weather forecast for our chosen date doesn't look good anymore. All the predictions from the Swiss centre, the

American centre and the local centre totally contradict each other. It is impossible to make a well-informed decision. We analyse the satellite images. We will be subject to airplane weather, and a tropical depression is building up around the Bay of Bengal. Where the hell is that? And why would it impact on our little party? Well, yes it would, and yes it will. All teams now aim for May 22, summiting on May 23, but it is difficult to assess if that is just a group think effect, where the word spreads from tent to tent, or is a rational, well-informed decision. Can anything be rational at this stage and in these circumstances?

As a consolation Serki serves banana pie for dessert. Then we get out the strobe lights and have a bit of a dance, which lifts our morale for a good night's sleep. We watch *Ocean's Twelve* and *Ocean's Thirteen* almost in one go. Very intellectual!

I read card number six by the light of my head torch. We are both starting to count the days. It's over halfway now. It's dangerously close to the date for returning home, and we are still unsure when we are going up.

Day Twenty-five

Today the pain from little friends is finally bearable and I move around the camp vigorously. Over the previous two days I spent most of my time in my tent in a foetal position, sometimes wiping tears from my cheeks. I felt completely helpless and tried reading a book to focus my mind on something other than the pain. I create a dream. I so want to walk through the winding streets of Montmartre in the height of the summer, holding Steve's hand. I decide a long weekend trip to Paris will be my thank you present to him for all the support he has provided me over the last four and a half months. I close my eyes and see myself eating chocolate croissant, drinking latte for breakfast, and drinking wine and eating gourmet food in the evening. I am wearing a skirt, which the warm wind blows softly. It feels so good.

The wait for our weather window is unbearable for some. In fact, some expeditions just pack up and leave. But for me it is a blessing as I muster the will to have a fair crack at it. I am so far along now.

Today is the first windless day in weeks. Over the last couple days teams have lost tents higher up, and we are glad to be lower down at 5,300 metres

(17,388 feet). With the current jet stream pattern we are getting sandwiched between high winds before May 20 and the mountain closedown at the end of May. Last year a big avalanche caused the mountain to be closed on May 26, eleven days from now.

Day Twenty-six (my birthday)

My backside has healed a bit, just in time. I go on a beautiful walk in the morning. From Pumori base camp one can see the beautiful pyramid of Everest from the north and south side, a picture-postcard shot. In the afternoon we watch *As Good As It Gets* with Jack Nicholson and listen to hailstones beating hard against the tents as the jet stream lingers and causes unstable weather in the afternoons. Our guides say the season is strange this year, with only a handful of summits to date. It is getting really late in the season for a lot of teams and our summit attempt might get crowded. Tomorrow will be a big decision day for the whole camp. Let's see.

I open my birthday card. It's about my beautiful body. I ponder over my hairy legs, my bruised arms and shins, my sickly spots all over, puffed eyes, greasy hair and blackened nails. Hmm!

After dinner comes a wonderful surprise, a birthday cake with candles. What a setting to complete thirty-seven years of age. I receive several presents, one of which, chocolate digestives, I pass on to Vivian as a thank you gift for being such a great companion. We dance around the table and in the Sherpa kitchen tent, and are loud and merry long into the night.

Day Twenty-seven

I suffer terrible food poisoning overnight. In the morning I vomit vigorously in front of the mess tent and pass out. The team catch me every time so I don't hurt myself. I have lost my supper and my birthday cake in the process. I feel like shit, weak and unable to move. I spend the whole day on the floor of the mess tent with a bucket of water, a bowl of boiled rice and an empty bucket just in case it all comes back again.

The decision is made that we are moving up tonight, the final rotation, with hopes of a summit bid. We are going straight up to camp two because the weather looks good for May 23. I force myself to pack because we are leaving early in the morning. I am too weak to climb so the guides assign a Sherpa to carry my backpack and turn around with me if I cannot continue. That sounds like a sentence. I tell myself I have to make it at least to camp one, where an emergency stay can be organized.

I make two last phone calls. One, with Steve, is full of compassion, love and wishing me well. I don't know why, but I call my sister. We rarely speak and are not close, yet she picks up immediately as if expecting the call. I tell her that we are moving … yes, all the way to the top … yes, into the death zone … yes, Saturday night will probably be the summit night.

She then says, sobbing, 'Ania, we love you, and we are so proud of you. You have achieved so much already. Please promise me that if it is too dangerous, you will turn around. You don't need to get to the top.'

My throat tightens and I cannot speak. We are both crying. She knows she might be talking to me for the last time. She wants to see me again. After hanging up I sit in my dark tent crying.

When I wanted somebody to give me a choice after the first rotation, there was nobody there. Now I am totally ready for whatever will happen. I am going up.

Just before snoring time I open the card for the summit days. It says, 'Go for it! Whatever happens, I am proud of you for all the things you have achieved.'

I think to myself 'The congratulations for not doing it are not necessary … not yet.' *I am up for it.*

Day Twenty-eight

I am ready to roll at four. I cannot eat anything for breakfast, but at least the mint tea stays down this time round. We circle the altar and I concentrate on every step of the way. Slowly I make my way through the icefall. It takes me an hour longer than the rest of the team to reach camp one. I am weak. I have no pride when my Sherpa pushes my backside across little crevasses and sets of ice staircases. I know I am struggling and need a proper break. Bill asks me to strip down. I take off all my extra layers because I know how hot it can get. We both decide that I should keep going forward.

I make it to camp two. How? I just don't know because I have not eaten for well over thirty-five hours now. As I say to a friend in an email on my return to England, 'I made it. Don't know how really, but perhaps it should be left in the unknown domain ... not to be repeated ever again for sure.' An hour before reaching camp two, I catch up with Cindy. It's weird because she is normally so strong and fast. I can immediately see that she is suffering from sunstroke and staggering strangely. In an instant I switch from patient to nurse. I make her sit down, drink and eat a little. I wave to my emergency Sherpa and give her the radio to call camp two. She gets help down, and we all make it to camp safely. With all the breaks, it takes me eleven hours. I feel totally ecstatic that I am here and do not vomit on the way. I collapse into my sleeping bag with a wide grin on my face and don't move until dinner. I am so glad that we are staying here for a full day before going up to camp three. I have some plain pasta with oil for dinner. It is rather tasteless, but I eat like mad. It's the only way to have a chance.

Day Twenty-nine

I do nothing but eat and sleep, gathering strength. Tonight we are trying for the next camp.

Day Thirty

Despite the good rest yesterday, on leaving camp I know I won't make it up the Lhotse Face today. I just can't move fast enough. A panicky thought rattles around my mind.

I gave it so much, and it might all just slip through my fingers and disappear.

I end up way behind the team and crawl up to the rock at the bottom of the Lhotse Face. I don't want them to start moving up. I need rest. I need some time to pull myself back together. *Please, please, please.*

Scott looks up, looks at us, and walks to one side with Bill. I am sitting on a rock, drinking and eating an energy bar. They conclude it is too windy to go up today, so we are turning back to camp two. I jump with joy. I have another day to recover! Everybody is dragging their feet. There are angry looks and faces all around, yet I am ecstatic. I run down and sit in my tent. And then a random thought flies into my consciousness.

What if my illness isn't a one-off and I am out of strength for good?

I make myself go to the mess tent to face the guides. I start crying, saying I was so slow today and I am undoubtedly the weakest person on the team. I am not sure about my abilities.

Scott cuts through my wailing. 'Have you made the decision in your head that you are turning around?'

I explode, 'Absolutely not.'

'Good. You just keep going as you are. For what you have been through you are doing just fine.'

I return to my tent and meditate.

Day Thirty-one

We leave for camp three at five. It takes me six hours, which is the upper limit, but I feel the weakness from yesterday isn't there. The day is absolutely beautiful. I remember the way up from the second rotation and just do my best to stay alive and keep going up and up and up. I climb on my own. Through the clear air I can see in the distance my team[7] slowly transform into our row of tents. This is my destination—I just have to get up there, I can almost touch it. Camp three does not really exist. There are tent platforms cut out of the Lhotse Face, and one has to be on crampons even when going to the toilet. There are many accidents in this camp so we take great caution.

As evening draws in we are rewarded for our efforts with the most beautiful sunset. The leisurely moving clouds and orange ball of the sun play frivolously. We have a cup of tea and a Ramen noodle soup each; I have some energy bars to fill the gap. My appetite is back, but there is not much to eat. We sleep on oxygen at minimum flow for a very short night. In fact it is a nap rather than a night. Vivian tells me that my peripheral oedema is back. Good job I don't have a mirror. He has lost his handsomeness somewhere as well.

---

[7] Everybody in our group is marked on the outside of our packs, so it is easy to spot each other on route.

Day Thirty-two

The move to camp four is dangerous and strenuous; it takes seven hours because, in some places, we are queuing and moving really slowly. The whole of base camp is here. There are around eighty climbers hoping for a summit, together with all the Sherpa support crews. I find Yellow Band and Geneva Spore challenging and disturbing. The crampons make a scratching sound on the rock, which breaks under our weight and falls on climbers below. The weather is stable and almost windless. We can still hear the jet stream relentlessly buffeting the top of the mountain. The tropical depression is moving in from the north. Our window is narrow. For the whole day I can't figure out how to adjust the oxygen mask, goggles and sun glasses, so I am sometimes without eye protection and risking snow blindness. I make that decision consciously, fully understanding the consequences.

I arrive at the South Col at twelve thirty and crash. To my surprise I am third with Vivian and Cindy still way behind me. Don't know how again! But this morning is my strongest time on the mountain so far. I am tired, but I feel good and my thinking is totally clear. As I approach camp four, comfortably set on a flat saddle the size of two football pitches, I see the 900-metre (2,952-feet), vertical, intimidating pyramid of Mt. Everest. I stand there for a while in thought. All the effort up to now does not count. There is more to endure, much more. I turn my eyes away.

After lunch of Ramen noodles again, I can't sleep, even on oxygen. Everything is a challenge when you are in your down suit with a mask on your face and a 3.5-kilogram bottle that you take everywhere with you. I have some snacks. The oxygen you breathe from the bottle is very dry, so our throats feel like they are full of barbed wire. Vivian points out that I have something wrong with my cheeks. They look strangely red and rubbed.

Until around six the weather is marginal, and we feel certain that we will stay at camp overnight and another day. However, at seven thirty everything goes quiet, and we start to prepare for the estimated fourteen-hour round-trip to the summit. We leave at nine o'clock and join the queue slowly moving up a gully to the balcony. I am chewing my ginger chews, deliciously tangy and keeping me alert. My feet are frozen and I inform Pemba, my summit Sherpa, who simply says, 'Keep them moving.' But of course! Even standing upright is difficult. I have to keep moving my feet inside my giant high-altitude boots. I make a deal with myself. If my feet don't warm up in an hour, I will turn around. The top is simply not worth ten toes. It does not matter that I am so close. I will turn around. I keep squeezing the parts of me I cannot feel anymore. Slowly, the pain of blood flowing back into capillaries spreads from toe to toe. I am relieved.

I am surprisingly aware and understand, at some deep level, everything that is going on with my body. I perfectly understand my surroundings. I know I am totally vulnerable in the death zone above 8,000 metres (26,246 feet). I have oxygen for twenty-one hours of life. I can see people turning around, being lead on short ropes. I can see people sitting motionless on the snow. I sense impatience and an unhealthy tension building in some climbers as they abandon their security ropes and risk everything, bypassing everybody in high exertion and panting parallel to us all. For me, it's fine. I have no pains anywhere, and the pace is slow, but we are moving. And most of all, I am warm. I just need to plod on.

I walk on pure passion for life, nature, love and an invisible but strong relationship with this mountain. I feel so privileged to be here.

Day Thirty-three (May 23, 2010)

It takes me by surprise, but, yes, I arrive at the so-called balcony. Here total chaos rules as everybody tries to get a new oxygen bottle. I feel like I'm in a Turkish market with everybody shouting at everybody else. I have some water, two energy bars and a ginger chew. They taste so good. In ten minutes I resume the climb. I am feeling good and do not want to wait for too long.

At the same time, in my home town my mum is squeezing a rosary in one hand and a shamanic stone in the other, not knowing what would be more helpful to me in the death zone. She is reciting in her head the positive thoughts I asked her to think that night: 'Ania is warm. It's all okay. Ania is safe. She is doing well. She is warm. It's all good.' My mum walks from church to church with that mantra and finally collapses after a sleepless night. She lives pure fear for twenty four hours.

We are waiting to ascend the south summit. There are some seriously steep bits here and the climbing is tough going. We stand in total darkness with a wonderful display of stars above us. It's such an amazingly quiet night. Slowly, through the black of the night, a tiny pink line grows through the middle.

Wow, it must be four thirty already.

I watch in amazement as, with every passing second, the moon quietly dances with the sun. I feel the warming rays on my battered body. I smile and feel the warmth from within. The pace up the south summit is amazingly slow, which allows me to breathe through my nose, which is very comforting. I concentrate on every step in the snow and ice, and every pull on the rope.

On the south summit I get my third and final bottle of oxygen, which will have to take me to the top and back to camp four. We move on after a short break and a couple of sips of water. I stand over nothing at approximately 8,790 metres (28,838 feet).

I actually don't feel that tired at all. I feel great. I have no fear.

I can see the famous Hillary Step in front of me. It is quite a sight. I am not surprised that people turn around from there. It is a pure wall of granite.

We are getting close to the ultimate turnaround time, which we have set for ten o'clock for our team. I have been climbing for well over ten long hours. Temba and I look at each other and press on with continued determination. I have lost track of my team. Suddenly, Scott, Denise and Paul appear to my left. I shout out to them, asking if I should continue in front of them. Scott just waves for me to keep going.

'I feel really bad, not sure I can make it this year,' he shouts.

Paul is waiting for his oxygen bottle.

On the Hillary Step we go over a rock, which is like a horse saddle. I sit, quite comfortably, with 7,000 metres (22,965 feet) of space behind me, clipped to a thin nylon rope. I cannot quite reach the other side of it, so I just kind of lower myself with my right leg above my head, swing my leg over the abyss behind me, and regain a stable standing position. I still can't see the summit. It rings in my head again that only from the top of Hillary Step can I say that I actually have a chance. I pause.

I have a chance.

It takes twenty more minutes. There I am, on the crowded top of

Sagarmatha[8] with stunning views all around me. Happy people are shouting, and the wind is picking up from the north. I reach the top at eight forty-five in the morning on May 23, 2010. The north side is foggy, so we can't quite see Tibet. I realise that I'm the first in my team to get to the top. Is that a joke or what? Two days ago I could hardly move.

Bill comes up to me after twenty minutes. 'Ania, I am really proud of you. You did so well today.'

We hug and exchange the pure joy of companionship and common success. I'm not crying. I'm not even feeling emotional. I'm trying to take it all in. I'm trying to comprehend that I am on the top of Mt. Everest.

I can go home now. This simple thought comes to mind.

Every step I take from now on will take me closer to home. Home isn't my flat. It is some kind of abstract concept of the strength and welcome of Steve's open arms.

I am surprised to learn that I have been on the top for an hour before the last member of our team joins us. Vivian does not even say a word—he's too exhausted. I start descending because the weather is changing fast. I do not know why, but my cheeks are hurting and my eyes are in a bad state. I can't see clearly and I am losing my peripheral vision. By the balcony, we are in a total whiteout, with wind battering us severely. At some point I feel the three vertebrae between my shoulder blades lock up. I squeeze my lips to stifle a scream. It starts hurting badly. Every arm wrap I have to do, every bend of my body to clip the carabiner, is sending rays of pain from the source to every cell of my body. My only thought now is to get down to camp four and lay down. I am speeding down. I can only sustain a limited amount of that pain. I am passing people with cerebral oedema who can no longer make sense of reality. Everybody is tended to, some have frostbite. I spot our Sherpa team assisting with a rescue. I am keen to keep going as my eyes are getting worse and I am now getting a muscular cramp in my upper back. In a narrow point, waiting for those ahead of me to pass, I sit down and instantly doze off. I wake up immediately and never sit down again. It is so easy to just fall asleep and never wake up again here. I start crying simply from pain and

[8] 'The forehead of the sky,' as Mt. Everest is called in contemporary Nepalese. The name depicts its perfectly.

have to take off my glasses because they are freezing up. That does not help my eyes.

Between the racing clouds I spot the reassuring view of the tents on the South Col. I can see how easily Everest's biggest disaster to date in 1996 could happen, when nine climbers died 200 metres (660 feet) from their tents because of the weather conditions. One moment I could see the tents; the next, I could see nothing. I squeeze the rope harder. I reach camp four, wailing from pain after eighteen and a half hours of climbing above 8,000 metres (26,246 feet). I realize I have not even had a pee for almost a day! I am met with a cup of tea in a small metal cup. I slurp it with wild pleasure. It's tea mixed with tears, the best cup of tea in my life. I get to my tent and wriggle into my sleeping bag. I hear nothing. I feel nothing. I'm not there.

Day Thirty-four

I wake up and cannot open my eyes. They are awfully red. A crust of white puss that has dried up in the oxygen-starved air has glued the lids together. I spit on a glove and start rubbing. I manage to open one eye, although I feel like I am peering through mud. Maybe it will get better throughout the day? I put on my sunglasses and start breaking camp after a pack of oats. I can hardly move from the pain in my back. Vivian takes a picture of my face, and I don't recognise myself. It is not the face of a victor who has just succeeded in conquering the highest mountain on Earth. It is the face of a feeble creature, totally beaten up, battered by almighty nature. I look like a Polish hooligan after five rounds with Mike Tyson. I delight in the broken and battered feeling of success. Once again, the back of my throat becomes uncontrollably wet and bitterly salty. It will take even more from me to get back down safely.

Outside it's still a whiteout, snowing and windy. We can't tell up from down or north from south. Visibility is zero. Again, I follow a snake of people down a rope. Every clip onto the rope and every arm wrap causes me excruciating pain. Tears roll uncontrollably down my face. I disassociate myself from the parts of me that are in pain. There is two of me: the one that can hardly move, and the one which keeps going. I cannot see properly anymore, the oxygen mask constantly rubs my bleeding cheeks. I become like the

Salvador Dali picture of a woman with drawers hanging out of her beautiful body. I'm like a wonderful Picasso, deconstructed into basic elements, those I can still use and those that are far beyond utilization by now, but hopefully not beyond repair. The me in pain is climbing slightly to the left; the still able to walk me is clipped into the rope.

I reach camp three where we stop for a while. I just lay there on the cold ice, thinking I have two more hours of being disintegrated before camp two. I get some strong painkillers. With constipation as a side effect, my little friends will be back. We move on. There's more arm wraps, more rappelling and more pain. At the last pitch of the rope, hanging vertically, my neck is stiff as a board from supporting the locked vertebrae in my upper back. I know my right hand, acting as a brake on the rope as I descend, is my only hope. I breathe energy into the single limb that is saving my life. I adore it.

When we get to the bottom of the Lhotse Face, I collapse and lay prostrate for a good thirty minutes before moving again and stumbling towards camp two. As I approach the camp I long to be whole again. I want someone to help me humanise the Picasso of pain and flesh. I think I will become one again in Steve's arms. I want to go home.

I'm so happy that I don't need to use my arms anymore. They just dangle alongside my body, bobbing in free movement against my hips. I can feel my belly button hurting, and I suspect an infection from not washing and from strapping the backpack buckle tightly round my waist to give some relief to my shoulder.

I am so happy to finally reach the kitchen tent, where all seven of us sleep together. My neck is completely stiff now and my left side has totally seized up. We all take off our boots together on the count of three. The smell somewhat tranquilises our senses. We have not washed for over six days now. After dinner we start our synchronized snoring concert. The alarm is set for two fifteen in the morning.

Day Thirty-five

In the morning my vision has improved. The oedema has come off my face, but the back pain is still there. Yes, my little friends are back, and my belly button is joining in the fun with a bleeding infection. Bill cannot wake up and mumbles a proposition that, if I need a day's rest, he would stay with me.

I laugh out loud. 'No thanks. I am going down, NOW.'

He is tired as he stayed behind yesterday and saved the life of a British climber named Mike, with severe cerebral oedema, abandoned by his team. He almost carried him down. Mike is later helicoptered from camp two (first landing ever), straight to Kathmandu hospital. We have a piece of bread each for breakfast and leave camp.

My lighter clothes have been sent to base camp by mistake. I am wrapped in a full down suit, which is just too hot for here. I reach an easy ladder and am gripped by terror. Hold on, I am not scared, or at least I should not be. This is an easy ladder. I step aside and think. I am extremely hot, sweat is streaming down my back, and my breathing and pulse are way too fast. My overheated body must have caused the fear to emerge. It amazes me how the body, head and heart are so closely connected. It's one. I calm my breathing and my pulse rate comes down. I open my suit to cool off, and then confidently cross over the ladder. With this incident I gain greater awareness of the humming harmony of mind, body and soul. All these facets need to be given the freedom to develop in order to help you reach your full potential. Many people tend to focus on one aspect of themselves, but I believe that the only way forward is to achieve a balance between all three.

I am relieved I am no longer wearing the oxygen mask. The last descent through the icefall is slow, hot and painful. I get some more drugs. My cheeks hurt, but my vision has fully returned, although everybody tells me it's a good thing I don't have a mirror. On the safe part of the glacier, a welcoming committee with Coca-Cola, cookies, and a big 'Congratulations' banner greets us. We have a short party, and the last thirty minutes of the walk are full of cheering, shouts and happy faces. We get to base camp for lunch and the loudest-ever music that shakes the tent in celebration. Sitting in a chair by the table and eating proper food for the first time in seven days makes me realize that I need to redefine the word 'tiredness.' Now I know exactly what it means. I have never felt this way before. I don't think I will ever use the word 'tired' to describe my condition back in civilisation. In the evening, though, we still find the energy to dance with all our Sherpa, the kitchen staff and some random guests. It goes on late into the night.

Day Thirty-six

We start packing and breaking up camp. I go to the doctor again. This time it's my cheeks and eyes. I have a severe bacterial infection from the leather part of the oxygen mask, and the bacteria has travelled to my eyes. It is not snow blindness.

Right. More antibiotics. Oh, yes!

I cannot take off my sunglasses. My eyes are so sensitive and my face is very inflamed. There are two wide-open wounds on my cheeks leaking dark yellow something, and a thick, red swelling surrounds my eyes. I hope it will recover soon. As I am struggling so much with my neck and eyes, I decide to get a helicopter out of base camp with some of the others. Before we board a frozen body from two years ago is taken out, it was recovered from near camp one.

What took us eleven days to climb up, takes eleven minutes to fly back down. The first breath of warm, summer air and the first sight of a tree take me completely by surprise. I embrace the thick, moist air. I sleep like a log. My hair and nails explode into new growth. It takes a month for them to become normal again. My face is healing rapidly. I am going home.

✳✳✳

We go to a bar. People ask for money at the end of the round of food. I look at the waiter in astonishment. What is money? I have just been on an eight-week all-inclusive holiday and have become accustomed to the notion that everything I needed could be obtained by a simple question and a smile.

Back in Kathmandu, we celebrate in the RumDoodle restaurant and every bar we can find. We indulge in salad, fresh water and ice cream. We break all the rules of being in a Third World country. I have my first Illy coffee, which tastes orgasmic. I have my first glass of champagne of the trip. After only two sips I ask the guys to put me in a taxi because I am totally, utterly drunk. I don't even remember the name of the hotel. This turns out to be one of my last alcoholic drinks, as I give up alcohol altogether on my return to London.

Only as the aircraft takes off from Delhi to take me home do I realise just how high I was less than a week earlier. When the giant jet takes off, I say to it: 'You are not even at camp two yet.' As the engines roar in the background, I say, 'Come on, camp three.' As I am sent deeper into my seat with the ascent, I say, 'You can give me more! Eight thousand metres. South Col.' The plane climbs higher, and I say, 'I have been higher than this. Don't embarrass yourself.' It finally gets to the 8,848 metres (29,028 feet) of Everest and stays at around 9,500 metres (31,168 feet) for most of the flight across two continents. Oh, my God! I was high. Incomprehensible!

When Steve picks me up at Heathrow I don't feel his hug, I don't feel anything. I am disassociated. Instead of a romantic evening, we report to A&E and spend three hours there while I have my behind examined. After the constipation and eleven hours of flying, it's pretty bad again. I landed on Tuesday night, so luckily I have five days before having to go to work.

It takes me three days to recognise my emotions. It takes me five days to comprehend the English reality of a small seaside town. It takes me three weeks to appreciate lovemaking again. It takes me three months to fully remember things. It takes me nine months to fully physically recover and regain pre-Everest strength. I write to all those who supported me:

Dear All, Almost a month ago, I stood on the top of the world, attempting to take it all in. I must confess that it is still sinking in as I slowly come to terms with completing the Seven Summits challenge, climbing the highest peak on every continent over the last four and a half years. As I suffered numerous infections (like never before on any mountain), I had a mentally weak moment halfway through the seven-week climb. I have seen frozen bodies being taken down and our team saved two lives. I have learnt a tremendous amount about myself, humanity, and authentic leadership.

Getting to the top is just the beginning of the real work, where one has to take full responsibility for oneself and stay fully alert, as in the death zone. Being in the grip of the elements and my own pain, with no control whatsoever over what happens next, I learnt not only to appreciate, but to enjoy such vulnerability. The more I made myself available to existence, the more existence was available to me. On my return, people congratulated me on the great thing I have just accomplished. From my perspective, I just took millions of small steps.

It's not about the giving

It took me eight months to fully come back down from Mt. Everest. My body was in pieces and for weeks everything ached getting out of bed in the morning. I didn't mind, though, as I felt it was a small price to pay for the inner knowledge I had gained.

When I presented myself back in Poland, my mum looked totally stunned at the airport and commented: 'Oh my God, you look so normal'. She couldn't take her eyes off me for hours as if seeing me for the first time. The reception I got from my colleagues on my return to work, and the congratulatory messages from friends and acquaintances, were overwhelming.

I am very grateful for all the support and recognition I received both during and after my journey. Although Steve and I split up nine months after I returned from Nepal, I am indebted to him for his unconditional support. I have not yet opened the 'When the going gets tough' card that he gave me before Everest – to my surprise, my thirst for the mountains has not been quenched, so I will keep this card for another venture.

But my mission is not yet complete. Almost a year after standing on the top of the world, I am packing again to return to Nepal and take part in the opening ceremony of the Peace School, dedicated to Wanda Rutkiewicz and Jerzy Kukuczka, the Polish Himalayists. I feel apprehensive about suddenly becoming a 'surrogate' mother to two hundred kids, especially when I can't even speak their language.

I have taken every opportunity to raise money for the school and I continue to do so. Everything I have raised has gone towards the school project. Epic Change and the Clinton Foundation have contributed as well. The first school will be opened on April 29, 2011. There are thirteen more to go and I need all the backing I can get. You can help by buying this book, recommending it to your friends and to libraries – 30% of the profit will go towards the schools. If you feel that you can help in any other way please write to pinnacleinspirations@gmail.com.

At the beginning I thought charity was all about the 'giving' and that I needed to motivate people to want to share. Now I know that the act of giving provides only a diminishing satisfaction. It is making a difference that stays with one forever. It is seeing the unlimited opportunities created for two hundred smiling faces aged between five and twelve in a school that is about to open. Thank you for taking part!

About the author

A nia Lichota was raised in Poland during the communist era. In her childhood she used to sell tomatoes and other family farm produce in a market. She later worked as an accountant in her father's shipping business, and by the age of eighteen she had set up her own metals trading and small appliances import company. In 1996 Ania left Poland to study at the London School of Economics. She currently holds four degrees: MSc in Management and Marketing, Social and Organizational Psychology; MBA and PhD in International Management via distance learning in the US. As a citizen of Eastern Europe, Ania could not hold a passport until she was aged eight, but since then her passion for travelling has taken her to sixty countries around the world.

A business management professional, Ania has lived and worked in Poland, Estonia, Russia, Germany, Romania, Italy, France, Czech Republic, the Netherlands, US, Mexico, South Korea, Taiwan, Hong Kong, Singapore and the United Kingdom, where she currently works as a global change program manager in an investment bank. She speaks four languages. More recently she has attained a licence in neuro-linguistic programming and has gained experience as a life and executive coach. Ania accepts public speaking engagements on topics including leadership and personal development.

As an adjunct to her outdoor pursuits and life in London, Ania has become an active supporter of charities, raising money for UNICEF and, more recently, for a project to build a school in a remote village in Nepal. She has served as a trustee on the board of the Attlee Foundation in London and currently chairs a large charity for the Polish community in London.

Ania's mountaineering career started as a hobby in her youth. It became a more serious pursuit in 2006 when she set her sight on the Seven Summits — to climb the highest peak on each of the world's seven continents. She completed the challenge in May 2010 after reaching the summit of Mt. Everest.

She has won awards for climbing and charitable efforts, and has been named Woman of the Year by the Polish press in London.

For more information please visit www.anialichota.com.